THE BASIC MARINE
AQUARIUM

The marine Aquarium is, as yet, a plaything, a mere toy; but it is destined to become . . . far more . . . . We shall yet have tropical Aquaria, in which the temperature and qualities of the sea between the tropics will be so successfully imitated, that the . . . fish gleaming with unusual dyes — metallic azure, and silvery crimson — will dart and glide . . . as in their own tropic ocean.

H. Noel Humphreys
Ocean Gardens, 1857

THE BASIC MARINE AQUARIUM

A Simplified, Modern Approach to the Care of Saltwater Fishes

CAROL E. BOWER

Director, Institute for Aquarium Studies
A Division of Sea Research Foundation, Inc.
Hartford, Connecticut

With a Foreword by
James W. Atz, Ph.D.
American Museum of Natural History
Sea Research Foundation

CHARLES C THOMAS • PUBLISHER
Springfield • Illinois • U.S.A.

Published and Distributed Throughout the World by
CHARLES C THOMAS • PUBLISHER
2600 South First Street
Springfield, Illinois, 62717, U.S.A.

© *1983 by* CHARLES C THOMAS • PUBLISHER

ISBN 0-398-04736-7

Library of Congress Catalog Card Number: 82-10253

With THOMAS BOOKS *careful attention is given to all details of manufacturing and design. It is the Publisher's desire to present books that are satisfactory as to their physical qualities and artistic possibilities and appropriate for their particular use.* THOMAS BOOKS *will be true to those laws of quality that assure a good name and good will.*

Contribution No. 36, Sea Research Foundation, Inc.

All proceeds from the sale of this book support the research
activities of the Institute for Aquarium Studies.

Printed in the United States of America
CU-R-1

Library of Congress Cataloging in Publication Data

Bower, Carol E.
    The basic marine aquarium.

    Bibliography: p.
    Includes index.
    1. Marine aquariums.   I. Title.
SF457.1.B68 1982   639.3'42   82-10253
ISBN 0-398-04736-7

In memory of my father,
Bernard Bower

FOREWORD

T HIS book will show you how to bring another world, the world of water, into your home. It also will show you how to operate one of the essential tools scientists use to learn about that world. It is remarkable that a simple piece of apparatus like an aquarium has made possible the development of a hobby giving pleasure to thousands upon thousands of people and, at the same time, has enabled biologists and medical men to discover many important things about life.

People have kept freshwater fishes and other aquatic animals alive in glass aquaria for at least 200 years and marine ones for about 150. In spite of all these years of practice, however, aquarium keepers (including the scientists among them) have yet to master their own special techniques; through the years, successful aquarists have been the ones who did the right things—but almost always for the wrong reasons!

Carol Bower is unusually well qualified and situated to change all this and to help put the operation of aquaria on a scientifically sound basis. She is the director of a scientific institute with a mission that is unique among research organizations: the understanding and improvement of the methods used to maintain aquatic life in captivity. In this institute, Bower has carried out experiments and made discoveries that have thrown new light on the management of marine aquaria. She is also an expert communicator who can describe a technique clearly and accurately, all the while explaining in simple terms how and why it works the way it does. Bower combines scientific objectivity with personal sensibility in an especially harmonious way, and this is probably the reason why hers is the first book on fish keeping to give the supersensitivity of fishes the emphasis it deserves.

In 1937 when I began my twenty-five years of service at the New York Aquarium, the tropical fish hobby was struggling to give birth to America's first marine pet fish craze. The main problem, as everyone saw it, was to find a way to set up a practical miniature saltwater circulation, since it was well recognized that, unlike many fresh-water fishes, marine ones would not thrive in a standing aquarium. The solution seemed to be to design a cabinet-sized version of the large water systems found in public aquariums, the places that had been exhibiting marine life to millions of people for the past three-quarters of a century. Everyone also agreed that seawater systems had to be corrosion-proof and that even stainless steel would eventually corrode and poison aquatic animals. Plastic and glass tubing was commercially available in the 1930s, but the nonmetallic pumps on the market were too large and expensive. A hard-rubber centrifugal pump seemed the most likely solution, and much time and effort were spent in trying to fabricate a small, reasonably priced water pump out of this inert but refractory material. Although some of the new miniatures pumped well enough, they invariably cost far too much. The disappointed would-be marine hobbyists did not know it, but a simple solution to their pumping problem sat right under their noses. The common, all-glass or plastic air-lift was well-known to most hobbyists, and any sanitary engineer could have told them how to redesign these inefficient aquarium devices to improve their water-moving capacity. Not until some twenty years later, when home aquarists had abandoned the multipartite water system of the public aquarium as a model and had returned to the unitary home aquarium, modified to provide its own water circulation, did the keeping of marine fishes at home really come into its own.

As this personally witnessed, historical fragment shows, small marine aquaria have had a convoluted history. Progress has been slow and erratic with many false starts and the exploration of many blind alleys. In her book, Carol Bower has brought together many of these diverse threads and has woven them into a straightforward, how-to manual. She has put together the kind of handbook that not only hobbyists but also experimental biologists and laboratory technicians will need, inasmuch as the latter seldom have the time or inclination to learn any more about their aquaria than is necessary to operate them properly. For those readers who wish to check sources of technical information, she has provided numerous detailed footnotes, separated from the text in order not to distract the general reader.

This versatile book has been written with both layman and scientist, amateur and professional, in mind. It will guide both the beginner and the advanced hobbyist, as well as the most absent-minded professor or the technician with the most wettable thumb.

James W. Atz
American Museum of Natural History
and Sea Research Foundation

PREFACE

IN 1978 Sea Research Foundation, Inc., a nonprofit organization dedicated to public education and research, established the Institute for Aquarium Studies, a laboratory with a single goal: to advance aquarium keeping through scientific study. By means of controlled experimentation, the Institute's staff has been able to examine, resolve, and clarify many questions and misconceptions about the changes that occur in marine aquariums, to develop new methods for improving the environments of captive fishes, and to evaluate the usefulness of common techniques and commercial products.

This book is a distillation of the information derived from our studies and those of other researchers, and is intended to serve as a practical, nontechnical guide mainly for hobbyists, but also for teachers and those who are involved with the collection, distribution, and sale of ornamental marine fishes. In it, I hope to dispel the myths and unshroud the mysteries that have been a persistent source of confusion to most aquarists. To enable readers to pursue subject matter in greater depth, I have provided references to most of the sources of scientific information. Any statements or recommendations that are speculative or based on personal experience either are noted as such or are not accompanied by literature citations.

This book deals mainly with the care of captive reef fishes, but a few invertebrates that can be kept successfully with fishes are also mentioned. The type of aquarium discussed is not a "natural system" or a "miniature ocean"; rather, it is almost entirely an artificial system in which few, if any, natural balances exist. Natural seawater is not used, nor are the methods of physical, chemical, and biological control the same as those in the sea. The basic aquarium is a no-frills system that is relatively simple and economical to set up and maintain; the only equipment and care required is that which is essential to keeping fishes in the best possible state of health.

Of all the factors that determine whether the inhabitants of a marine aquarium live or die, thrive or just survive, water quality has often been singled out as the only matter of prime importance. In my view, however, a marine aquarium is an integrated system in which no isolated factor can be considered more influential than any other. Thus, all the physical, chemical, biological, nutritional, psychological, and social conditions that affect the well-being of captive fishes are given equal emphasis. Keeping a marine aquarium successfully is simply a matter of recognizing and understanding all these conditions, and then putting this knowledge into practice.

Hartford, Connecticut   CAROL E. BOWER

ACKNOWLEDGMENTS

I AM grateful to several colleagues and friends, whose gifts of time and creativity contributed so much to this book. James W. Atz, of the American Museum of Natural History and Sea Research Foundation, Inc., graciously accepted the prodigious task of criticizing the entire manuscript not once but twice, and edited some of the chapters as many as five times. He brought to my attention many valuable literature references, sternly but patiently prodded me into eliminating jargon and redistributing my injudiciously placed punctuation marks, and transformed more inelegant and unintelligible phrases than I care to admit into comprehensible and polished sentences. I think Jim must have brooded upon and labored over the wording of the final draft almost as much as I did. David T. Turner, of Sea Research Foundation, Inc., Institute for Aquarium Studies, contributed immeasurably to the design and execution of many of the research projects described in the text, criticized and proofread the manuscript, and double-checked the calculations. Stephen Spotte, of Sea Research Foundation, Inc., Mystic Marinelife Aquarium, read the manuscript and contributed many substantive changes.

Lance Voboril, of Aquarium Designs Ltd., helped to compile the information in Table 16; he and Barry J. Forbes made many helpful comments on the manuscript, from the viewpoints of aquarium retailer and hobbyist, respectively. Allan Grant prepared most of the photographs, and Cathie Derrick drew Figures 43, 52, and 53; the other line drawings are my own. Denton J. Lane generated Tables 9 and 10 by computer.

I am particularly indebted to William E. Kelley, of Sea Research Foundation, Inc., who had the forbearance to criticize the early drafts of the manuscript. Bill truly deserves credit for co-authorship of the entire volume, because every chapter is based on philosophical premises that I adopted from him, and each contains practical information that is the product of his unique inventiveness and talent for identifying and solving the problems that have eluded others. It is unfortunate that Bill has so rarely recorded his own thoughts and observations; I believe that over the past two decades, he has contributed more to the advancement of the art and science of marine aquarium keeping than any other individual, chiefly by providing counsel to aquarists and researchers, myself included, who happen to be more prolific writers than he.

Finally, special acknowledgment should be given to the entire Board of Trustees of Sea Research Foundation, Inc., without whose encouragement and support of the Institute for Aquarium Studies and belief in the priority of research this book never would have been completed.

CONTENTS

THE BASIC MARINE
AQUARIUM

Chapter 1

INTRODUCTION: MEETING THE NEEDS OF CAPTIVE FISHES

In a world older and more complete than ours they move
finished and complete, gifted with extensions of the senses we
have lost or never attained, living by voices we shall never hear.

Henry Beston
The Outermost House, 1928

TO keep an animal successfully in an artificial habitat it is helpful to know about the animal's abilities, limitations, and needs,
and about its life in its natural environment. A basic understanding
of the biological and psychological characteristics and needs of reef
fishes can be critical to the establishment and maintenance of a
tropical marine aquarium.

CHARACTERISTICS OF FISHES

A fish is a cold-blooded animal that lives in water, has a
backbone, breathes with gills, swims with fins, and has a scaly,
slime-covered body. There are, of course, exceptions. Certain
species can regulate their body temperatures, some breathe with
lungs or other air-breathing devices, a few have no fins, and several
have no scales. Moreover, some "fishes" are not fishes at all. Starfish,
jellyfish, and shellfish such as clams and lobsters are not fishes,
because they lack backbones; they were named at a time when the
term "fish" was used to described any animal that lived in water, and
their common names have been retained.

Just as all plants and animals on land are not alike, all fishes are
not alike, either. In addition to their obvious differences in shape,
size, and color, fishes also vary in their physical, chemical, nutritional, and psychological requirements. Generally speaking, fishes

3

that come from unstable, changeable environments are tolerant of environmental changes, whereas those that inhabit highly stable places often can hardly adjust to changes of any kind.

In the wild many animals that cannot adjust to environmental changes can move to other, more suitable locations when local conditions become unfavorable. During cold winters, for example, some birds fly south and some fishes migrate to warmer waters. Captive animals do not have this option. They are totally dependent on their captors to provide healthful environmental conditions. Because of the stability of their natural habitat, captive coral-reef fishes require a highly stable aquarium environment. The specific needs of these fishes — how they compare with those of familiar land animals, how they are fulfilled in the ocean, and how they should be met in captivity — are subjects about which every would-be aquarist should know.

PHYSICAL, CHEMICAL, AND NUTRITIONAL NEEDS

Marine fishes are adapted to life in seawater. Although they have the same basic needs as land animals, such as food to eat, water to drink, and oxygen to breathe, these needs must be met very differently in the sea from the way they are met on land. Fishes are in intimate contact with their surrounding medium, water, and they rely on it to control many of their body processes. The ocean is the protector of the animals that inhabit it and has been called "the easiest place in the world to live,"[1] because it supports life with degrees of consistency and dependability unknown anywhere else on our planet. On the contrary, air is a harsh medium in which to live, and animals cannot survive on land without several types of special protective devices.

Water

Water is more essential to life than any other substance. It constitutes about 70 percent of the weight of the human body and up to 96 percent of the body weight of some marine animals. The supply of water on land is so highly unpredictable and variable that much of the physiology and behavior of land animals concerns acquiring and conserving water.

Marine animals never have to search for water, because they are surrounded by it. Instead of the dead, waterproof skins needed by land animals to prevent them from drying out, fishes have delicate, living skins filled with sensitive nerve endings, and they need their slimy coating of mucus to protect them from scratches and to act as a barrier against invasion by disease-causing microorganisms. Fishes have no eyelids; the cleansing and lubricating functions of these structures are unnecessary in the sea, since they are carried out by the water in which the fishes live.

Because of the vulnerability of its eyes and skin, a fish cannot be handled in the same way as a land animal. Contact with anything but another wet, nonabrasive surface can be extremely damaging, so a fish should never be removed from water in a net. Methods of capturing and handling fishes without injuring them are described in Chapter 10.

Salts

All natural waters contain dissolved inorganic substances called *salts* or *minerals*. The major difference between freshwater and seawater lies in the quantity of salts each contains; with about 3.5 percent of its weight consisting of salts, seawater is 3,000 times more salty than most drinking water.

The most abundant salt in seawater is sodium chloride or common table salt, but the ocean contains many other salts in various concentrations. It is likely that natural seawater contains every known element on earth. Some are present in large quantities and are called *major elements;* others that occur in tiny, barely detectable amounts are called *trace elements.*

Salts or minerals are important to all forms of life, because they play an important role in the chemical reactions that are the basis of life. Calcium, for example, is necessary for the normal growth of bone, muscle, and teeth, and iron helps carry oxygen in the blood. Only 21 mineral elements — 7 major elements and 14 trace elements — are known to be essential to animal life (Table 1), but there is little information on the requirements for these elements by fishes.

Table 1

ESSENTIAL MAJOR MINERALS AND TRACE MINERALS
FOR HIGHER ANIMALS. THE REQUIREMENTS
OF MARINE FISHES HAVE NOT BEEN ESTABLISHED.

Major minerals	*Trace minerals*
Calcium	Chromium
Chlorine	Cobalt
Magnesium	Copper
Phosphorus	Fluorine
Potassium	Iodine
Sodium	Iron
Sulfur	Manganese
	Molybdenum
	Nickel
	Selenium
	Silicon
	Tin
	Vanadium
	Zinc

From Miller and Neathery (1977)[2]

Land animals obtain essential minerals from the food they eat. Fishes probably derive most of their mineral requirements from food, too, but the matter is complicated because fishes have the ability to absorb minerals from their external environment. For this reason, there is some controversy regarding the need for trace elements in artificial seawater. Marine fishes have been cultured successfully in simple seawater formulations that do not contain special trace-element additives. It therefore seems likely that trace elements are not needed in artificial seawater, provided that the fishes receive well-balanced diets.

The maintenance of a proper salt and water balance is an important aspect of the everyday lives of fishes. The blood and body fluids of most marine species are considerably less salty than seawater. As a consequence, marine fishes continuously lose water through their gills by *osmosis*, the movement of water across a membrane from the less salty side to the more salty side. This same process is responsible for the wilting of salad greens after salting. If osmosis proceeded without regulation, marine fishes would rapidly become dehydrated. To overcome this problem, marine fishes drink large volumes of seawater, but they then must eliminate the excess salts they ingest at the same time. This is accomplished mainly by specialized salt-secreting cells in their gills and by fecal excretion. Pathways of salt and water regulation in a typical marine fish are shown in Figure 1.

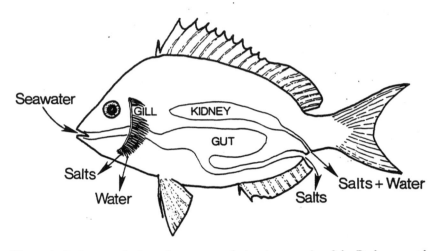

Figure 1. Pathways of salt and water regulation in a marine fish. Redrawn and modified from Wedemeyer et al. (1976).[3]

Fishes from different marine habitats have different capacitites to adjust to changing salinities. The salt concentration of seawater in the tropics varies little throughout the year; it is therefore not surprising that reef fishes have limited internal mechanisms for adjusting to changes in salinity. Small changes in the saltiness of seawater may cause severe distress to such fishes. A sharp decrease in saltiness causes a sudden influx of water into their bodies, and a sudden increase causes rapid dehydration.

Unlike the stable salt concentration of tropical seawater, the saltiness of aquarium seawater is sometimes highly variable. Improper preparation of artificial seawater or the use of an inaccurate instrument to measure the salt concentration often results in unsuitable water. Because water evaporates continuously from a well-aerated aquarium, the seawater in it becomes progressively more salty with each passing day. Each time a fish is transferred from one aquarium to another, it faces the danger of exposure to water that has a different salt concentration from that in which it was originally kept. The proper ways to mix artificial seawater and to measure and adjust its salt concentration are discussed in Chapters 4 and 6. A method of acclimating fishes to a different salt concentration is described in Chapter 11.

Oxygen

Oxygen is one of the gases in air. It is used by all animals to "burn" food in order to release energy. Before oxygen can enter the bloodstream of any animal, it must first be dissolved in water. It would be most impractical to have the respiratory surfaces of land animals exposed directly to the external environment, because air would rapidly dry up and destroy these special membranes. To conserve water and obtain oxygen at the same time, land animals have internal lungs that are connected to the outside by a complicated series of tubes and passages. As air is inhaled through these passages, it is warmed, cleaned, and moistened; when it finally reaches the innermost parts of the lungs, oxygen can dissolve into the wet film on the surface and then diffuse through it and into the blood.

The breathing structures of fishes do not have to be protected from the external environment. Seawater contains abundant oxygen that is already dissolved and ready for use. Oxygen enters the ocean at its surface, where air dissolves into the water, assisted by wind and waves. *Gills,* the equivalent of lungs in a typical fish, are in direct contact with water. As illustrated in Figure 2, a fish takes water into its mouth and then forces it over its gills. The gill tissue, like the innermost lung tissue, is filled with microscopic blood vessels. As the water flows over the gills, oxygen diffuses into the bloodstream, and carbon dioxide and other wastes are carried out and washed away.

It is often written that water can dissolve only a fraction of the oxygen present in air, and that warm water and saltwater cannot dissolve as much oxygen as cold water or freshwater, implying that fishes inhabiting warm seawater are at a disadvantage with respect

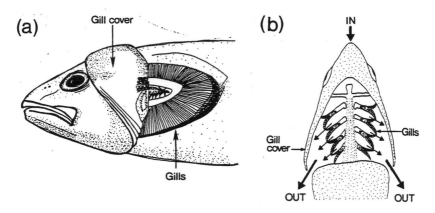

Figure 2. The gill system of a typical fish. (a) Position of the gills. (b) Cut-away view of a fish from below, showing the pattern of water flow over the gills. Water is taken into the mouth, forced over the gills, where dissolved oxygen diffuses into the fish's blood and carbon dioxide and other wastes diffuse out, and is then expelled. Redrawn from various sources.

to the availability of oxygen. Although these statements are true, the implications are not. Fishes do not require as much oxygen as land animals, because their energy requirements are lower; thus, the amount of oxygen in warm seawater is more than adequate to meet the demands of reef fishes.

An aquarium lacks the wind and waves that help to dissolve oxygen into the ocean, and the oxygen that dissolves into a calm-surfaced, covered aquarium usually is consumed by the fishes more rapidly than it is replaced. To ensure that the supply of oxygen never becomes depleted, a marine aquarium must always be equipped with devices to introduce air and to keep the water in motion. The aeration of aquarium water is discussed in Chapters 2 and 3.

Temperature

Of all the factors that determine where life can exist, temperature is one of the most important. All chemical processes carried out by living cells depend on temperature, and proceed only within narrow limits. A rise in body temperature increases the rate at which an animal lives, or the rate at which it uses up food and oxygen; a decline in temperature decreases its rate of living. When an animal's limits of temperature tolerance are exceeded, cell destruction and death eventually take place.

The temperature of air can change very rapidly, so land animals need temperature-control devices and ways to keep out excessive heat and cold. Birds and mammals are *warm-blooded* — they can maintain a constant body temperature regardless of the external temperature; moreover, they have insulation such as fur, feathers, or thick layers of body fat to conserve heat. They have internal mechanisms for dissipating heat when it becomes too hot, and for producing heat when it becomes too cold; they also can move to a warmer or cooler place.

Fishes are *cold-blooded* animals. Because they cannot generate or dissipate body heat, their internal temperature is controlled by the temperature of the water in which they live. Fortunately, changes in water temperature occur slowly, and the larger the body of water, the more slowly its temperature changes. The temperature of air may increase by 30°F (17°C) or more in the course of one day, whereas it takes an entire summer to heat the ocean that much in regions with the most extreme seasonal variations in temperature. In most parts of the ocean seasonal temperature changes are smaller, and in the equatorial waters where most reef fishes live, the yearly change is usually less than 3.5°F (2°C).

The coral-reef environment is so stable with respect to temperature that reef fishes tend to be less able to tolerate changes in temperature than fishes from other ocean habitats. The volume of water in an aquarium is miniscule when compared with that of the ocean, and changes in room temperature produce rapid changes in the temperature of the aquarium water. To maintain a constant temperature aquariums should be situated in rooms that do not become exceedingly hot during the summer, and they should be equipped with thermostatically controlled heaters. Precautions also should be taken to avoid the thermal stress or shock to fishes that may occur upon their transfer to a new aquarium, or as a result of water replacement. Temperature control of aquarium water is discussed in Chapters 2, 3, and 4, and procedures for temperature acclimation are described in Chapter 11.

Food

Tropical ocean waters lack the extremes of weather that so often determine the availability of food on land, and there is an abundant supply of food around the coral reef throughout the year. Algae form the basis of the food supply in the sea, just as green-leaved plants do on land. Both possess the unique ability to manufacture their own food, using energy from the sun, carbon dioxide, and mineral nutrients.

Microscopic algae are eaten by near-microscopic animals, which, in turn, are consumed by larger animals, and so on. A sequence in which organisms feed upon other, usually smaller, creatures, is called a *food chain*, with each species in the chain constituting one link. Marine food chains may have only two links or many, but they almost always begin with algae. Countless individual food chains mingle and intersect at nearly every link, forming complex systems called *food webs*. Food webs represent a kind of insurance for marine animals; if one link in any given chain becomes depleted, animals higher in the chain have alternative sources of food.

Food chains and webs exist only to a very limited extent in a marine aquarium, because algae and small invertebrates seldom flourish under typical aquarium conditions. A successful aquarium is one in which its inhabitants feed *with*, not *on* one another. Although captive fishes will feed on any suitable organisms that happen to grow and multiply in an aquarium, no marine aquarium is self-sustaining nutritionally.

Providing the correct diets for reef fishes may be an aquarist's most difficult task because, as far as fishes are concerned, the needs of only a few freshwater species are known. Most information about the feeding habits of reef fishes comes from observations of them in the wild and from analyses of their stomach contents, and these accounts are limited. Although some fishes have such highly specialized diets that they refuse all but a single type of food, most species, particularly when they are acquired as juveniles, will adjust readily to artificial diets in captivity. The key to meeting the nutritional needs of reef fishes, in the absence of information about their specific requirements, is to offer the greatest possible variety of foods.

Recommendations about suitable foods and feeding techniques are provided in Chapter 12.

Pollutant-free Water

To survive and reproduce all living creatures require an environment that does not contain dangerous amounts of poisonous substances. The ocean is no longer the pollution-free environment it once was; mercury, PCBs, DDT, and other toxic industrial wastes and pesticides have been found in the tissues of animals collected even from the deepest and most remote parts of the ocean.

The ocean does, however, have some self-purification capabilities. Because of the immense volume of water it contains, animal wastes and other pollutants are diluted and dispersed rapidly from their sources. Biodegradable wastes are decomposed by bacteria into simple substances that are taken up by algae and subsequently recycled into food chains; those not subject to biological breakdown either become incorporated into bottom sediments or remain in dilute form in the water, from which they may be absorbed by algae or microscopic animals and then passed on to larger animals in food chains and webs.

An aquarium is like the ocean regarding the fate of pollutants, some being decomposed and others not, but it differs from the ocean in a few important ways. Regardless of size, an aquarium contains a small volume of water with respect to the weight of animal life it supports; thus, animal wastes and foreign pollutants are not diluted even a small fraction as much as they are in the sea. Sufficient algae to remove the products of bacterial decomposition rarely, if ever, are present, so these substances can accumulate and reach harmful concentrations. Toxic chemicals, such as those present in tobacco smoke, insecticides and other aerosols, may dissolve into aquarium water from the air.

In addition, the metabolic activities of aquarium inhabitants cause the water to become acidic, a condition that is unhealthy, because the natural environment of reef fishes is alkaline. Captive fishes can poison themselves with their own wastes. The major excretory product of fishes is ammonia, and ammonia is poisonous even in trace amounts. In the ocean, ammonia is diluted instantaneously and then taken up by algae or converted by bacteria to less toxic substances (see Chapters 3 and 5), but these beneficial organisms are practically absent from a new aquarium. The accumulation of ammonia most likely causes "new-tank syndrome," in which the fishes introduced into an aquarium often become diseased and die during the first month or two.

It is now recognized that pollution control is a most critical aspect of aquarium operation and maintenance. Provision must be made to (1) establish and maintain a large population of ammonia-consuming bacteria, (2) remove foreign pollutants that enter from the air, (3) remove nonbiodegradable waste products, and (4) prevent the water from becoming acidic. Methods and equipment for pollution control are described in Chapters 2, 3, 5, and 6.

PSYCHOLOGICAL AND SOCIAL NEEDS

Reef fishes are very sensitive to their environment physiologically, and they appear to be equally sensitive psychologically. Meeting the physical, chemical, and nutritional needs of captive reef fishes does not guarantee their survival in an aquarium; creating the proper psychological and social environment is equally important. Some practical applications of fish behavior or psychology are given in Chapters 8 through 12.

Sensory Capabilities of Fishes

The first step in attempting to interpret an animal's behavior is to understand its sensory capabilities, that is, its ability to receive environmental stimuli. Fishes have highly developed sense organs. They can discriminate among different colors and, because of the usual placement of their eyes (one on each side of the head), they can see what is in front of, beside, above, below, and even behind them. Fishes also have marvelous sensory capacities for smell, hearing, touch, and taste. They can find their way to distant areas guided mainly by their sense of smell and can discern the body scents of other species. Many fishes produce sounds and respond to the sounds made by other fishes. Free nerve endings scattered throughout their skin endow fishes with sensitivity to the slightest touch. Finally, the taste buds of fishes are not located only in their mouths; they may be on the body, lips, barbels, and even fins.

In addition to keenness of the traditional five senses, fishes also have other unique senses. The *lateral-line sense,* roughly speaking, combines hearing with touch. The lateral line is visible as a conspicuous row of scales, each with a pore, that runs along each side of a fish's body. It is sensitive to low-frequency vibrations in water that are not sound waves and therefore are not detectable by ear. Such vibrations are created by disturbances in the flow of water around a solid object, or by the movements of another fish. The lateral line thus enables even a blind fish to avoid contact with the walls of an aquarium and to "feel" the presence of other fishes in total darkness. Certain fishes, such as the torpedo rays and some stargazers, can emit powerful electrical impulses into the water, thus creating electrical fields around themselves. Disturbances in these fields may help the fishes to navigate through cloudy water or to detect prey. Some fishes are so sensitive to electrical fields that they will follow a magnet as it is moved along the side of an aquarium. Others emit such powerful electrical impulses that they are capable of stunning other fishes in an aquarium.

Clearly, captive fishes are far from oblivious to what is going on inside and outside the aquarium. Their combined senses enable them to perceive what is going on around them with remarkable acuity. They are easily frightened by rapid movements and by sudden strong stimuli, such as turning the lights on or off, and by the vibrations caused by heavy footsteps, tapping on the aquarium glass, or slamming down the aquarium cover.

Fish Behavior and Social Interactions

A single area of a coral reef may support more than a hundred different species of fishes. There are, in fact, more different kinds of fishes in the tropical-reef environment than in any other type of aquatic habitat. Because of the numbers and diversity of fishes and other animals, life on and around a coral reef must be highly competitive. Under such circumstances, reef fishes have developed complex and individualized behaviors and life-styles.

One important characteristic of reef fishes is their specialization in ways of feeding. Reef fishes may be very particular about the foods they eat, and also in the times when they feed. Some eat only animal matter, some only algae, and others eat a combination of both. Some are active only during the daylight, some only at dawn and dusk, and others only at night. The specialized mouthparts of certain species are manifestations of their feeding behavior; for example, some have anteater-like snouts for picking tiny organisms out of crevices, and others have teeth fused into hard beaks for crunching on coral.

Reef fishes also are specialized in their relationships with other animals. Some swim only in schools, and others are strictly loners. Some form colonies in individual burrows in the bottom rubble, and others live in close association with totally unrelated animals. Anemonefishes reside within the deadly tentacle rings of sea anemones; pearlfishes live inside the bodies of sea cucumbers or star fish; some cardinalfishes find shelter within shells of large conches; and shrimpfish hide among the long, venomous spines of sea urchins.

This leads to another important point about the life-styles of reef fishes: most species require some form of shelter or refuge. The small, brightly colored fishes that are most popular with hobbyists often have high, flat bodies, rather than the familiar torpedo-like shape of most fishes. Such compressed fishes rarely leave the reef to swim in open water. Their body shape enables them to slip into cracks and crevices within the reef when they are frightened or threatened by a predator. Shelter, in the form of aquarium decorations, is a necessary constituent of a psychologically healthy environment for captive reef fishes, but its importance is often overlooked, even by experienced aquarists.

The decor in an aquarium, in addition to providing hiding places for very timid fishes, provides territorial markers for the more aggressive individuals. Many species not only cling close by the reef but also establish well-defined territories from which they rarely stray and from which they aggressively exclude other fishes. The spatial requirements of captive fishes are thus important considerations for their successful maintenance. A psychologically healthy aquarium must contain adequate space and decor for the establishment of territories, and should include a combination of individuals and species that can coexist peacefully. Aquarium decor and the spatial requirements of fishes are discussed more fully in Chapters 2 and 9.

IS A MARINE AQUARIUM RIGHT FOR YOU?

A marine aquarium is more expensive to set up and maintain than a freshwater tank. At today's retail prices one might expect to spend nearly $200 for a 20-gallon (76-liter) set-up, not including the cost of the fishes, which range in price from a few dollars to more than $100. Initial expenditures can be reduced by buying equipment second-hand or at discount stores, and by purchasing sea salts in bulk instead of in small packages, but fishes always should be purchased only from reputable dealers.

The day-to-day maintenance of marine and freshwater aquariums is surprisingly similar, as far as time and effort are concerned. However, because of the potentially harmful changes that occur in seawater, a few important water conditions, namely pH and salt concentration, must be measured and adjusted regularly. Moreover, reef fishes, being more specialized in their habits and life-styles, demand more attention than freshwater species, particularly when it comes to feeding them.

Use of the proper equipment and careful control of water quality will contribute much to the successful keeping of reef fishes, but another factor is equally important. The best aquarist is one who is *sympatico* with his or her fishes — willing to try to view life from their point of view, and to do whatever is needed to ensure their safety, regardless of personal inconvenience. This means being patient enough to dangle bits of food on a thread to encourage a new fish to eat, and caring enough to avoid unnecessary cruelties such as prodding timid fishes from their hiding places or moving them in nets.

Anyone who domesticates a wild animal or keeps any kind of pet has a moral obligation to provide his captive with the best possible care. Tropical marine fishes present a greater challenge than most other animals, because they are so different from us and are therefore more difficult to relate to, and because they are such delicate creatures. A marine aquarium may not be right for everyone, but for those willing to accept the challenge, the maintenance of reef fishes can be one of the most aesthetically pleasing and personally satisfying endeavors of one's lifetime.

PART ONE
THE BASIC AQUARIUM

Chapter 2

BASIC EQUIPMENT

> Only the following basic statement need be repeated here: the ideal solution . . . is not to provide an exact imitation of the natural habitat, but rather to transpose the natural conditions in the wild, bearing in mind biological principles, into the artificial ones . . . .
>
> Heini Hediger
> *Man and Animal in the Zoo: Zoo Biology*, 1969

> Artificial sea-water is now much used, and the formula for its preparation is given by several authors. But I do not advise the uninitiated to experiment in its composition. Aquarium dealers sell the necessary powders, mixed in proper proportions, and will give full directions for its use.
>
> George B. Sowerby
> *Popular History of the Aquarium*, 1857

> . . . I wasted my money years ago, when we were all in the dark as to the true principles of Aquarium science.
>
> Shirley Hibberd
> *The Book of the Marine Aquarium*, 1860

THE basic equipment for a successful marine aquarium consists of a sturdy water-tight enclosure, an effective system to filter and aerate the water, a suitable environmental medium (artificial seawater), decor to shelter the fishes, and the apparatus needed to monitor the quality of the water and to keep the aquarium clean. The preferred types of equipment and their functions are outlined below. Instructions for their use are given in later chapters.

THE ENCLOSURE AND RELATED EQUIPMENT

The Aquarium

Functions

The aquarium provides a safe, attractive enclosure for captive marine fishes.

Recommendations

Construction. Use a standard all-glass or plastic-and-glass aquarium that has no metal parts.

Size. The desired size of the aquarium will depend on the numbers, species, and adult sizes of the fishes to be kept in it. It is important to consider that marine fishes require more space than freshwater species, for reasons that are explained in Chapter 9. Large aquariums are more expensive to set up and maintain, but they are less likely to become overcrowded, and they also are relatively easy to care for. An aquarium with a capacity of 20 or 30 gallons (76 or 114 liters) is recommended for the novice aquarist.

Shape. When a choice is available for aquariums of the same or similar capacities, always choose the tank with the greatest surface area. Surface area is more important than volume for two reasons. First, a large surface area enables more effective filtration and air exchange. Second, extra bottom surface area allows for the use of more decor, enabling more fishes to establish suitable territories. As shown in Table 2 and Figure 3, "low" models have more surface area than "high" models, even though both hold the same volumes of water, and some small aquariums have more surface area than larger tanks.

The Cover

Functions

The aquarium cover keeps the fishes *in* and foreign matter *out*. It

Table 2

DIMENSIONS AND BOTTOM AND TOP SURFACE AREAS OF STANDARD, ALL-GLASS AQUARIUMS

Volume[a]		American units				Metric units			
gal	L	Length (in)	Width (in)	Height (in)	Surface area (ft²)	Length (cm)	Width (cm)	Height (cm)	Surface area (cm²)
5½	21	16	8	10	0.9	40.6	20.3	25.4	824
10	38	20	10	12	1.4	50.8	25.4	30.5	1,290
15	57	24	12	12	2.0	61.0	30.5	30.5	1,861
20H	76	24	12	16	2.0	61.0	30.5	40.6	1,861
20L	76	30	12	12	2.5	76.2	30.5	30.5	2,324
24	91	24	12	20	2.0	61.0	30.5	50.8	1,861
29	110	30	12	18	2.5	76.2	30.5	45.7	2,324
30H	114	24	12	24	2.0	61.0	30.5	61.0	1,861
30L	114	36	12	16	3.0	91.4	30.5	40.6	2,788
40	151	48	13	16	4.3	121.9	33.0	40.6	4,023
55	208	48	13	20	4.3	121.9	33.0	50.8	4,023
65	246	36	18	24	4.5	91.4	45.7	61.0	4,178
70	265	48	18	20	6.0	121.9	45.7	50.8	5,571
80H	303	48	13	30	4.3	121.9	33.0	76.2	4,023
80L	303	60	13	24	5.4	152.4	33.0	61.0	5,029
90	341	72	13	22	6.5	182.9	33.0	55.9	6,036
100	379	72	18	18	9.0	182.9	45.7	45.7	8,359
125	474	72	18	22	9.0	182.9	45.7	55.9	8,359
135	511	72	18	24	9.0	182.9	45.7	61.0	8,359

[a]"H" indicates "high" model; "L" indicates "long" or "low" model.

Figure 3. A "low-model" aquarium (top) is preferable to a "high model" (bottom), because it provides more surface area for filtration, air exchange, and the establishment of territories. Both models hold the same volume of water.

reduces the rate at which water evaporates from the aquarium, and helps to minimize temperature changes.

Recommendations

The cover should be made of glass or plastic, and should fit loosely enough to allow good ventilation. A method for modifying standard aquarium covers to reduce water leakage and salt build-up around the edges is described in Chapter 4.

The Light

Functions

The light illuminates the aquarium for good viewing by the fishes and by their observers. It also provides radiant energy to promote the growth of algae.

Recommendations

Direction of Incoming Light. Light should enter the aquarium from above. Side or bottom lighting has been shown to stress fishes,[1] and therefore should be avoided.

Type of Light. Fluorescent lights are preferable to incandescent lights because they are more efficient; they provide more light energy per watt consumed, and they generate relatively little heat. Plant-stimulating lights such as Sylvania Gro-Lux® and Penn-Plax Sea-Lux® fluorescent tubes have been recommended for stimulating algal growth, but they produce less intense light than standard fluorescent lamps, and they also may impart unnatural colors to the aquarium fishes and decorations. For general lighting purposes Duro-Test® Vita-Lite®, or Sylvania Warm White Deluxe fluorescent lamps are recommended.

The Aquarium Stand

Functions

The stand raises the aquarium to a height suitable for viewing, and at the same time supports its entire weight.

Recommendations

Standard tank stands made of wrought iron or formica-covered wood are recommended. Tables or other supports may be used only if they are *sturdy* — each gallon (3.8 liters) of water weighs 8.4 pounds (3.8 kilograms) — and *level*. A warped or uneven surface under the tank causes unequal distribution of weight and can result in leaks or cracked glass. Heated surfaces, such as the top of a radiator or television set, are not suitable. Fishes may become frightened if the aquarium is placed too near the floor (they probably react to the movements above them), so the stand should have a height of at least 30 inches (76 centimeters).

The Heater

Functions

A heater with a thermostatic control maintains aquarium water at a temperature that is above room temperature.

Recommendations

Construction. An immersion heater with a built-in thermostat

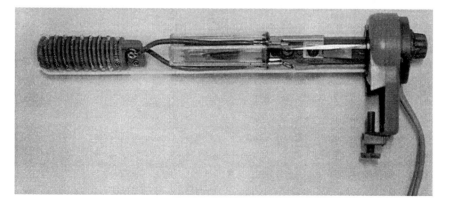

Figure 4. A typical immersion heater, with a heating element enclosed within a glass tube and a built-in thermostatic control dial.

and control dial is recommended (Fig. 4). This device consists of a heating element enclosed within a glass tube; a long tube that extends almost to the surface of the filter bed is preferable to a short tube. When the water temperature falls, a temperature-sensitive metal strip in the thermostat bends and engages with another metal strip, completing an electrical circuit that heats the water. When the desired temperature is reached, contact is broken and heating stops. The contact points corrode with time and may fuse together, causing the water to overheat. It is therefore important to buy a heater with replaceable parts, and to clean or replace the contact points regularly to prevent malfunction. Heater adjustments and maintenance are discussed in Chapters 4 and 6, respectively.

Wattage. In rooms in which air temperature is always above 65°F (18°C) about 2 watts are needed for each gallon (3.8 liters) of water to be heated. In unheated rooms, use 5 watts per gallon. Recommended wattages for standard aquariums in both heated and unheated rooms are given in Table 3.

THE FILTRATION/AERATION SYSTEM

The Undergravel Filter

Functions

The undergravel filter consists of a perforated base plate and two or more vertical airlift tubes (Fig. 5). The base plate forms a false bottom upon which the filtrant (gravel) rests, and the airlift tubes channel a flow of air and water from beneath the filter plate to the surface. The functions of an undergravel filter are explained in detail in Chapter 3.

Recommendations

The base plate must be strong enough to support the weight of the filtrant without collapsing or breaking. It also should contain large numbers of evenly spaced holes or slots of a diameter that allows water to flow freely but does not permit filtrant grains and other solid matter to fall through.

The airlift tubes should be at least 1 inch (2.5 centimeters) in

Table 3

RECOMMENDED TOTAL WATTAGES OF HEATERS TO BE USED IN AQUARIUMS OF VARIOUS CAPACITIES KEPT IN HEATED ROOMS (MINIMUM TEMPERATURE 65°F or 18°C) OR UNHEATED ROOMS

The figures represent the individual or combined outputs of standard commercial heaters.[a]

Aquarium capacity		Total watts	
Gallons	*Liters*	*Heated rooms*	*Unheated rooms*
5½	28	25	25
10	38	25	50
15	57	25	75
20	76	50	100
24	91	50	100
29	110	50	150
30	114	50	150
40	151	75	200
55	208	100	275
65	246	125	325
70	265	150	350
80	303	150	400
90	341	200	450
100	379	200	500
125	474	250	625
135	511	275	675

[a]Aquarium heaters are available in 25-, 50-, 75-, 100-, 150-, and 200-watt sizes.

diameter for aquariums of 20 gallons (76 liters) or less, and larger for aquariums with greater volumes. Unfortunately, in constructing undergravel filters for large aquariums, most manufacturers increase the number of 1-inch airlift tubes, instead of increasing the diameters of the two corner tubes, although the latter arrangement is both more efficient and more attractive.

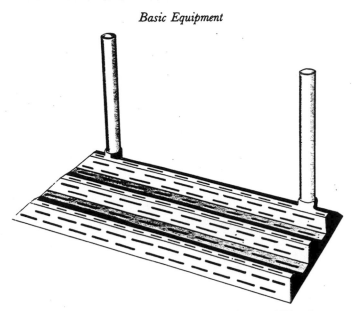

Figure 5. An undergravel filter plate with two airlift tubes.

The Filtrant

Functions

The filtrant, a layer of gravel or crushed shell, rests on the base plate of the undergravel filter. The filtrant has three important functions: (1) it traps suspended particles and removes them from the water; (2) it provides surfaces upon which filter bacteria can grow; and (3) it prevents the aquarium water from becoming extremely acidic. These functions are explained more fully in Chapter 3.

Recommendations

Type of Filtrant. The filtrant for marine aquariums should consist entirely of crushed oyster shell or of gravels such as calcite, dolomitic limestone (dolomite), and limestone. Crushed oyster shell is available from farm suppliers, and the various gravels are sold at aquarium stores. All of the above filtrants contain the minerals calcium carbonate and magnesium carbonate; carbonates help to control the pH of the aquarium water. Silica (quartz) gravel and colored glass gravels are not suitable filtrants for marine aquariums, because they contain no available carbonates.

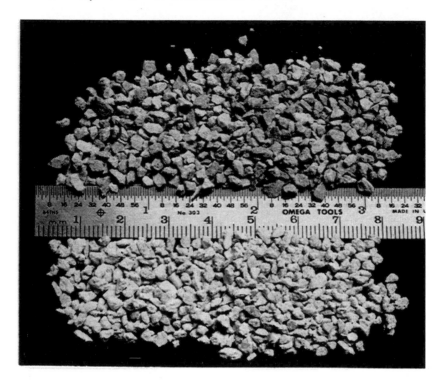

Figure 6. The filtrant used in a marine aquarium should be composed of carbonates and should be graded to grain sizes of 1/16 to 3/16 inches (2 to 5 millimeters). Dolomitic limestone is shown at the top, and Florida Crushed Coral® at the bottom.

Size of Filtrant Grains. The filtrant should be graded uniformly to a U.S. standard mesh size of 6 × 16 (6 × 14 Tyler mesh). This is equivalent to grain sizes of about 1/16 to 3/16 inch or 2 to 5 millimeters (Fig. 6). Some authors suggest using a coarse lower layer of filtrant and a fine upper layer, but fine particles are not recommended; they can sift down and clog the holes in the filter plate, and can result in the build-up of unsightly debris on the filtrant surface.

Depth of the Filter Bed. The layer of filtrant on the base plate, called the *filter bed,* should be about 2 inches (5 centimeters) deep in a 20-gallon (76-liter) aquarium, 3 inches (7.6 centimeters) deep in a

40-gallon (150-liter) aquarium and so on. Deeper beds may be installed but may require extra air pumps to ensure adequate flow of water through the filtrant.

Amount of Filtrant. Filtrants usually are sold by weight. Approximately 8 pounds (3.6 kilograms) of gravel will form a filter bed 1 inch (2.5 centimeters) deep covering 1 square foot (929 square centimeters) of surface. Table 4 gives the approximate weights of filtrant needed to form filter beds of various depths in aquariums of standard capacities and dimensions.

Table 4

APPROXIMATE WEIGHT OF FILTRANT
IN POUNDS (KILOGRAMS)
NEEDED TO FORM FILTER BEDS OF VARIOUS DEPTHS
IN STANDARD, ALL-GLASS AQUARIUMS[a]

Aquarium capacity[b] (gal)	Depth of Filter Bed							
	2 in (5.1 cm)		3 in (7.6 cm)		4 in (10.2 cm)		5 in (12.7 cm)	
5½	14	(6)						
10	22	(10)	34	(15)				
15	32	(15)	48	(22)				
20L	40	(18)	60	(27)				
20H	32	(15)	48	(22)	64	(29)		
24	32	(15)	48	(22)	64	(29)		
29	40	(18)	60	(27)	80	(36)		
30H	32	(15)	48	(22)	64	(29)		
30L	48	(22)	72	(33)	96	(44)		
40	69	(31)	103	(47)	138	(62)		
55	69	(31)	103	(47)	138	(62)	172	(78)
65	72	(33)	108	(49)	144	(65)	180	(82)
70	96	(44)	144	(65)	192	(87)	240	(109)
80L	86	(39)	130	(59)	173	(78)	216	(98)
80H	69	(31)	103	(47)	138	(62)	172	(78)
90	104	(47)	156	(71)	208	(94)	260	(118)
100	144	(65)	216	(98)	288	(131)	360	(163)
125	144	(65)	216	(98)	288	(131)	360	(163)
135	144	(65)	216	(98)	288	(131)	360	(163)

[a]*See* Table 2 for aquarium dimensions.
[b]"H" indicates "high" model; "L" indicates "long" or "low" model.

Air Diffusers

Functions

Air diffusers are small blocks or cylinders of porous material that break or *diffuse* the airstream from the air pump into small bubbles (Fig. 7). The bubbles create a flow of water to the surface, facilitating air exchange, and when inserted into airlift tubes, the diffusers aid in circulating water through the filter bed. The importance of water circulation is discussed in Chapter 3.

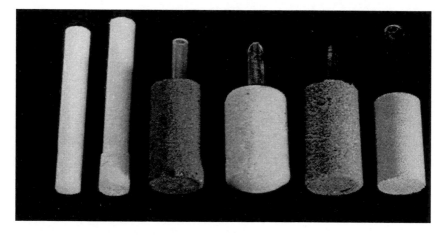

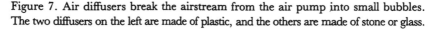

Figure 7. Air diffusers break the airstream from the air pump into small bubbles. The two diffusers on the left are made of plastic, and the others are made of stone or glass.

Recommendations

A stream of air released as fine bubbles moves more water than the same volume of air released as coarse bubbles. Unfortunately, diffusers that produce very fine bubbles offer the greatest resistance to air flow from the air pump. They reduce the volume of air entering the water, and subsequently reduce the volume of water moved. The back pressure created by such air diffusers can wear out an air pump in a very short time.

Plastic air diffusers (e.g., Dispos-a-stone™ by Aquology Corp.) produce relatively fine bubbles with minimal back pressure. Since all diffusers eventually become clogged, probably with salts or organic matter, it is necessary to keep extras on hand and to replace them frequently. A procedure for checking air diffusers is given in Chapter 6.

The Air Pump

Functions

The air pump delivers compressed air to the aquarium. This air powers the filters and circulates and aerates the water.

Recommendations

A high-capacity vibrator pump, such as the one illustrated in Figure 8, is recommended for aquariums up to 20 gallons (76 liters) in volume. Additional pumps should be used with larger aquariums.

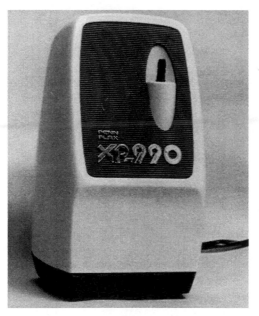

Figure 8. A vibrator-type air pump supplies air to circulate and oxygenate the water in an aquarium.

The Box Filter

Functions

The plastic box filter is a container that usually is filled with activated carbon and placed inside the aquarium.

Recommendations

An inexpensive box filter, such as the one shown in Figure 9, functions as well as larger, more expensive types, and is easily hidden behind decor.

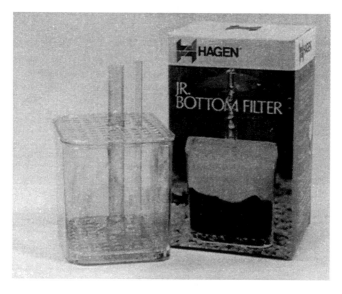

Figure 9. An inexpensive box filter.

Activated Carbon

Functions

Granular activated carbon (not to be confused with ordinary charcoal) removes a variety of undesirable substances from aquarium water. These substances include metals, antibiotics and other medications, organic plant and animal wastes, nonbiodegradable materials that turn the water yellow, and many foreign chemicals that inadvertently get into the water. There is some evidence that activated carbon stimulates the growth of algae by removing growth-inhibiting metabolites from the water.[2]

Recommendations

Activated carbons that are made from bituminous coal, peat, and palm kernel shell charcoal are superior to those made from coconut shell and other materials.[3] Use only products that are packaged in glass or plastic containers, and keep the containers sealed tightly, because activated carbon can pick up harmful pollutants from the air (Fig. 10).

Figure 10. Activated carbon should be stored in air-tight glass or plastic containers to prevent the adsorption of pollutants from the air.

Polyester Filter Fiber

Functions

Polyester filter fiber is placed above and below the activated carbon in the box filter to keep small particles of carbon from entering the water and to filter out debris.

Recommendations

Polyester filter fiber is sold at aquarium stores (Fig. 11). The same material may be purchased less expensively as "polyester batting" at dry goods stores (it is used for stuffing quilts and pillows).

Airline Tubing

Functions

Flexible and rigid airline tubing are used to connect the air pump with other components of the aeration/filtration system.

Recommendation

Use standard tubing of 3/16-inch (4.8-millimeter) diameter.

Gang Valves

Functions

Gang valves (Fig. 12) are placed between the air pump and the air diffusers or box filter to regulate the flow of air and to direct air where it is needed.

Recommendations

Brass or plastic gang valves are suitable for marine aquariums, although brass valves can corrode and "freeze up" if exposed to ex-

Figure 11. Polyester filter fiber.

cessive humidity or salt spray. Each air pump should have its own set of gang valves. One outlet on each set of gang valves is needed to channel air to each diffuser and to the box filter, so be sure to buy a set with enough outlets for your particular needs. It is a good idea to buy a set of valves with one or more extra outlets; these can be used, without disturbing the normal flow of air to the aquarium, to bleed off excess air, or for aeration purposes outside the aquarium.

Figure 12. A set of gang valves is needed to direct the stream of air from the air pump to the air diffusers and box filter.

THE SEAWATER MEDIUM

Artificial Sea Salts

Artificial sea salts, when mixed with tap water, produce a medium, *artificial seawater,* that is capable of supporting captive marine fishes. Artificial seawater may be considered superior to natural seawater in five respects.

1. Artificial sea salts are less expensive to ship and are easier to store than natural seawater, because they are dry and compact.

2. Artificial seawater can be used immediately after it is prepared; unlike natural seawater, it does not require filtration or storage in the dark before use.

3. Artificial seawater does not contain the harmful microorganisms or pollutants that are sometimes present in natural seawater.

4. Because artificial seawater can be prepared anywhere that a supply of clean, fresh water is available, it is possible to keep marine fishes at a great distance from the ocean.

5. The artificial sea salts produced by a given manufacturer usually have a constant composition. This means that the fishes will not be subjected to fluctuations in water quality that may result

when natural seawater, particularly that collected from near-shore areas, is used.

Recommendations

About two dozen brands of artificial sea salts are available for use by aquarists. Although one salt formulation might appear to be much the same as the next, there is considerable variation among the compositions of salts by different manufacturers. The composition of most formulations is proprietary and therefore is not given on package labels; moreover, there are no regulations governing purity. The fact that certain aquarium stores sell certain brands of salts is no guarantee of the quality of the products; more often than not, it merely reflects effective marketing and competitive pricing.

The vast majority of artificial sea salts are, however, suitable for general aquarium application; if they were not, their manufacturers would rapidly be out of business. Still, there are a few ways that an aquarist can judge various salt formulations *before* using them in an aquarium. First, artificial sea salts need not be carbon copies of natural sea salts. As noted in Chapter 1, all elements found in natural seawater are not essential to fishes; moreover, certain components of natural seawater build up naturally in aquariums, so they are not needed in the original salt formulation. Second, the texture of artificial sea salts should be considered. Artificial sea salts are blends of individual salts. Because the concentration of one salt in the final mixture may be one million times greater than that of another, uniform blending is essential to ensure that all salts are distributed equally. Well-blended sea salts contain salt crystals and grains of uniform sizes that will not settle out after packaging and shipping. Poorly blended sea salts produce artificial seawater of inconstant composition. Third, the purity of artificial sea salts sometimes can be judged by their color. Pure salts are clean looking and white. Colored particles may indicate contamination. Manufacturers' claims that their formulations are made with reagent-grade, ultra-pure chemicals should be taken "with a grain of salt." Products composed strictly of highly pure salts would be prohibitively expensive (at least 20 dollars per pound), and their production is both unnecessary and unlikely. Finally, packaged sea salts should have a low moisture content — they should be dry and free-flowing. Mixtures with the consistency of wet snow are difficult to dissolve, and they usually produce artificial seawater with an initial pH value that is too high.

The ultimate criteria in choosing an artificial sea salt formulation are the reputation of its manufacturer and its persistence on the market for many years. Do not be misled by grandiose advertising claims for a new product; instead, choose a product that has a long history of successful use. One such sea salt formulation is shown in Figure 13. The composition of a typical artificial seawater medium is given in Table 5.

Figure 13. Artificial sea salts. Photo courtesy of Aquarium Systems, Inc.

Trace-element Additives

Functions

Trace-element solutions and powders supposedly provide captive

Table 5

COMPOSITION OF SALTS IN A TYPICAL ARTIFICIAL SEAWATER MEDIUM

Salt	Amount (grams per liter)
Sodium chloride	24.087
Magnesium chloride	5.111
Sodium sulfate	4.019
Calcium chloride	1.131
Potassium chloride	0.681
Sodium bicarbonate	0.197
Potassium bromide	0.098
Boric acid	0.027
Strontium chloride	0.025
Sodium fluoride	0.003

From Lyman and Fleming (1940)

fishes with essential minerals that either are not present in or become depleted from artificial seawater.

Recommendations

If packages of artificial sea salts contain separate containers of trace elements, use them. If they do not, there is no need for concern. Because the benefits to marine fishes of trace elements *in the water* have not been established (see Chapter 1) the value of such additives is doubtful. Simple salt mixtures without trace elements seem to support fishes as well as complex mixtures with trace elements. Certain trace elements may promote the growth of algae, but some of them become complexed by organic substances in the water, and others are removed by activated carbon.

Chlorine Neutralizer

Functions

Chlorine neutralizer, sodium thiosulfate (Fig. 14) removes the residual free chlorine from treated tap water. Water to which chlorine neutralizer has been added does not require "aging" before use.

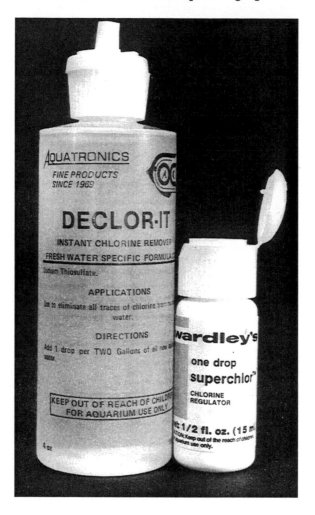

Figure 14. Liquid chlorine neutralizers remove the residual free chlorine from chlorinated tap water.

Recommendations

According to a recent study, commercial products such as Jiffy DeClor (Wasco Products, Inc.), Declor-It (Aquatronics), Chlorine Remover (Fritz Chemical Co.), Aqua-D-Chlor® (Hartz Mountain),

Superchlor (Wardley Products Co.), and Superchlor Plus (Wardley Products Co.) are effective chlorine removers.[5] These products should be used according to the manufacturer's instructions.

Baking Soda

Functions

Baking soda (sodium bicarbonate) is added to aquarium water as needed to maintain the proper alkaline pH value.

Recommendations

Household baking soda, sold in supermarkets and drugstores, is suitable for use in marine aquariums. Sodium carbonate (washing soda) tablets and solutions, which are sold in aquarium stores as "pH adjuster," are not recommended, because they may raise the pH rapidly to exceedingly high values (see Chapter 3, Fig. 21).

EQUIPMENT FOR WATER TESTING

The only water quality characteristics that need to be measured regularly are salt concentration, temperature, and pH. These are measured, respectively, with a hydrometer, a thermometer, and a pH test kit, which are described below.

Hydrometer

Functions

A hydrometer is an instrument used to measure the concentration of salts in seawater. A description of a hydrometer and its proper use is given in Chapter 6.

Recommendations

The most accurate hydrometers are calibrated to national (NBS) standards and can be purchased only from scientific supply companies. Of those available from aquarium suppliers, large ones with expanded scales are the most useful and easiest to read (Fig. 15). Combination hydrometer-thermometers are not recommended, because the thermometers are usually inaccurate.

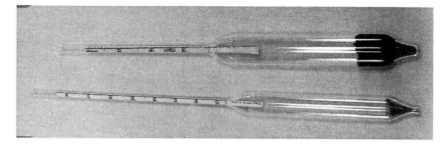

Figure 15. A hydrometer with an expanded scale (bottom) is more accurate and easier to read.

Thermometer

Functions

A thermometer is used to measure the temperature of the water.

Recommendations

The most accurate thermometers have silver-colored mercury indicators and can be purchased from stores that sell photographic supplies and equipment. Thermometers with red alcohol indicators are inaccurate. A dial-type photographic thermometer and a glass thermometer with a mercury indicator are illustrated in Figure 16. Metal thermometers should not be left in aquariums for long periods of time, because they may corrode or release poisonous substances into the water.

pH Test Kit

Functions

A pH test kit is used to determine if the water is appropriately

Figure 16. A dial-type photographic thermometer (top) and a glass thermometer with a mercury indicator (bottom).

alkaline. Testing for pH is discussed in Chapter 6.

Recommendations

According to a study on the accuracy of commercial pH test kits, most of the kits sold at aquarium stores do not perform well in seawater.[6] Kits that employ phenol red indicator solution are not recommended, because more sensitive and reliable indicators are now available. In tests conducted at the Institute for Aquarium Studies, the kits manufactured by Aquarium Systems, Kordon, and New Technology performed accurately. The former two kits were found superior, however, because they employ dry chemicals instead of liquid reagents, and therefore have very long lives.

AQUARIUM DECORATIONS

Aquarium decorations should be selected with one thought in mind: the security of a shelter is essential to the well-being of most tropical marine fishes. When frightened or threatened, reef fishes retreat to the safety of holes and crevices within the coral reef. The most functional aquarium decorations, therefore, contain the most available hiding places.

Long, flat rocks positioned vertically, thickly branched corals, and dense groupings of plastic plants are ideal aquarium decorations. Large shells are also suitable, but care should be taken to ensure that no remnants of the dead mollusks are left inside. (Saw off the pointed ends of conch shells, to clean them out and to allow water to circulate through them.) When decorating an aquarium, *think big*. Small, round rocks and corals placed sparsely on the bottom may look attractive to some observers, but they offer no shelter to fishes. Several small pieces can, however, be attached together with aquarium sealant to create interesting and functional decorations.

MISCELLANEOUS EQUIPMENT

The following items, shown in Figure 17, are useful for a variety of purposes.

Plastic Buckets

New plastic buckets, marked with graduations in gallons or liters, are needed for mixing and transferring the seawater. They also may be used for acclimating new fishes to the water in a different aquarium. Metal buckets and old plastic buckets that have held detergents or other toxic substances are not suitable for aquarium use. To prevent confusion, it is helpful to write FOR AQUARIUM USE ONLY with a permanent marking pen on new buckets and other utensils.

Plastic Baster and Eyedropper

A plastic gravy baster and a glass or plastic eyedropper are useful for removing debris from the tank bottom and for dispensing food to the fishes.

Sponges

New, clean cellulose sponges are needed to clean the aquarium

Figure 17. Some utensils that are useful for cleaning and maintaining an aquarium include sponges, nets, a plastic bucket, measuring spoons, a gravy baster, a plastic siphon hose, silicon sealant, and a barbecue fork.

glass. An aquarium sponge on a long wooden handle is especially useful for cleaning the glass in deep tanks.

Barbecue Fork

A long-handled barbecue fork is a good tool for stirring the filter bed in order to keep the filtrant grains from becoming packed together by debris (see Chapter 6).

Aquarium Nets

Nets are useful for removing unwanted matter from the water and for rinsing certain foods. Nets never should be used to remove live fishes and soft-bodied invertebrates from the water (see Chapters 1, 10, 11).

Plastic Siphon Hose

A plastic siphon hose is used to drain or fill an aquarium. A 5-foot (1.5-meter) length of ½-inch (13-millimeter) diameter, noncollapsible polyethylene tubing works well.

Styrofoam® Chest or Ice Bucket

Styrofoam is an excellent insulator against temperature changes. Ice chests and ice buckets are useful for transporting marine fishes, especially in hot or cold weather.

Aquarium Sealant

Colorless, nontoxic sealants of silicon rubber, such as those manufactured by General Electric and Dow/Corning, are useful for fixing leaks in aquarium tanks and for various other applications that require a flexible, waterproof bond.

AUXILIARY AQUARIUM

It is often useful to have an extra aquarium (10 to 15 gallons or 38 to 57 liters in capacity) available for isolating new fishes or treating diseased fishes with medications. This aquarium should be equipped, set up, and maintained in the same way as the main aquarium. The cost of an auxiliary aquarium can be minimized by using a plain plastic cover and small fluorescent strip light (sold at hardware stores) in place of an aquarium hood, and by using decor such as rocks and flowerpots, instead of expensive corals.

Chapter 3

THE AQUARIUM AS A CONTROLLED ENVIRONMENT

If a few fish were confined in a vessel of water, and the water remained unchanged, they would soon droop and die.

George B. Sowerby
Popular History of the Aquarium, 1857

. . . take a piece of whalebone, or a porcupine quill, dip it into the water a reasonable depth, and move it backwards and forwards quickly. This causes the entanglement of air at the surface, which serves to oxygenate the water and destroy impurities.

Shirley Hibberd
The Book of the Marine Aquarium, 1860

THE ability of a marine aquarium to support life depends on the careful control of environmental conditions. Like other animals, marine fishes consume food and oxygen and excrete carbon dioxide and other chemical wastes. The volume of water in an aquarium is small, and if no controls were exercised, it would rapidly become polluted and unfit for fishes. In a well-managed aquarium, high concentrations of carbon dioxide and poisonous wastes rarely are problems. This chapter explains the basic mechanisms of environmental control in marine aquariums, and provides information that will help you when you set up your aquarium and introduce the first fishes into it.

CONTROLS BY THE FILTRATION/AERATION SYSTEM

The filtration/aeration system moves water through the aquarium in a characteristic pattern. As illustrated in Figure 18, compressed air from the pump is broken into small bubbles by the air diffuser. These bubbles combine with water to form a mixture that is lighter than water alone. It rises up the airlift column and spills out at the surface. As the air-water mixture rises in the column, water from beneath the filter plate enters the lift tube, mixes with the bubbles, and moves upward. Meanwhile, water moves downward through the gravel, through the holes in the filter plate, and to the space beneath the filter plate, where the same process is repeated. In this way, aquarium water is circulated continuously, from top to bottom, and always through the filtrant.

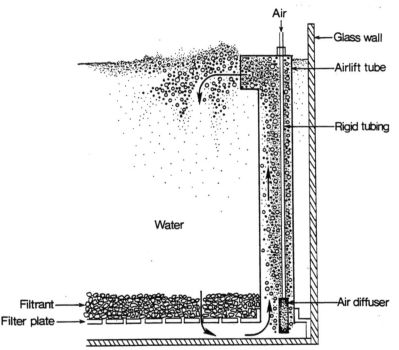

Figure 18. The pattern of water circulation in an aquarium with an undergravel filter. See text for explanation.

The water circulation pattern created by an air-powered undergravel filter has five effects that help keep the aquarium fit for life. They are aeration, particle removal, bacteriological filtration, temperature regulation, and pH control.

Aeration

At the points of contact between air bubbles and water, and between the water surface and the air above it, oxygen enters the aquarium water and carbon dioxide leaves it. The greater the volume of air that enters the water, the more rapidly oxygen and carbon dioxide are exchanged.

The accumulation of high concentrations of carbon dioxide in aquarium water is undesirable for two reasons. First, carbon dioxide combines with water to form carbonic acid, which tends to make the pH less alkaline. Second, high concentrations of dissolved carbon dioxide make it difficult for some fishes to excrete their own carbon dioxide waste; carbon dioxide can be eliminated from their blood (at their gills) only when the concentration in their blood is *higher* than the concentration in the water. If the concentration of carbon dioxide in the water is higher, the fishes no longer can excrete it, causing their blood to become acidic and decreasing the ability of their blood to hold oxygen. Eventually, the fish may suffocate.

Recently, "power" undergravel filters have come into vogue with marine aquarists. These devices employ a mechanical water pump, rather than an air pump, to circulate the water. Mechanical water pumps are expensive and are not essential to the successful maintenance of an aquarium. Although I do not recommend them, their popularity merits a few words of caution regarding the aeration of aquariums in which they are used.

It is a common observation by hobbyists and aquarium retailers that aquariums equipped with mechanical water pumps (either the type that attaches to the top of an airlift column, or cannister types) without supplemental aeration are characterized by chronically low pH. Although the cause of this problem has not been determined experimentally, the following explanation seems reasonable.

Most aquarium covers fit closely. The exchange of air under the cover with air outside the aquarium occurs only through small spaces around the edges of the cover. An air pump continuously injects fresh air into the aquarium. When the bubbles break at the surface, they force air out from under the cover, and prevent carbon dioxide from accumulating in the air over the water surface. Since mechanical water pumps do *not* force air into an aquarium (they merely move the water from one place to another), the air under the cover is comparatively stagnant. Once it becomes filled with carbon dioxide, no more of the gas can leave the water. As a result, the concentration of carbon dioxide in the water increases and the pH falls.

Two steps can be taken to prevent the aeration problem inherent with the use of mechanical water pumps. First, the tank can be left partially uncovered. Second, air can be introduced into the aquarium through a diffuser connected to a small air pump. Either measure will prevent the accumulation of stagnant air, laden with carbon dioxide, over the water surface, and will alleviate the problems of low pH and high concentrations of dissolved carbon dioxide in the water.

Particle Removal

As water flows through the filter bed, solid wastes, bits of uneaten food, and other small particles become trapped among the filtrant grains. This action keeps the water clear.

Bacteriological Filtration

In nature all elements are recycled by plants and animals; that is, the elements contained in a whole organism or in its metabolic wastes are used as food by other organisms. The use of manure as fertilizer is one example of such recycling; animal wastes are used for growth by plants, the plants are eaten by other animals, and so on.

The cycling of the element *nitrogen* is of particular importance to aquarists, because certain compounds that contain nitrogen are highly toxic to fishes. Proteins, which are major constituents of the foods of fishes, contain nitrogen, and the waste products of fishes are organic and inorganic substances that also contain nitrogen.

The *nitrogen cycle* in the ocean is illustrated in Figure 19. Marine animals excrete nitrogen as organic wastes or as inorganic *ammonia*. Bacteria in the water decompose the organic wastes to ammonia, and ammonia either is used for growth by algae or is converted by other bacteria to *nitrite* and *nitrate*. These substances also are taken up by algae; alternatively, they may be converted by bacteria into even simpler substances, such as nitrogen gas. As noted in Chapter 1, microscopic algae are consumed by microscopic animals, and microscopic animals are eaten by larger animals that form links in food chains and webs. Thus, the nitrogen in the ocean is passed from

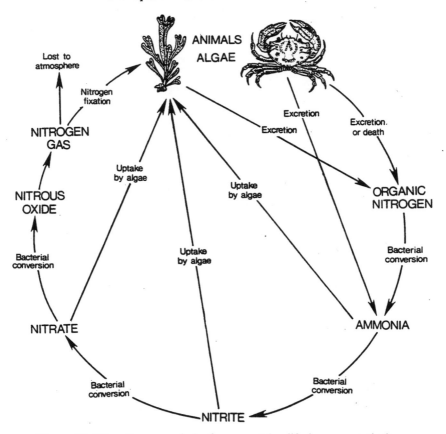

Figure 19. The nitrogen cycle in the ocean (simplified representation).

algae to animals and back again, and no single nitrogenous substance, whether organic or inorganic, ever reaches very high concentrations in the water.

The fate of nitrogen is somewhat different in an aquarium than it is in the ocean. Nitrogen enters an aquarium in the food that is fed to the fishes. Most of the food is eaten and the rest falls to the bottom. Fishes excrete ammonia at their gills, and uneaten food and organic fish wastes are broken down by bacteria to form ammonia. The ammonia is converted to nitrite and then to nitrate by bacteria, and here ends the similarity between ocean and aquarium. Typical aquariums do not contain large numbers of microscopic algae or seaweeds that use ammonia, nitrite, and nitrate for growth, and very little nitrate, if any, is converted by bacteria to nitrogen gas. Consequently, more nitrogen enters an aquarium than can be removed; it is only partially recycled, and most of it ends up as nitrate dissolved in the water. The changes in the forms of nitrogen in an aquarium therefore occur in a sequence rather than a cycle, which reaches a "dead end" with nitrate.[1] The *nitrogen sequence* in an aquarium is illustrated in Figure 20.

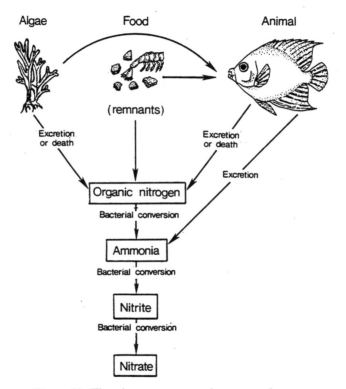

Figure 20. The nitrogen sequence in an aquarium.

The conversion of ammonia to nitrite and nitrate by bacteria in an aquarium is called *bacteriological filtration*. Most of the bacteria that perform these conversions are attached to the surfaces of the filtrant grains. The role of these filter bacteria in maintaining a healthy environment for captive fishes cannot be overestimated, because ammonia is extremely poisonous to fishes. In the absence of filter bacteria, the ammonia excreted by captive fishes would accumulate rapidly to lethal concentrations. The establishment of bacteriological filtration in a new aquarium is discussed in detail in Chapter 5.

The pattern of water circulation created by the filtration/aeration system is critical to maintaining large populations of filter bacteria. Because most of these bacteria are attached to the filtrant, the flow of water *through* the filtrant ensures that dissolved ammonia, nitrite, and organics will reach them efficiently, along with dissolved oxygen that they require to convert ammonia to nitrate.

pH Regulation

The subject of pH is difficult to discuss, because its effects on the marine fishes are poorly understood and because, unlike dissolved oxygen, salt, or ammonia, it is not a chemical substance that can be added to or removed from aquarium water.

The term *pH* refers to a scale of numbers that corresponds mathematically to "the negative logarithm of the concentration of hydrogen ions in a solution." The concentration of hydrogen ions in a solution determines whether the solution is acidic or basic; the higher the concentration of hydrogen ions, the greater the acidity.

The pH scale ranges from 0 to 14. A value of 7 is neutral (neither acidic nor alkaline), values below 7 are increasingly acidic, and those above 7 are increasingly alkaline or basic. The pH values of some familiar substances are given in Figure 21. The pH of a solution is also a measure of its relative acidity; thus, 8.0 and 8.5 are both alkaline values, but 8.0 is more acidic than 8.5, and 8.5 is more alkaline than 8.0.

It is more convenient to discuss acidity and alkalinity in terms of pH than in terms of the actual concentration of hydrogen ions to which the pH value corresponds. It is simpler, for example, to say that a solution has a pH of 7.9 than to say that it has a hydrogen ion concentration of 0.0000000126 moles per liter.

Because the pH scale is based on logarithms (complex mathematical functions), its numbers are not related by simple arithmetic. A pH value of 8, for example, is *not* twice as alkaline (or half as acidic) as pH 4. Instead, a change of one pH unit represents a ten-fold change in acidity or alkalinity. Thus, pH 7 is ten times more acidic than pH 8, and pH 6 is ten times more acidic than pH 7 and 100 times more acidic than pH 8. The number of times the acidity or alkalinity of a solution increases or decreases with changes from 0.1

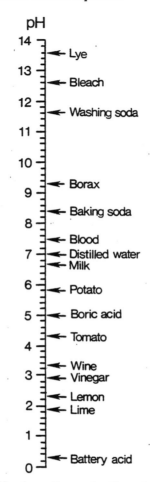

Figure 21. The pH values of some familiar substances.

to 1.0 pH unit is given in Table 6. One can see that a pH decrease of only 0.3 pH unit (from pH 8.3 to pH 8.0, for example) indicates that the acidity of the solution has doubled. From this, it should be clear that what appear to be minor changes in pH are actually very large changes in acidity or alkalinity.

The pH of tropical ocean water averages about 8.2 and is mildly alkaline. This value is remarkably stable, and is maintained by many interacting chemical and biological factors. The pH of aquarium water can be highly variable. The life processes of aquarium animals and filter bacteria release acidifying substances

Table 6

CHANGES IN ACIDITY OR ALKALINITY THAT RESULT FROM pH CHANGES OF 0.1 To 1.0 pH UNITS[a]

Magnitude of change (in pH units)	Number of times acidity or alkalinity increases or decreases	Percent change
0.1	1.26	26%
0.2	1.58	58%
0.3	2.00	100%
0.4	2.51	151%
0.5	3.16	216%
0.6	3.98	298%
0.7	5.01	401%
0.8	6.31	531%
0.9	7.90	690%
1.0	10.00	900%

[a] An *increase* in pH *increases* the alkalinity and *decreases* the acidity. A *decrease* in pH *decreases* the alkalinity and *increases* the acidity.

into the water, causing a gradual decline in pH.

Although the effects on marine fishes of a gradual decline in pH have not been studied experimentally, low pH generally is thought to be undesirable. When the pH of seawater falls, the concentration of dissolved carbon dioxide increases, making it difficult for fishes to excrete their own carbon dioxide wastes and possibly causing short-term stress. Also, it has been reported in a few studies that the cultivation of some invertebrates at pH values below 8.0 causes inhibition of growth[2] and increases susceptibility to poisoning by nitrate.[3] In a study conducted in South Africa, it was found that larval marine fishes were not harmed by acidification of the water until pH values were lowered below 6.0.[4] This implies that it may not be necessary to keep the pH of aquarium water at values approximating those in the ocean, but unfortunately, the period of exposure to low pH was only 24 hours, and the effects of longer exposures were not determined.

Although there is no conclusive evidence that exposure to pH values lower than those normally encountered in the ocean is harmful to fishes, there also is no conclusive evidence to the contrary. Until questions about the effects of pH and changes in pH on fishes are answered through experimentation, one can only assume that the safest pH value for aquarium water is approximately 8.2, the value of the water in which marine fishes evolved and to which they presumably are best adapted for survival.

Natural seawater and some artificial seawater formulations contain dissolved substances called *carbonates* that help maintain a stable pH through a process called *buffering*. Carbonates are destroyed by the acids that are excreted by fishes and filter bacteria; thus, although pH changes occur more gradually in carbonate-rich waters than in waters without carbonates, even aquarium seawater eventually loses its ability to regulate pH.

As noted in Chapter 2, the filtrants recommended for use in marine aquariums are composed chiefly of carbonates. It is widely thought that the use of such filtrants, alone, will keep the pH of aquarium water at 8.2, because the carbonates can dissolve and neutralize the acids. Of all available carbonate filtrants, "dolomite" gravels usually are described as the most effective.[5]

In a test conducted at the Institute for Aquarium Studies, we found that previous assumptions about buffering by carbonate gravels and other filtrants were not true.[6] We set up identical aquariums, and stocked them with the same weights of fishes. The filtrants we tested were crushed oyster shell, limestone gravel (Florida Crushed Coral), and dolomitic limestone gravel (dolomite). A noncarbonate filtrant, silica gravel, was used as the control. As shown in Figure 22, the decreases in pH in all the aquariums were similar until values below approximately 7.8 were reached. At this value, differences in the performances of the various filtrants became apparent. In tanks containing crushed oyster shell, pH values never fell below 7.8 to 7.9. In tanks with limestone filtrant, pH values stabilized at 7.7 to 7.8. The pH floor maintained by dolomite was only 7.4 to 7.5. In aquariums containing silica gravel, the pH never stabilized, and when the experiment was terminated after 90 days, values below 6.0 had been reached.

This study demonstrated for the first time that no commonly used carbonate filtrant will maintain the pH of aquarium seawater at

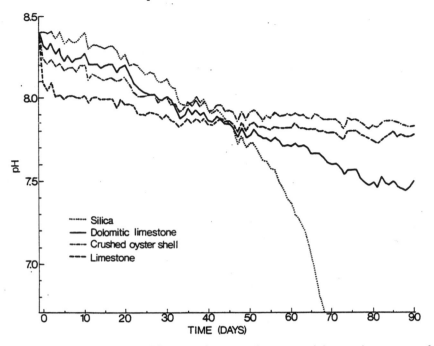

Figure 22. Changes in pH in marine aquariums containing various types of filtrants. See text for explanation. From C.E. Bower et al. 1981. Aquaculture, 23: 221-217. Courtesy of Elsevier Scientific Publishing Co.

values above 8.0. We concluded, however, that carbonate filtrants, regardless of their types, always should be used in marine aquariums for two reasons. First, they probably prevent the pH from ever decreasing to values below neutrality. Second, they provide a built-in safety factor to prevent sudden decreases in pH. Since silica gravel afforded no protection against acidification, we recommended that it not be used as a filtrant in seawater aquariums. Although pH values were not compared in aquariums with and without under-gravel filters, it is likely that a flow of water through the filtrant is essential to the regulation of pH and to the prevention of extreme acidification of aquarium water.

Temperature Regulation

Warm water has a tendency to rise, while cold water sinks. For this reason, the water at the surface of a pond or any other stagnant body of water is usually warmer than the underlying water. The continuous circulation of water by the filtration/aeration system ensures uniform temperature throughout the aquarium, and prevents the formation of "hot spots" near the heater or at the surface.

CONTROLS BY THE AQUARIST

The undergravel filtration/aeration system is a simple and effective means for controlling many environmental conditions in a marine aquarium. There are, however, a few environmental variables that cannot be controlled in part or at all by the filter. These variables — salt concentration, alkaline pH, and the build-up of wastes other than ammonia and nitrite — must be kept in check by the aquarist.

Salt Concentration

The average salt concentration or salinity of the ocean is about 34 to 35 parts per thousand. As discussed in Chapter 1, a fish living in water that is saltier than its own internal fluids is presented with problems concerning its salt and water balance. The saltier the water, the more energy the fish must expend to prevent dehydration.

Water evaporates continuously from all aquariums, especially well-aerated ones, and the result of evaporation is an increase in the salinity of the water. In a covered aquarium, one can expect the salinity to increase by about 2 parts per thousand (0.0005 to 0.001 specific gravity unit) each week; in an uncovered tank, the change is much greater. Most fishes can adapt to a fairly wide range of salinity values, provided that the changes in salinity occur gradually. Still, it is advisable to allow as little variation as possible, since even slight changes in the salt concentration may be stressful to fishes.

Because the salinity of aquarium seawater is always on the rise, it is a good practice to start with and to maintain a salt concentration that is lower than normal, about 30 to 32 parts per thousand. (This is equal to a specific gravity of about 1.020 to 1.021 at temperatures of 73 to 79°F or 23 to 26°C.) When the salinity is maintained at a lower value, the burden on a marine fish of water conservation and salt elimination is lessened, and exposure to values higher than those normally occurring in the ocean is prevented. Procedures for determining and maintaining the salt concentration of aquarium seawater are given in Chapter 6.

pH Control

The recommended pH value for aquarium seawater is 8.2, with an acceptable range of 8.1 to 8.3. As pointed out earlier in this chapter, the use of carbonate filtrants will keep the seawater alkaline (above pH 7) but will not prevent the pH from declining to values below 8.1. The safest and most simple way to maintain the proper alkaline pH in aquarium seawater is to add common baking soda (sodium bicarbonate) to it on a regular basis. As shown in Figure 21, a baking soda solution in fresh water has a pH value of about 8.2. Procedures for measuring the pH of aquarium seawater and adjusting it with baking soda are given in Chapter 6.

Removal of Nonbiodegradable Wastes

Solid animal wastes, dead organisms, and uneaten food never actually are removed from an aquarium by filtration devices. They simply are removed from sight by entrapment in the filtrant, or they are decomposed by bacteria to form soluble, invisible substances and particulate debris. Along with nitrate, the concentrations of other substances, such as sulfate, phosphate, and dissolved organic matter, increase to abnormally high values in aquarium seawater. The concentrations of some major salts and trace elements also are known to increase. All of the substances mentioned above are *nonbiodegradable* — they are not subject to further breakdown by microorganisms.

The effects of the accumulation of nonbiodegradable substances on captive marine fishes have received little study. Low concentrations of nitrate appear to be toxic to some invertebrates,[3,7,8] but fishes do not seem to be harmed by it until exceedingly high concentrations — in the order of 1,000 times higher than those found in the ocean — are reached.[9] It was reported recently that juvenile clownfish (*Amphiprion ocellaris*) maintained in water containing the high concentrations of nitrate that are typical of long-established aquariums (approximately 375 to 525 parts per million) exhibited poor coloration and restricted growth, though their survival was not affected.[10]

The concentrations of dissolved phosphate and sulfate that accumulate in aquarium water do not appear to be toxic to marine life,[11] but very little research has been conducted on this subject.

Dissolved organic substances, which are produced from the decomposition of food and animal wastes, also accumulate in aquarium water. Some of these substances give the water an unpleasant yellowish color. Almost nothing is known about the toxicity of dissolved organic compounds to marine animals, in part because they are too numerous to isolate and identify, and partly because it is difficult to separate their effects from those of the other accumulated substances. There is some evidence that dissolved organic matter in aquarium water may inhibit growth,[11] and it is commonly observed that captive marine fishes become more active and have better appetites after organic substances have been removed from the water.

Although phosphate, sulfate, nitrate, and dissolved organic matter do not appear to be particularly hazardous to the health of marine fishes in the short run, any long-term sublethal effects that they may exert have not yet been measured. As is the case with low pH, however, until these substances are proven unequivocally to be harmless, it makes good sense to control their accumulation, if only because they represent conditions to which marine fishes are never exposed in nature.

Filtration with granular activated carbon is the easiest and most effective way to remove dissolved organic substances from water, and it is particularly useful for keeping the water sparkling and colorless. The types of organic substances that are removed by activated carbon were listed in Chapter 2, and the proper use and maintenance of an activated carbon filter are described in Chapters 4 and 6.

The concentrations of nitrate, phosphate, sulfate, and accumulted salts in seawater are not reduced by filtration with activated carbon. In fact, there is no known physical or chemical method of selectively removing these substances from seawater. The most reliable way to restore the composition of aquarium seawater to its near-original quality is to discard some of the water regularly and to replace it with new artificial seawater. This procedure is described in detail in Chapter 6, and the problems it corrects are illustrated in Figure 23.

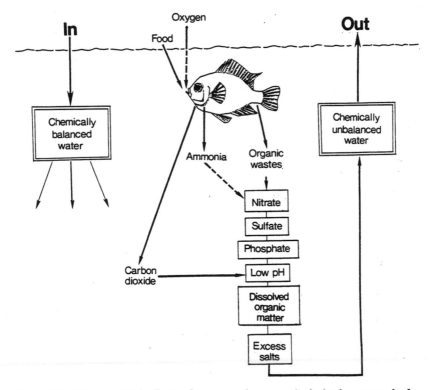

Figure 23. The beneficial effects of water replacement include the removal of accumulated inorganic and organic substances and the restoration of a properly alkaline pH.

Chapter 4

SETTING UP A NEW AQUARIUM

Before filling the tank with sea water, it becomes necessary to select the position which it is to occupy . . . . Now, there are generally several positions at the disposal of the aquarium-keeper, and in nine cases out of ten he selects the very worst that can possibly be found.

Reginald A.R. Bennett
Marine Aquaria, 1889

A bee-glass, with a bit of sponge thrust into the orifice, is a convenient form of filter, but if such a thing is not at hand, take an *old* flower-pot, and wash it quite clean, thrust a piece of sponge through the hole in the bottom, and throw into it a handful of powdered charcoal.

Shirley Hibberd
The Book of the Marine Aquarium, 1860

ELECTRICAL SAFETY

ELECTRICAL current always present a hazard near water and is especially dangerous near salt water. To ensure electrical safety around an aquarium, certain precautions should be taken. Always use electrical outlets located above or several feet away from the aquarium. Any electrical connections that may be exposed to salt spray from the aquarium should be coated with a thick layer of silicon sealant, to prevent them from getting wet and shorting out. Always disconnect the aquarium light and heater before putting your hands in the water.

PROCEDURES FOR SETTING UP

Resealing the Tank Rim

The plastic rim or border around the upper edges of standard all-glass aquariums often is not sealed very tightly to the glass. As a result, the spray from bursting bubbles can creep between the rim and the glass, and salt water will run down the outer glass. This water forms pools around the lower rim of the tank that are often mistaken as signs of leaking; it dries and leaves behind unsightly crusts of salt. This problem can be prevented easily, before the aquarium is set up, by using the following procedure for resealing the tank rim.

1. Gently pry the top tank rim loose from the glass, and remove it. It may come off as a single rectangular unit or as four separate pieces, depending on the brand and model of the aquarium.

2. Using a single-edged razor blade, carefully remove all the old sealant from the upper glass surfaces. Scrape any remaining sealant from the groove inside the plastic rim with the tip of a screwdriver or any other suitable tool.

3. Wipe the glass edges of the tank and the inside of the plastic rim with acetone or isopropyl (rubbing) alcohol to remove grease and oils. Silicon sealant will not adhere properly to dirty or oily surfaces.

4. Run a thick, continuous line of sealant along the top edge of the aquarium glass. Set the plastic rim in place on top of the tank, and press it down firmly to spread the sealant and create a tight seal.

5. Allow the sealant to dry for at least 24 hours before adding water to the the aquarium. You can tell that certain sealants have dried when they no longer have a sour, vinegarlike odor.

Cleaning the Aquarium

Rinse the aquarium and any decorations to be used in it with tap water. Coarse (kosher) salt or baking soda may be used for scouring, and sponging with a mild bleach solution will remove most stains. If soap must be used, choose a mild, nondetergent product such as Ivory® soap. Always remember to rinse the aquarium thoroughly after cleaning with salt or soap.

Checking for Leaks

Place the aquarium on a sturdy, level surface, such as a countertop beside a sink. Try to rock the aquarium to be sure that all four corners are simultaneously in contact with the supporting surface. Add tap water to about one-third the aquarium's capacity. If no leaking is apparent after several minutes, fill the aquarium to the top, and examine it again for leaks. If no leaks appear, drain the aquarium with a bucket or by siphoning. The use of a siphon hose is described in Chapter 6. *Caution: never lift or try to move an aquarium that contains more than one inch (2.5 centimeters) of water.*

Painting a Background

Many "backgrounds" for small tanks can be purchased at aquarium stores. They usually consist of sheets of patterned metal foils, plastic, or coated papers, or paintings or photographs of undersea scenes, that can be taped to the outer back glass of the tank. In my estimation, commercial backgrounds are unnatural and unattractive; in addition thay are not very practical, because they can be ruined if they get wet or coated with salts.

Every aquarist — even one with no artistic talent — can create a permanent and natural-looking aquarium background. The only materials needed are latex interior housepaint and a paintbrush, roller, or sponge.

The outside back glass is prepared for painting by wiping with alcohol to remove grease or oil. The paint is then applied directly to the glass. Only the *outside* glass should be painted; paint should never be applied to the inside of an aquarium.

Single colors (e.g. dark blue or green) are easy to apply with a brush or roller, and produce simple, uniform backgrounds. Those who wish to be more creative might try the following technique, which employs several colors and shades.

1. Mix a few different paints (e.g. blue, green, yellow, and white) to produce the desired colors, and pour each into one compartment of a cupcake pan.

2. Wet a cellulose sponge with water, and wring it out.

3. Dip a flat edge of the sponge into the paint (do not saturate the sponge), and blot it against newspaper until the excess paint is removed.

4. *Dab* the paint against the glass. The paint will adhere in a pat-

tern duplicating the texture of the sponge. Apply one color at a time. After each color has dried, begin with another, and continue until the entire surface is covered.

5. Keep in mind that painting an aquarium glass is the opposite of painting on walls or paper; the colors that are applied *first* are those that will be seen when viewed through the front glass. Thus, you may wish to begin with lighter shades and then fill in the gaps with darker shades to create an illusion of depth.

Any mistakes you make can be wiped away with a wet cloth and then repainted. In fact, you may wish to experiment on a small section of glass to perfect your technique, and then wash it off and begin again.

Selecting a Suitable Location

The aquarium should be situated away from direct sunlight, drafts, radiators, and heating or cooling ventilators. A heated and air-conditioned room that receives some natural daylight is preferable to an unheated, uncooled room without windows. Controlled room temperature lessens the burden on the aquarium heater and prevents the water from overheating during hot weather. Windows minimize the possibility of stressing or shocking the fishes in the morning and evening, when artificial lights are turned on and off. If possible, the aquarium should not be placed directly opposite a window, because reflections off the glass make viewing the aquarium difficult.

Leveling the Aquarium

Set the aquarium on its stand, and place a carpenter's level on the upper tank rim (Fig. 24). Check the levelness from left to right, and from front to back. The tank must be perfectly level, to prevent unequal weight distribution. Insert wooden shims (small wedges) between the tank stand and the floor — not between the stand and the aquarium — to correct any irregularities.

Installing the Undergravel Filter and Filtrant

1. Follow the manufacturer's instructions for installing the

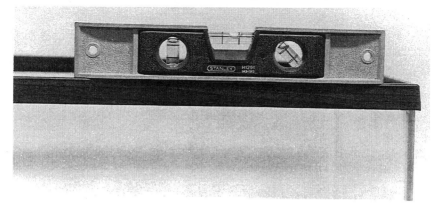

Figure 24. The off-center bubble in the carpenter's level indicates that this aquarium is not perfectly level, and that the right side is higher than the left side.

filter plate and airlift tubes. The lift tubes should open just *below* the water surface. Estimate this height, and trim the tubes if they are too tall. Some lift tubes come equipped with top elbow joints that can be used to direct the flow of water. The use of these joints is optional, as some create turbulence that can decrease the flow of water out of the tubes.

   2. Pour some gravel into a clean plastic bucket, and flush it with tap water until the run-off water is almost perfectly clear (Fig. 25). Wash all the filtrant.

   3. Cover the entire surface of the filter plates with the appropriate depth of washed gravel. The amounts of gravel needed for standard aquariums of various dimensions were given in Table 4 in Chapter 2.

   4. Install rocks, corals, and any other heavy pieces of decor. Weighty decor should always be added before the water, because they may displace large volumes of water.

Filling the Aquarium with Water

   Spread a sheet of heavy plastic (e.g. a new trash bag) over the entire surface of the filtrant. This will prevent the filtrant from becoming displaced when water is added. Pour warm tap water (100°F or 39°C) into the aquarium, until the tank is filled to about 1 inch (2.5 centimeters) below the upper rim.

   Be sure to keep track of how much water (in gallons or liters) you add. Know-

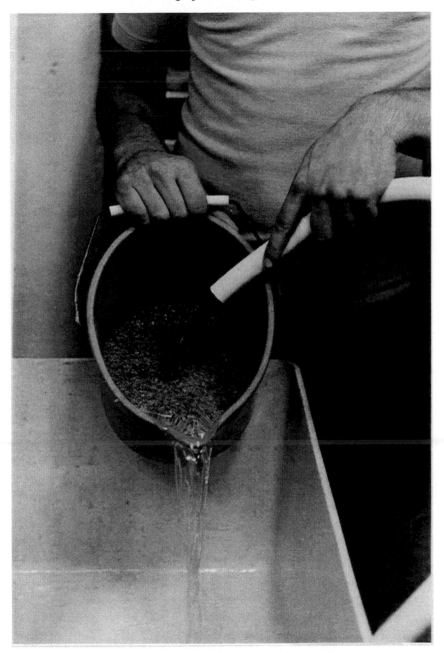

Figure 25. New filtrant should be flushed with tap water until the run-off water is almost completely clear.

ing the exact volume of water in your aquarium will be essential later on, when you have to determine how much artificial sea salt to add, how much extra salt or fresh water is needed to adjust the salt concentration, how much baking soda is needed to adjust the pH, or how much of a particular medication should be added to the tank.

Filtrant and decor displace water, so the actual volume in the aquarium may be 10 to 15 percent less than the aquarium's dry capacity. Remove the plastic sheet from the bottom before continuing.

Connecting the Aeration and Pumping Apparatus

1. Attach the air diffusers to rigid airline tubing with short (½-inch or 13-millimeter) lengths of flexible tubing. Flexible tubing is easier to work with if it is first softened by a dip in hot water.

2. Insert the rigid tubing and diffusers down the airlift tubes, until the diffusers rest on the tank bottom. Cut the top of the rigid tubing to about ¼ inch (6 millimeters) above the tank rim.

3. Using flexible tubing, connect the top of the rigid tubes to the gang valves, and the gang valves to the air pump. Be sure to use enough tubing to allow the gang valves and pump to be placed at a level *above* the water surface. This will prevent water from spontaneously siphoning out of the aquarium and into the pump.

4. Open all the gang valves, including the extra valve (the "bleeder"), and plug the pump into an electrical outlet. Close the bleeder valve slowly, until all the diffusers produce a smooth, strong stream of bubbles. Do not close off the bleeder valve completely; it protects the pump from back pressure in the event that the diffusers become clogged.

5. Adjust the valves supplying air to the diffusers, so that the bubble streams from all the diffusers are equal. Thumb-screw controls on the valves that are difficult to turn should be lubricated with petroleum jelly (Vaseline®). Hissing from the bleeder valve can be stopped by inserting a short length of a pipe cleaner into the hole from which air is escaping.

Adding Chlorine Neutralizer

Following the manufacturer's instructions, add to the water the correct amount of chlorine neutralizer for the volume of water in your aquarium. If the sea salts you use contain chlorine neutralizer (sodium thiosulfate), this step is unnecessary.

Adding Artificial Sea Salts

Pour directly into the water the amount of salts recommended by the manufacturer for the *measured* volume of water in your tank. Stir the water to make the salts dissolve more rapidly. If salts settle out on the gravel surface, stir them up into the water; they will dissolve eventually, with or without stirring. The water will be cloudy until the salts have dissolved completely.

Sea salts in open bags absorb moisture from the air. They become hard-packed, do not dissolve completely, and produce artificial seawater with a pH that is usually too low. Extra salt should therefore not be left exposed to air. Transfer small quantities to glass jars with tight-fitting lids. Large quantitites may be stored in covered plastic "jelly buckets," which can be purchased second-hand and very inexpensively from large bakeries and doughnut shops.

Measuring and Adjusting the Salt Concentration

When the water becomes perfectly clear, indicating that the salts are fully dissolved, the salt concentration should be measured. Directions for using a hydrometer to measure the specific gravity of the water are given in Chapter 6.

If the specific gravity value is too high, the water is too salty and more tap water must be added. Use Tables 9 or 10 in Chapter 6 to determine how much more water is needed. Add the water, allow it to mix, and then redetermine the specific gravity. Some manufacturers package salts to yield a higher salinity than the value recommended in this book. Consequently, the aquarium may be overfilled after the specific gravity has been adjusted. Excess artificial seawater can be removed from the aquarium and stored in a clean, covered plastic bucket until it is needed. Stored artificial seawater should be aerated for several hours before it is added to an aquarium.

If the specific gravity value is too low, it indicates that the water is not salty enough. Use Table 11 (U.S. measure) or Table 12 (metric measure) in Chapter 6 to determine how much more sea salt is needed. Add the salt to the aquarium, and after it has dissolved, remeasure the specific gravity.

Installing and Adjusting the Heater

1. Insert the heater tube into the aquarium water, and attach it to the tank rim according to the manufacturer's instructions. Wait five minutes before continuing, to allow the air in the tube to reach the water temperature.

2. Measure the water temperature with a thermometer. If it is still warmer than desired, wait for it to cool before continuing.

3. If the water temperature is within one degree of the desired value, plug in the heater, and turn the dial on the thermostat control (Fig. 26) until the indicator light in the glass tube goes on. Then turn the dial back a bit, until the indicator light flickers on and off. At this setting, the current water temperature will be maintained.

Figure 26. The thermostatic control dial on the heater can be rotated to turn the heater on or off.

4. If the water temperature is too low, plug in the heater, turn the dial until the indicator light goes on, and then turn it a little further in the same direction so that the light stays on, indicating that the water is being heated. Check the water temperature a few times each hour. If the heater shuts off before the desired temperature is reached, turn the dial to make the light go on again. When the desired temperature is reached, follow the directions given in the last part of step 3, above.

5. For the first week that the aquarium is set up, check the water temperature frequently, to make sure that the thermostat is functioning properly. If the temperature varies by more than a few degrees, return the heater to its place of purchase for replacement.

Installing the Box Filter

1. Remove the cover from the box filter, leaving the base plate and attached plastic tube in place on the bottom. Drop in a few glass marbles or a handful of filtrant. This will weight the box to keep it from floating.

2. Pack a thin layer of filter fiber on top of the weighting material.

3. Pour some activated carbon into a metal strainer or an aquarium net, and rinse it under tap water to remove dust and fine particles. Add the carbon to the box until it forms a layer approximately 2 inches (5 centimeters) deep.

4. Loosely pack another layer of filter fiber over the carbon, and replace the cover. Be sure that no loose strands of filter fiber hang out of the box; fishes can ingest them and choke on them. An assembled box filter is illustrated in Figure 27.

5. Submerge the box filter in the aquarium, and shake it to release any trapped air. Place the box on the bottom of the aquarium, preferably hidden behind a large rock or coral.

6. Connect one end of a length of flexible airline tubing to the air stem on the filter box and the other to a gang valve; then adjust the gang valve to produce an uninterrupted stream of bubbles.

Modifying the Aquarium Cover

Standard aquarium canopies are constructed to lie flat across the

Figure 27. An assembled box filter containing gravel for weight (bottom) and activated carbon (center), sandwiched between two layers of polyester filter fiber.

top of the tank rim. Saltwater spray collects on the inside of the cover, runs to the edges, and drips down the outside glass, creating puddles of water and crusts of dried salt. In addition, many aquarium covers do not contain holes to permit the entry of the airline tubing and the heater. Modifications of the cover to correct these deficiencies are described below.

Trimming the Cover to Prevent Dripping

1. Remove the fluorescent light fixture from the aquarium

canopy, and set the canopy on top of the tank.

2. With a pencil or a piece of chalk, mark the points at the front and rear of the cover that align with the right and left *inner* edges of the tank rim. Connect these points with a ruler to form straight lines.

3. Using a hack saw or a coping saw, trim off the plastic outside the lines.

4. After trimming, the cover should rest on the inner lip of the tank rim at the rear, and on top of the tank rim at the front. Any water that collects on the cover now will roll to the rear and then back into the aquarium. The position of a typical aquarium cover before and after trimming is illustrated in Figure 28.

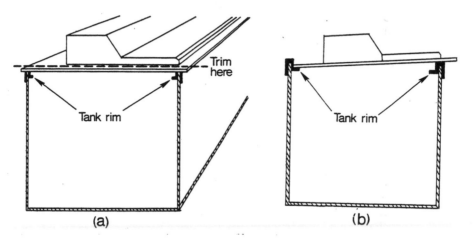

Figure 28. The seating of a standard aqarium cover before (a) and after (b) modification to prevent water from dripping down the glass.

Cutting Slots for the Airline Tubing and Heater

1. Arrange the airline tubes and the heater in their desired positions along the back rim of the aquarium. Then slide the aquarium cover into place, until it rests against the heater.

2. With a pencil or felt-tip marker, mark the areas on the cover (usually a flexible plastic strip) where cut-outs for the airline tubes and heater are needed.

3. Use scissors to cut slots in the soft plastic, but be conservative in making the cuts; a small slot can be enlarged, but overcuts are difficult to correct. If the type of heater illustrated in Figure 4

(Chapter 2) is used, be sure to cut the slot to the diameter of the glass heater tube, which is much smaller than the plastic control fitting at the top of the assembly. Figure 29 illustrates a tank cover modified to accommodate a heater and three pieces of airline tubing (one for the box filter and two for air diffusers).

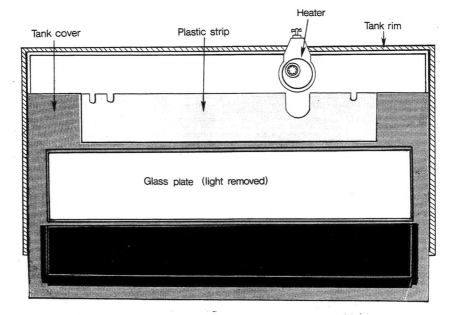

Figure 29. Top view of an aquarium with its cover partially displaced to show the slots that have been cut to accommodate three airline tubes and a heater.

Measuring and Adjusting the pH

The pH of artificial seawater usually stabilizes within a few hours after it is mixed, provided that it is well aerated. Following the instructions of the manufacturer, measure the pH of the seawater with your pH test kit, and add baking soda to the water if the pH is too high or too low. Information about testing for pH and adjusting the pH with baking soda are given in Chapter 6.

"Conditioning" the Aquarium

As discussed in Chapters 1 and 3, a new aquarium does not contain large numbers of the filter bacteria that remove ammonia from the water. Most fishes introduced into a new aquarium would quickly succumb to poisoning from the ammonia that they excrete into the water. The "conditioning" of a new aquarium — the establishment of filter bacteria in it — is the subject of the next chapter.

Chapter 5

CONDITIONING A NEW AQUARIUM

It is evident . . . that the artificial water must be at first totally deficient in one very important element, namely, the animalcules with which water in its natural state abounds, and which are necessary for the sustenance of many marine animals.

George B. Sowerby
Popular History of the Aquarium. 1857

If a little real sea-water, even a pint or two, can be obtained to mix with the artificial, the ripening of the latter will be considerably hastened . . . . As the water acquires age, like good wine, it increases in strength, and after some months use, will maintain creatures in health that would perish in a day in water recently prepared.

Shirley Hibberd
The Book of the Marine Aquarium, 1860

The reason for adding a small quantity of natural sea-water to that manufactured chemically lies in the fact that sea-water contains some mysterious ingredient which up to the present has defied analysis, but which may be considered analogous to what is known as the vitamins contained in food.

E.G. Boulenger
The Aquarium Book, 1925

A MARINE aquarium that has just been set up as described in Chapter 4 is a potentially dangerous home for fishes and other sea creatures. It is not safe until bacteriological filtration (Chapter 3) has been established. The *conditioning period* for a new aquarium is defined here as the time it takes to establish bacteriological filtration. More specifically, it is the interval required to grow enough filter bacteria to ensure that the ammonia excreted by the fishes or produced by the decomposition of organic nitrogenous wastes and uneaten food will never reach toxic concentrations in the water.

From the foregoing statements, it may seem that the conditioning period presents a "Catch 22" situation: on the one hand, fishes cannot be introduced into a new aquarium, because the absence of filter bacteria creates the risk of ammonia poisoning; on the other hand, filter bacteria will not grow in an aquarium unless they have a source of ammonia on which to "feed," and an aquarium without fishes or other inhabitants essentially is ammonia-free. There are, however, simple ways to establish bacteriological filtration in a new aquarium without endangering the health of the fishes that are introduced first. One particularly effective method is described later in this chapter.

THE NITROGEN SEQUENCE IN A NEW AQUARIUM

As noted in Chapter 3, most of the nitrogen excreted by aquarium animals is not recycled, as it is in the ocean; rather, it is changed by bacteria from one chemical form to another, with nitrate as the end product. Ammonia is excreted directly into the water by aquatic animals, including fishes. It is not a solid waste that sinks to the bottom and gets trapped in the filtrant; it is highly soluble and is invisible.

Very low concentrations of ammonia — many times lower than those that can be detected by the human sense of smell — are toxic to fishes. Although very few studies have been conducted on the toxicity of ammonia in seawater, marine fishes appear to be as susceptible to ammonia poisoning as are freshwater fishes, and freshwater species have been studied extensively. Less than 0.1 part per million (ppm) of ammonia or *one drop dissolved in approximately 132 gallons (500 liters) of water* can kill many sensitive species of fishes, and even lower concentrations can cause permanent gill damage.[1] Exposure to ammonia also has been associated with the occurrence of disease in fishes,[2,3] and it has been shown that prolonged exposure to ammonia concentrations as low as 0.03 ppm can decrease the resistance of fishes to invasion by pathogenic bacteria.[4]

A newly set-up marine aquarium contains very few filter bacteria — too few to prevent the ammonia excreted by even one small fish from accumulating to harmful levels. Such an aquarium is termed *unconditioned.* To determine exactly what happens to the ammonia ex creted by fishes in an unconditioned aquarium, the following experiment was performed in our laboratory.

Experimental Findings

Eight 10-gallon (38-liter) aquariums were set up exactly as described in Chapter 4, but without box filters containing activated carbon. The water temperature was maintained at 77°F (25°C), and the salinity at 30 parts per thousand (specific gravity 1.020). Each tank was stocked with two marine fish about 1½ inches (4 centimeters) long. The species we used has comparatively high tolerance to ammonia. Just before the fish were introduced, we measured the concentrations of ammonia, nitrite, and nitrate in each tank, and continued to make daily measurements for the next eight weeks.

The changes in the concentrations of ammonia, nitrite and nitrate during our study are shown in Figure 30. As expected, ammonia appeared immediately, and had reached harmful concentrations after only a few days. The ammonia levels did not decrease to safe values until more than three weeks had passed, indicating that it takes this long for ammonia-consuming filter bacteria to become established in a new aquarium. Concentrations of nitrite began to rise on the tenth day, showing that some ammonia was being converted to nitrite, and concentrations peaked on day 35. At this time, nitrite-consuming bacteria began to flourish; nitrite had decreased to negligible values by the beginning of the seventh week, and concentrations of nitrate (the product of nitrite conversion) rose sharply during the same period.

The nitrogen sequence in a new aquarium was thus found to have three distinct steps. These steps were characterized by (1) a rise and fall in ammonia that lasted about three to four weeks, (2) a rise and fall in nitrite that lasted about six weeks, and (3) a progressive increase in nitrate, which might be expected to continue indefinitely.

AMMONIA, NITRITE, AND THE CONDITIONING PERIOD

If the reader is familiar with any modern marine aquarium

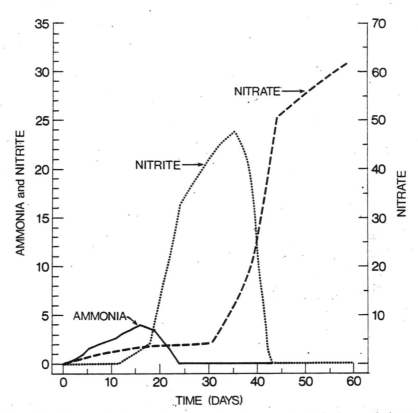

Figure 30. Changes in the concentrations of total ammonia, nitrite ion, and nitrate ion in a new aquarium. Concentrations are expressed as parts per million (milligrams per liter). See text for discussion.

guides or has spoken with a retailer or an experienced hobbyist, he or she probably has been told that an aquarium is not safe or fully conditioned until both ammonia and nitrite concentrations have fallen to values near zero. This common recommendation is based on the assumption that nitrite is only slightly less toxic than ammonia to fishes. Nitrite is, in fact, extremely toxic to freshwater fishes, and because no studies had been conducted with marine fishes until recently, it was believed that nitrite was equally toxic in seawater.

In 1977 three research teams, working at universities in Montana, California, and Rhode Island, reported that the addition of sodium chloride (common table salt) to freshwater decreases the toxicity of nitrite to freshwater fishes.[5-7] In one of these studies, it was found that salmon, a type of fish that can live in freshwater or seawater, can withstand at least 50 times more nitrite when kept in seawater than can be tolerated in freshwater.[6] The protective effect of seawater against nitrite poisoning was demonstrated with marine fishes in 1980, when a South African scientist reported that several different species of larval marine fishes were not harmed by concentrations ranging from approximately 70 to 1,750 ppm nitrite, depending on the species tested.[8] The concentration of nitrite that can kill highly sensitive fishes in freshwater after only a few days of exposure is a mere 0.6 ppm.[9]

These reports, along with others that have followed, show that nitrite toxicity is not an important consideration in the maintenance of marine fishes in captivity. At Instant Ocean Hatcheries in Florida, where several species of tropical reef fishes are farmed commercially, researchers found that the tomato anemonefish (*Amphiprion frenatus*) was not killed or even stressed by exposure to concentrations of nitrite as high as 12.7 ppm.[10] Clearly, the completion of the nitrogen sequence in a new aquarium, which is characterized by the conversion of all ammonia and nitrite to nitrate, is not synonymous with the completion of conditioning. By its new definition, which is different from that given by other authors, the conditioning of a new aquarium is complete when the filter bacteria are capable of removing all ammonia from the water. It should be pointed out that this definition is valid only for marine aquariums, and that freshwater aquariums cannot be considered fully conditioned until the filter bacteria are also able to remove all the nitrite.

STUDIES ON ACCELERATED CONDITIONING

In our study on the fate of ammonia in new aquariums, we found that about three to four weeks were required to complete conditioning and that the nitrification sequence did not reach its final stage until the beginning of the seventh week. In this study, however, we were particularly careful to prevent the introduction of filter bacteria into the aquariums; we chlorinated all the aquariums and filtration equipment before we began, and even rinsed the fishes in new seawater before transferring them to the experimental tanks. Consequently, our findings probably express the longest possible time it takes to complete conditioning and the nitrification sequence *under the given conditions*. (Conditioning takes much longer at lower temperatures, for example.)

To condition an aquarium rapidly, instead of letting nature take its course and waiting out the four-week period, two things must be added to a new aquarium: a large population of filter bacteria, and enough ammonia to promote the growth of the filter bacteria. Many different sources of bacteria and ammonia have been recommended for speeding up the conditioning of a new aquarium. They are listed in Table 7. In our laboratory we conducted experiments to determine which sources of bacteria will accelerate conditioning the most rapidly.[11] We tested the following sources: three commercial additives (Bio-Life II, Fritz-Zyme No. 2, and Nitro-Quik); different amounts of wet and dried gravel from a long-established seawater aquarium; wet gravel from a long-established freshwater aquarium;

Table 7

SOURCES OF BACTERIA AND AMMONIA THAT HAVE BEEN USED TO CONDITION NEW MARINE AQUARIUMS

Bacteria	Ammonia
1. Naturally occurring in air, soil, and water.	1. Present as a minor contaminant of artificial seawater.
2. Introduced on the bodies of fishes.	2. Produced from the decay of food (clam juice, minced fish, etc.).
3. Introduced with water from an established aquarium.	3. Excreted by aquarium animals.
4. Introduced with gravel from an established aquarium.	4. Added as a pure chemical or solution (liquid ammonia, ammonium chloride, ammonium sulfate, etc.).
5. Added in the form of commercial liquid or freeze-dried preparations of bacteria.	

and water from an established seawater aquarium. The ammonia was provided by equal-sized fish in each tank.

As shown in Figures 31 and 32, the conditioning period was not shortened by adding any of the commercial products or gravel from a freshwater aquarium. The addition of seawater (20 percent by volume) from an established seawater aquarium shortened the conditioning period by only four days. The most dramatic effect occurred when one-tenth of the gravel in the new aquariums had been transferred from the filter bed of a long-established marine aquarium; the concentration of ammonia never increased, and conditioning was completed in just a few days. One interesting result of this experiment was the observation that gravel which had been removed from a conditioned seawater aquarium, air-dried for 13 weeks, and then added to new aquariums also accelerated the con-

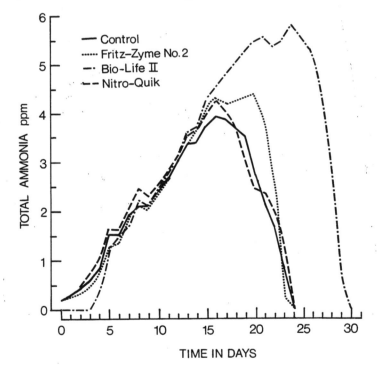

Figure 31. The concentrations of ammonia in new marine aquariums into which various commercial additives were introduced to accelerate conditioning. The control contained no additives. See text for discussion. Modified from Bower and Turner (1981).[11]

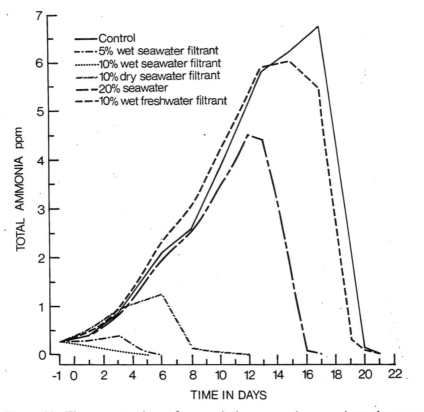

Figure 32. The concentrations of ammonia in new marine aquariums that were "seeded" with filtrant or water from conditioned aquariums. See text for discussion. Modified from Bower and Turner (1981).[11]

ditioning period. When filter beds in the new aquariums consisted of 10% dry conditioned gravel and 90% new gravel, the conditioning period lasted only 11 days. This showed that some ammonia-consuming bacteria can survive drying out. Thus, even the old, dry gravel from a dissembled aquarium can be used to help condition a new aquarium, provided that it has not been washed before being used again.

One additional point must be emphasized about using gravel from an established aquarium to provide bacteria for a new aquarium. Filter bacteria are extremely sensitive to environmental changes. It has been demonstrated that bacteria from conditioned aquariums do not perform well if they are transferred to aquariums having lower temperatures or higher or lower pH values or salt concentrations than those to which they are adjusted.[12, 13] For this reason *seed gravel* (gravel used to introduce filter bacteria into a new tank) should always be taken from an aquarium that has the same water quality characteristics as the water in the new aquarium.

Because it is possible to shorten the conditioning period or eliminate it entirely, the common recommendation that delicate reef fishes should not be introduced into a new aquarium until several weeks have passed no longer is appropriate. Moreover, it is not necessary to test the water for ammonia or nitrite. The following procedure outlines the most simple and effective way to condition a new aquarium rapidly.

HOW TO CONDITION A NEW AQUARIUM

Seeding the Aquarium with Filter Bacteria

1. Set up your aquarium as described in Chapter 4.

2. After the temperature, salt concentration, and pH have been adjusted to appropriate values, return to your aquarium retailer and obtain some gravel from one of the dealer's established *seawater* aquariums. Gravel from a tank that contains only invertebrates is preferable to gravel from a fish tank, because the latter may contain transferable disease organisms. The quantity of gravel you will need is approximately one-tenth of the amount already in your tank. If your aquarium contains 50 pounds (22.7 kilograms) of new gravel, for example, you will need 5 pounds (2.3 kilograms) of seed gravel.

3. Carry the wet gravel home in a clean plastic bag. Do not wash the gravel; washing may kill or remove the bacteria from its surfaces. Add the gravel directly to your tank, and stir the filter bed gently to mix it with the other gravel.

4. It is important that you add the seed gravel *after* your tank is filled and the water is properly adjusted. If the seed gravel is installed at the same time as the new gravel (before the seawater is mixed), the drastic changes in salt concentration that take place when the seawater is prepared might kill the beneficial bacteria.

Stocking the Aquarium During the Conditioning Period

The filter bacteria on the seed gravel require a constant supply of ammonia for their growth and reproduction. It has been shown that 40 to 70 percent of ammonia-consuming bacteria in pure cultures die after being deprived of ammonia for only five days.[14] Similarly, in our laboratory we have found that when all the fish have been removed from conditioned aquariums, the ammonia-consuming capacity of the filter bacteria is reduced by about 10 percent after one week, 50 percent after two to four weeks, 60 percent after eight weeks, and 90 percent after 16 weeks. Because filter bacteria are likely to die after being transferred to water that does not contain appreciable amounts of ammonia, it is important to introduce live animals into a newly seeded aquarium as soon as possible, preferably in less than one week. In this way, maximum bacterial survival is ensured, and the accumulation of ammonia after stocking is avoided.

Although little or no ammonia should accumulate in a properly seeded aquarium, it is safest to be conservative and to introduce only one or two ammonia-tolerant animals at first. Such animals include fishes such as the false clown anemonefish (*Amphiprion ocellaris*), the three-spot humbug or domino fish (*Dascyllus trimaculatus*), and the blue devil (*Pomacentrus coeruleus*), or a hardy invertebrate such as a small hermit crab. These animals are all desirable and attractive aquarium inhabitants; they adapt readily to the captive environment and prepared foods, and none grows very large.

Determining When Conditioning Is Complete

It is commonly recommended that aquarists purchase test kits for ammonia and nitrite, so that the concentrations of these substances can be monitored throughout the conditioning period. This recommendation has been based on two assumptions: that the conditioning period is extremely lengthy (six to eight weeks); and that the test kits are accurate. Neither assumption is true.

As explained earlier in this chapter, nitrite is relatively nontoxic in seawater, so an aquarium can be regarded as conditioned even though the water still contains nitrite. Moreover, if an aquarium is seeded with conditioned gravel from an established aquarium, little or no ammonia or nitrite will accumulate in the water.

According to a study performed in our laboratory, most commercial test kits for ammonia and nitrite are inaccurate.[15] Although certain test kits for nitrite work extremely well, only one ammonia test kit (SeaTest by Aquarium Systems) is sensitive enough to detect very low but toxic concentrations. Test kits for ammonia and nitrite therefore are not needed.

An aquarium that has been seeded with conditioned gravel and stocked with animals as recommended above will be completely conditioned in one week or less. Thus, approximately seven days after the first animals have been introduced, it is safe to populate the aquarium with more fishes and even with delicate species such as angelfishes and butterflyfishes.

INCREASING THE POPULATION OF A
CONDITIONED AQUARIUM

The activities of the filter bacteria in a conditioned aquarium are in balance with the quantity of wastes that are excreted by the aquarium animals. When the number of animals in the aquarium is increased, the established filter bacteria require time to adjust to the increased demand on them; they either multiply in numbers, or increase their consumption of the wastes.[16]

Complete adjustment may take a few days to several weeks, depending on environmental conditions, but one thing is clear: the greater the increase in the animal population, the longer the adjustment period will be, and the greater the possibility that ammonia may reach a harmful concentration before a new balance is established.

The number of fishes in an aquarium should always be increased gradually. A good rule of thumb is to add no more than twice the weight of animals already present during any one-week interval. If, for example, an aquarium was conditioned with two small fishes, two more small fishes or one larger fish may be added during the second week. Recommendations about the order of stocking and the numbers, sizes, and types of fishes that may be kept in the same tank are given in Chapter 9.

A NOTE TO AQUARIUM RETAILERS (AND MARINE AQUARIUM SOCIETIES) ABOUT SUPPLYING SEED GRAVEL

Providing your customers with conditioned seed filtrant is an important and valuable service that is as much to your advantage as to theirs. Loss of fishes from ammonia poisoning or from diseases that stem from ammonia stress does not occur in new aquariums that have been seeded, and novice aquarists that do not lose expensive fishes are not likely to become discouraged and to abandon the hobby.

If there is sufficient space in your establishment, the following procedure is recommended for establishing a disease-free source of "super-conditioned" filtrant, to be used exclusively for establishing new aquariums.

1. Set up an aquarium with a large surface-to-volume ratio (a 40-gallon or 151-liter tank is ideal), and install an undergravel filter with at least four airlift columns.

2. Cover the filter plate with carbonate filtrant (limestone, dolomitic limestone, etc.) to a little less than one-third the depth of the aquarium.

3. Fill the aquarium with newly mixed artificial seawater that is adjusted to the same temperature, salinity, and pH as the water in your fish tanks. Be sure to measure the exact volume of water you add.

4. Equip the aquarium with twice the number of air pumps you ordinarily would use for a tank its size, to ensure good circulation through the large volume of filtrant.

5. Transfer to the aquarium approximately 10 percent by weight or volume of filtrant from one of your established seawater aquariums, preferably one that contains only invertebrates. Never use filtrant from a tank that has been treated with any medication, particularly copper compounds.

6. For each 10 gallons (38 liters) of water in the tank, add a rounded ¼ teaspoon (about 1.5 grams) of ammonium chloride crystals. When dissolved, this amount will yield a concentration of approximatley 10 to 15 ppm ammonia. The filter bacteria will use this ammonia for growth. Ammonium chloride (USP or technical grade) can be purchased at some pharmacies or from suppliers of laboratory chemicals.

7. After the addition of the ammonium chloride, wait two weeks

to allow the bacteria to consume it. Then add ¼ teaspoon of ammonium chloride for every ten gallons every other day thereafter. Meaure and adjust the pH and the specific gravity of the water every week, and replace one-half of the water in the tank once a month.

8. Filtrant that is removed for seeding purposes should be taken from the top layer of the filter bed. Add new filtrant as needed, and mix it thoroughly with the remaining filtrant.

Chapter 6

BASIC MAINTENANCE PROCEDURES

There are undoubtedly greater difficulties attending the healthy maintenance of small marine tanks . . . than fresh-water ones, but some of these difficulties vanish before a little common-sense treatment and knowledge of the habits of the creatures we endeavor to keep . . . . Indeed, considering how altered are the circumstances under which they live, the wonder is that the inhabitants of aquaria give so little trouble.

J.E. Taylor
The Aquarium, 1881

Don't leave the water to itself until its volume is reduced about a third, as the creatures will thus run the risk of being pickled.

Reginald A.R. Bennett
Marine Aquaria, 1889

I F your aquarium has been set up properly, if adequate time has been allowed for establishing bacteriological filtration, and if it is not overcrowded (see Chapter 9 for recommendations about how many fishes to keep), it will require surprisingly little maintenance. Nevertheless, tropical marine fishes are often very sensitive to slight changes in water quality, and so it is essential to keep track of and control certain physical and chemical factors. The most important aspect of aquarium maintenance is that it be done with unfailing regularity. A few minutes each day can save hours of work and frustration later on.

DAILY CARE

Each morning and evening while you are feeding the fishes, check the aquarium for the following:

1. *The temperature* should be within 2°F (1°C) of the original setting.

91

2. *The water* should be clear and colorless, and the water level should be neither too high nor too low.

3. *The air diffusers* should be bubbling vigorously, and water should be emptying from the airlift columns just below the water surface.

4. *The air pump* should be operating quietly. An overheated air pump that hums or vibrates strongly usually indicates back pressure from clogged air diffusers.

5. *The animals* in the aquarium should be alive, healthy, and behaving normally. Observe them carefully for signs of stress or disease (see Chapter 13), and make sure that each gets its share of food (Fig. 33).

Figure 33. While feeding your fishes, inspect them carefully to make sure that they are in good health and are behaving normally.

6. *The aquarium bottom* should be free of excessive debris and large pieces of uneaten food.

Remove dead animals and pieces of uneaten food immediately, and make other adjustments as required. You may wish to use a

Date	Water	Air	Temp.	Specific Gravity	pH	Comments
Aug. 5	OK	OK	76	—	—	FISHES NOT EATING WELL
Aug. 6	OK	OK	77	1.022	8.0	ADDED FRESH WATER AND BAKING SODA. 25% WAT. CHG.
Aug. 7	OK	REPLACED DIFFUSERS	76	1.021	8.2	ALL OK
Aug. 8	OK	OK	76	—	—	ADDED NEW HERMIT CRAB

Figure 34. A "check sheet" is useful for keeping a record of the history of your aquarium and its inhabitants.

check sheet, similar to the one illustrated in Figure 34, to keep a permanent record of your aquarium and its inhabitants.

WEEKLY CARE

Because of normal biological and physical processes that cannot be controlled by the filtration/aeration system, the salt concentration and pH of aquarium water usually change as time passes. These variables should be measured each week, and corrections made as necessary.

Determining and Adjusting the Salt Concentration

A marine aquarium normally loses a significant amount of water each week by evaporation. When evaporation occurs from seawater, water leaves and the salts stay behind. Consequently, evaporation makes seawater more salty.

The salt concentration or *salinity* of seawater is defined as the weight in grams of total salts dissolved in exactly 1,000 grams of seawater; thus, salinity is expressed as grams per thousand grams, or *parts per thousand* (ppt). The salinity of the open oceans rarely is lower than 33 ppt or higher than 37 ppt, with an average value of 34 to 35 ppt. As noted in Chapters 1 and 3, it is desirable to keep the salinity of aquarium seawater at a value of approximately 30 to 32 ppt, to reduce the burden of salt excretion on the fishes and to prevent the water from becoming dangerously salty from evaporation.

There is no accurate, simple, and inexpensive way to determine salinity directly. The most convenient way for aquarists to measure the salt content of seawater is to determine its salinity indirectly, with a hydrometer.

How a Hydrometer Works

A hydrometer is a sealed glass tube with a broad, weighted bottom and a narrow stem that contains a scale of numbers on paper. It is constructed to float upright in water. Salt water is more buoyant than freshwater, so the saltier the water, the higher the hydrometer floats.

A hydrometer measures *specific gravity,* which is related to salinity in a round-about way. For our purposes, no complex definition of specific gravity is needed. In fact, one needs to know only two things about it:

1. Pure, freshwater has a specific gravity of 1. Salt water has a specific gravity greater than 1. The higher the specific gravity value, the saltier the water.

2. Temperature does not affect the concentration of salts in seawater, but it does affect the specific gravity. Warm water of a given salinity always has a *lower* specific gravity than cold water of the same salinity. For this reason, any specific gravity reading is meaningless if the temperature of the water is not known. The relationship between salinity and specific gravity at different temperatures is illustrated in Figure 35. At 77°F (25°C), for example, a specific gravity reading of 1.0210 represents a salinity of 31.5 ppt, whereas at a temperature of 86°F (30°C), the same specific gravity reading represents a salinity value of 33.5 ppt.

How to Use a Hydrometer

1. If the hydrometer is to be floated directly in the aquarium, unplug the air pump or disconnect the air diffusers, and wait for the water surface to become still. If the hydrometer is too tall to float in the aquarium without touching the gravel, transfer some aquarium water to a suitable container for measurement. Some aquarium stores sell hydrometer cylinders, clear glass vessels intended for this purpose.

2. Wipe the hydrometer thoroughly with a tissue or a paper

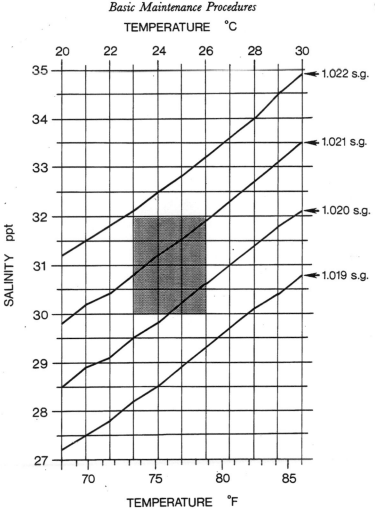

Figure 35. The relationship between the salinity and the specific gravity of seawater at different temperatures. Specific gravity varies with temperature, whereas salinity does not. Shaded area represents the preferred temperature and salinity ranges for marine aquariums. Prepared from data given by Zerbe and Taylor (1953).[1]

towel. The glass surface must be perfectly clean and free of grease to float properly. Hold the clean hydrometer at the top of the stem to avoid getting oil from your fingertips on its body.

3. Slowly, lower the hydrometer into the water, and wait for it to stop bobbing. Be sure that it is floating freely and is not in contact with any solid objects or with the walls of the aquarium or the mea-

suring vessel. Also check to see that no bubbles adhere to the hydrometer's surface.

4. Turn the top of the stem gently, until the numbers on the scale face you. Looking through the glass of the aquarium or measuring container from just below the water level, read the first number on the scale that appears just below the *meniscus*. The meniscus is the upward curve of the water against the glass wall of the hydrometer. The number you read is the specific gravity value. The location of the meniscus and the proper way to view a hydrometer is shown in Figure 36.

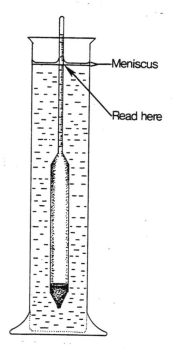

Figure 36. A hydrometer suspended in aquarium water in a glass hydrometer cylinder, with the proper reading point indicated. See text for explanation.

5. Use a thermometer to measure the temperature of the water in which the hydrometer is floating, i.e. in the aquarium or in the measuring container.

6. After measuring the specific gravity directly in an aquarium, don't forget to plug in the air pump or reconnect the air diffusers.

How to Read a Hydrometer

An enlarged view of a section of the specific gravity scale in a hydrometer is shown in Figure 37. Each of the ten divisions between

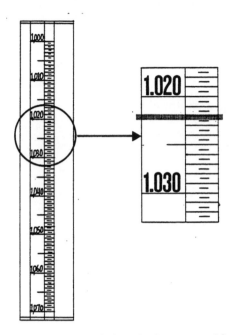

Figure 37. The specific gravity scale in a hydrometer, with an enlarged section shown at the right. Shaded area represents the meniscus. See text for explanation.

1.020 and 1.030 represents 0.001 specific gravity unit (1.021, 1.022, 1.023, etc.). The lines in the center of these divisions each represent 0.0005 unit (1.0205, 1.0215, 1.0225, etc.). If the meniscus, represented by the shaded area on the scale, were to fall on the scale as depicted, the reading would be 1.0225. With a little practice, you should find it easy to read a hydrometer to the fourth decimal place. It should be noted, however, that only the most accurate hydrometers have such finely divided scales.

How to Interpret a Hydrometer Reading

As mentioned previously, a hydrometer reading, together with a temperature reading, are used to relate specific gravity values to

Table 8

THE SPECIFIC GRAVITY OF SEAWATER
(SALINITY = 30 TO 32 PARTS PER THOUSAND)
AT DIFFERENT TEMPERATURES

| Temperature | | Specific gravity |
°F	°C	
72	22.2	1.0215
73	22.8	1.0215
74	23.3	1.0210
75	23.9	1.0210
76	24.4	1.0210
77	25.0	1.0205
78	25.6	1.0205
79	26.1	1.0205
80	26.7	1.0200
81	27.2	1.0200
82	27.9	1.0200
83	28.3	1.0195
84	28.9	1.0195
85	29.4	1.0195
86	30.0	1.0190

salinity values. Table 8 gives the specific gravity values for seawater having a salinity of 30 to 32 ppt at different temperatures. Locate the temperature of your water on the table, then compare your specific gravity reading with the value given for that temperature. Alternatively, you may wish to use the graph in Figure 35 for this purpose. If the specific gravity of your aquarium water is higher or lower than the value given in the table, you will need to adjust the concentration of salts in the water.

What to Do if the Specific Gravity Is Too High

If water has evaporated from your aquarium, the specific gravity reading will be higher than the optimum value for the water temperature, meaning that the water is too salty. A high specific gravity is corrected by adding *fresh water* (never *seawater*) to the aquarium.

1. Use Table 9 (U.S. measure) or Table 10 (metric measure) to find how much freshwater is needed to lower the specific gravity to the appropriate value. These tables tell you how many ounces or milliliters of water to add for each gallon or liter, respectively, of seawater in the aquarium, to change the specific gravity from the *measured* value to the *desired* value.

2. Locate the column headings giving values that pertain to your aquarium water. Where the columns intersect, note the number given in the table.

3. Multiply this number by the volume of seawater (gallons or liters) in your aquarium. The resulting number is the volume of freshwater you must add, expressed in liquid ounces or in milliliters.

For example, your 20-gallon aquarium contains 18 gallons of seawater. The temperature is 76°F, and the specific gravity is 1.0230. In Table 8, the correct specific gravity for this temperature is 1.0210. According to Table 9, you need 12 ounces of freshwater for each gallon of seawater. Since your aquarium contains 18 gallons of seawater, you will need 12 × 18 or 216 ounces (roughly 1 ¾ gallons) of freshwater.

4. To avoid stressing the animals in the aquarium, the specific gravity should not be lowered more than 0.001 unit each day. If the required change is greater, the water additions should be made in part on consecutive days. If, for example, the required change is 0.002 unit (from 1.0230 to 1.0210), add half the freshwater at once, and half on the next day; if the change is 0.003 unit, add one-third on the first day, one-third on the second day, and the remainder on the third day.

5. Tap water may be used to lower the specific gravity of seawater, but it should be treated with chlorine neutralizer if it comes from a chlorinated water supply. Adjust the temperature of the running tap water to the temperature of the aquarium water, and collect the proper volume in a clean plastic bucket. Add chlorine neutralizer if necessary.

Some authors recommend that, instead of using chlorine neutralizer, tap water should be "aged" (left standing in an open con-

Table 9

VOLUMES OF FRESH WATER (IN OUNCES)[a] NEEDED TO LOWER THE SPECIFIC GRAVITY
OF ONE GALLON OF AQUARIUM WATER FROM THE MEASURED VALUE TO THE DESIRED VALUE

Desired specific gravity	Measured specific gravity											
	1.0195	1.0200	1.0205	1.0210	1.0215	1.0220	1.0225	1.0230	1.0235	1.0240	1.0245	1.0250
1.0190	3	7	10	13	17	20	24	27	30	34	37	40
1.0195		3	7	10	13	16	20	23	26	30	33	36
1.0200			3	6	10	13	16	19	22	26	29	32
1.0205				3	6	9	12	16	19	22	25	28
1.0210					3	6	9	12	15	18	21	24
1.0215						3	6	9	12	15	18	21
1.0220							3	6	9	12	15	17
1.0225								3	6	9	11	14
1.0230									3	6	8	11
1.0235										3	5	8
1.0240											3	5
1.0245												3

[a]Some useful equivalents (in liquid measure) are:

    1 cup = 8 ounces
    1 quart = 32 ounces
    1 gallon = 128 ounces

Table 10

VOLUMES OF FRESH WATER (IN MILLILITERS) NEEDED TO LOWER THE SPECIFIC GRAVITY
OF ONE LITER OF AQUARIUM WATER FROM THE MEASURED VALUE TO THE DESIRED VALUE

Desired specific gravity	Measured specific gravity											
	1.0195	1.0200	1.0205	1.0210	1.0215	1.0220	1.0225	1.0230	1.0235	1.0240	1.0245	1.0250
1.0190	25	53	79	105	132	158	184	211	237	263	289	316
1.0195		26	51	77	103	128	154	179	205	231	256	282
1.0200			25	50	75	100	125	150	175	200	225	250
1.0205				24	49	73	98	122	146	171	195	220
1.0210					24	48	71	95	119	143	167	190
1.0215						23	47	70	93	116	140	163
1.0220							23	45	68	91	114	136
1.0225								22	44	67	89	111
1.0230									22	43	65	87
1.0235										21	43	64
1.0240											21	42
1.0245												20

tainer for one or more days) to dissipate the chlorine. It has been shown, however, that it takes five to six days with aeration and almost two weeks without aeration to expel the chlorine from tap water,[2] so it seems that aging is a comparatively impractical and ineffective method of chlorine removal.

6. Pour the freshwater slowly into the aquarium, and allow it to mix thoroughly with the seawater. Then remeasure the specific gravity, to make sure that the salt concentration has been adjusted properly.

What to Do if the Specific Gravity Is Too Low

In a tropical marine aquarium the specific gravity rarely becomes too low, unless too much freshwater was added during the preparation of the artificial seawater or to compensate for evaporation. The following procedure should be used to increase the salt concentration of newly mixed artificial seawater (to be used for a partial water change or in a tank that is in the process of being set up), or to raise the specific gravity of aquarium seawater that was mixed improperly.

1. Use Table 11 (U.S. measure) or Table 12 (metric measure) to find out how much more salt is needed to raise the specific gravity to the appropriate value. Table 11 gives teaspoons or tablespoons of salt needed to raise the specific gravity of 5 gallons of seawater, and Table 12 gives grams of salt needed to increase the specific gravity of one liter of seawater.

2. Locate the column headings in the table that give the *measured* and *desired* specific gravity values that pertain to your aquarium water. Where the two columns intersect, note the number given in the table.

3. Multiply this number by the volume of seawater (in liters if using Table 12, or in multiples of 5 gallons if using Table 11) that you want to make more salty. The resulting number is the amount of salt that must be added to produce the desired specific gravity.

For example, you have just prepared 10 gallons of seawater for a partial water change. The water temperature is 76°F, and the specific gravity is 1.0190. According to Table 8, the proper specific gravity of seawater at this temperature is 1.021; thus, the measured specific gravity is 1.019, and the desired value is 1.021. From Table 11, you find that you will need to add 7 teaspoons of dry artificial sea

Table 11

APPROXIMATE AMOUNTS (IN LEVEL TEASPOONS, *t*
OR TABLESPOONS, *T*) OF DRY ARTIFICIAL SEA SALTS NEEDED
TO RAISE THE SPECIFIC GRAVITY OF 5 GALLONS OF AQUARIUM
WATER FROM THE MEASURED VALUE TO THE DESIRED VALUE[a,b]

Desired specific gravity	Measured specific gravity						
	1.015	1.016	1.017	1.018	1.019	1.020	1.021
1.019	5 *T*	11 *t*	7 *t*	4 *t*	-	-	-
1.020	6 *T*	5 *T*	11 *t*	7 *t*	4 *t*	-	-
1.021	7 *T*	6 *T*	5 *T*	11 *t*	7 *t*	4 *t*	-
1.022	25 *t*	7 *T*	6 *T*	5 *T*	11 *t*	7 *t*	4 *t*

[a]Based on the assumption that 1 level teaspoon of unhydrated sea salt weighs approximately 7 grams, and that the addition of 5 grams of sea salt to one gallon of seawater at 77° F will raise the specific gravity by about 0.001 unit. (Determinations conducted with Instant Ocean®.)
[b]Some useful equivalents (in dry measure) are:
    1 tablespoon = 3 teaspoons
    ¼ cup = 4 tablespoons = 12 teaspoons
    ⅓ cup = 16 teaspoons
    ½ cup = 8 tablespoons = 24 teaspoons
    1 cup = 16 tablespoons = 48 teaspoons

Table 12

APPROXIMATE AMOUNTS (IN GRAMS) OF DRY ARTIFICIAL
SEA SALTS NEEDED TO RAISE THE SPECIFIC GRAVITY
OF ONE LITER OF SEAWATER FROM THE MEASURED VALUE
TO THE DESIRED VALUE[a]

Desired specific gravity	Measured specific gravity						
	1.015	1.016	1.017	1.018	1.019	1.020	1.021
1.019	6.0	4.5	3.0	1.5	-	-	-
1.020	7.5	6.0	4.5	3.0	1.5	-	-
1.021	9.0	7.5	6.0	4.5	3.0	1.5	-
1.022	10.5	9.0	7.5	6.0	4.5	3.0	1.5

[a]Based on the assumption that approximately 1.5 grams of unhydrated sea salt will raise the specific gravity of one liter of seawater at 25°C by about 0.001 unit. (Determinations conducted with Instant Ocean.)

salts per 5 gallons, or 14 teaspoons (¼ cup plus 2 teaspoons) per 10 gallons to produce the desired change.

4. If the seawater requiring adjustment is in an aquarium that contains fishes or invertebrates, *do not add the salt directly to the aquarium water.* The ingestion of undissolved salts can be extremely harmful to the animals. Instead, transfer some tank water to a bucket, dissolve the salts in this water, and then pour it slowly into the aquarium. Salts may be added directly to the water in a bucket or in an aquarium that is not stocked with live animals.

5. If the required specific gravity change is greater than 0.001 unit (e.g. from 1.0190 to 1.0120) add part of the salt on two or more consecutive days to avoid stressing the fishes in an established aquarium. If no live animals are present, all the salts may be added at once.

6. After the salts have dissolved completely and have mixed thoroughly with the seawater, remeasure the specific gravity to ensure that it has been adjusted properly.

Measuring and Adjusting the pH

As discussed in Chapter 3, the pH of aquarium seawater becomes progressively less alkaline, even though the filter bed is composed entirely of carbonate filtrant. This pH decline is due chiefly to the metabolic activities of the aquarium animals and the filter bacteria, which result in the liberation of acids and carbon dioxide into the water. Although carbonate filtrants usually keep the pH from declining to values below 7.5, no filtrant can maintain pH values of 8.1 or higher. In fact, as shown in Figure 22 (Chapter 3), filtrants have almost no effect when the pH of the water is above 8. Partial water changes help to maintain alkaline pH values, but their effects are usually transient.

The optimum pH values for tropical reef fishes are 8.1 to 8.3, which is the range of values in their natural environment. The effects of values outside this range are not clear, but it is quite likely that higher or lower values cause stress and therefore should be avoided.

How to Measure the pH

1. After the conditioning period is over, the pH value of aquar-

ium water should be measured once a week.

2. Precise determinations of pH require a pH meter, but studies in our laboratory showed that some pH test kits such as those illustrated in Figure 38, give accurate, reliable readings.

3. A pH test kit contains an "indicator" solution or powder that

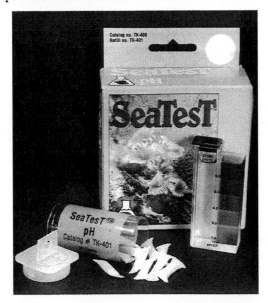

Figure 38. Saltwater pH test kits that employ an indicator powder (top) and an indicator solution (bottom). The indicator is added to a sample of aquarium water in a vial, and the resulting color is compared with standard colors.

produces characteristic colors when added to water having certain pH values. By comparing the color of the water sample with pH "color standards" provided with each kit, the pH of the water can be estimated. Test kits with transparent plastic or liquid color standards usually are better than those with opaque plastic standards or paper color charts, because the standard colors and the color of the seawater sample are easier to match.

4. Use the test kit according to the manufacturer's instructions. Try to estimte the reading to 0.1 pH unit.

5. If the pH of value of the seawater is too high, *do nothing*. It will decline to values within the preferred range after a week or two, as a result of the metabolic activities of the fishes and filter bacteria.

6. If the pH value is 8.1 or lower, it should be adjusted to a higher value by the procedure given below.

How to Raise the pH

Low pH is easily corrected by the addition of baking soda (sodium bicarbonate) to the water. Household baking soda, e.g. Arm & Hammer® brand, is inexpensive, suitably pure, and is available at most drugstores and supermarkets. Sodium carbonate, which is sold at aquarium stores in liquid or tablet form as "pH adjuster," also will raise the pH of aquarium water. It is not recommended, however, because it can raise the pH too high too quickly if it is not used with extreme care. The materials needed to raise the pH of aquarium water are illustrated in Figure 39.

1. Measure out one level teaspoon (about 5 grams) of baking soda for each 20 gallons (76 liters) of water in the aquarium.

2. Dissolve the baking soda in about 1 gallon (3.8 liters) of aquarium water (not tap water), in a clean plastic bucket, and pour the solution into the aquarium. *Never add dry baking soda to an aquarium that contains fishes or other animals.*

The addition of baking soda to seawater usually causes an initial decrease in pH, followed by a gradual increase. The more vigorously the water is aerated, the more rapidly the pH will rise. Do not be alarmed if the pH of the water is lower after the baking soda addition than it was initially; it will climb to higher values after several hours.

3. Wait at least 12 hours after adding the baking soda, and then

Figure 39. To adjust the pH of your aquarium water, you will need a plastic bucket, baking soda, and measuring spoons.

measure the pH. If it is still too low, repeat steps 1 and 2 each day, until the desired value has been reached.

BIMONTHLY CARE

Partial Water Changes and Related Maintenance

Once every two weeks, it is important to devote an hour or so to the simple maintenance that so often determines whether a marine aquarium is a glorious success or a dismal failure. As discussed in Chapter 3, partial water changes (i.e., removing some tank water and replacing it with newly prepared artificial seawater) are an important means for maintaining overall high water quality. A partial water change has three functions: it dilutes accumulated wastes and other substances, helps to restore the original balance of salts, and also helps to maintain a constant pH.

How Much Water to Replace

There are no simple ways to measure the amounts of dissolved organics and individual elements in seawater. The concentration of nitrate in an aquarium is a good indicator of overall water quality, because the accumulation of nitrate is accompanied by the accumulation of other undesirable substances. Unfortunately, most test kits for nitrate are extremely unreliable and inaccurate,[3] so routine testing for nitrate is not recommended.

Another useful indicator of water quality is the color of the water. The presence of greenish-yellow discoloration indicates that certain organic substances have accumulated in the water.[4] These "indicator" substances, however, are usually removed by filtration with activated carbon.

When an aquarium is stocked with animals in accordance with the recommendations given elsewhere (see Chapter 9), the rates at which nonfilterable, nonbiodegradable wastes accumulate can be estimated with a reasonable degree of accuracy. If stocking recommendations have been followed, the following volumes of water should be replaced every two weeks:

- 20 to 25 percent of the water in an aquarium with activated carbon filtration;
- 30 to 50 percent of the water in a tank without activated carbon filtration.

These volumes can be calculated, if the exact volume of water in the aquarium is known, or estimated visually, if the water volume was not determined previously.

An exception to the above rule can be applied to aquariums with activated carbon filtration that contain a rich growth of filamentous (hair-like) green algae. In such an aquarium, the requirement for water changes is lower, or about 30 percent once every month, provided that the water remains colorless and the animals appear healthy.

Procedure

1. *Measure and adjust the pH and specific gravity of the aquarium water,* as described earlier in this chapter.

2. *Test the air diffusers for blockage.* All air diffusers eventually become clogged, presumably with salts and organic matter that impede the air flow and create damaging back-pressure on the air pump. Determine how well the air diffusers are working:

a. Disconnect the flexible tubing from the rigid tubing that projects above the tank cover.

b. Lift the rigid tubing to raise the diffuser off the tank bottom, and blow into the tubing to make the diffuser bubble (Fig. 40).

c. It should take very little pressure to make the diffuser bubble vigorously. If it bubbles freely, lower the diffuser to the bottom and reconnect the air supply.

d. If your efforts leave you red in the face and produce only a weak stream of bubbles, the diffuser is blocked. Replace it immediately with a new one. The price of an air diffuser is insignificant when compared with the cost of repairing or replacing a pump that has been ruined by excessive back-pressure.

e. Some air diffusers can be rejuvenated by soaking them in acid or distilled vinegar and then boiling them for a few minutes. Follow the manufacturer's instructions for cleaning such diffusers. Rejuvenated diffusers never seem to perform as well as new ones, and also tend to become clogged more rapidly.

3. *Prepare new artificial seawater.* After deciding how much water you intend to remove from your tank, prepare the same volume of new artificial seawater in a clean plastic bucket. A trash can lined with a white, plastic trash bag is a suitable container for mixing large volumes.

a. Dissolve the salts in tap water that is just a few degrees warmer than the water in the aquarium, and add the appropriate amount of chlorine neutralizer, if necessary.

b. Connect an air diffuser to an extra gang valve or a spare air pump, and drop the diffuser into the water. Aeration will speed the dissolution of the salts and will help to stabilize the pH of the new seawater.

Figure 40. To check an air diffuser for blockage, disconnect the flexible tubing from the rigid tubing, and then blow into the rigid tubing to produce bubbles from the diffuser.

c. After the water has become clear, measure the specific gravity and make any necessary adjustments.

d. Artificial seawater to be used for a water change should always be prepared in a separate container and then added to the aquarium. *Never add dry sea salts to an aquarium containing fishes or other animals.* I have heard of instances in which fishes have mistaken the salt granules for food, ingested them, and later became extremely ill.

4. *Remove and clean the aquarium cover.* To prevent electrical shocks, unplug the heater and the aquarium light. Remove the light and cover from the aquarium, and wipe off any accumulated dust and salt with a sponge and warm water. Residues on the cover that do not dissolve in water usually will dissolve in full-strength white distilled vinegar. Be sure to rinse the cover thoroughly after vinegar is applied, to prevent this acidic substance from entering the aquarium water.

5. *Remove excessive algae from the aquarium.* Use a clean sponge or plastic algae scraper to remove unwanted algae from the glass (Fig. 41). Under most circumstances, algae should not be removed from rocks, corals, and other decor; it is an important food for many fishes, and its presence gives the aquarium a more natural appearance. If algal growth becomes excessive, however, and it is not being consumed by the fishes, remove some of the filamentous algae and discard it; if left "unharvested," it will eventually die off and contribute pollutants to the water.

6. *Stir the gravel bed to loosen debris.* The filter bed is the major site of bacteriological filtration in an aquarium. Filter bacteria live on the surfaces of gravels, as well as on the organic debris that accumulates between the grains. Excessive debris and mats of algae can "cement" the gravel grains together, restricting the flow of water through the filter bed and decreasing the efficiency of filtration. For this reason, as a regular maintenance procedure, the entire filter bed should be stirred gently to keep it open and unclogged.

The ideal utensil for stirring gravel is a stainless steel barbecue fork. Insert the fork into the gravel bed, taking care to reach all the way down to the filter plate, and move it slowly through the entire filter bed until all packed areas have been broken up (Fig. 42).

7. *Siphon water out of the aquarium.* The disturbance from stirring

Figure 41. Algae that obscure viewing can be removed from the aquarium glass with a non-abrasive sponge.

the filter bed will liberate some debris into the water. Use a plastic siphon hose, as illustrated in Figure 43, to drain water and debris from the aquarium into a bucket or trash can. Remove approximate-

Figure 42. Use a long-handled barbecue fork to break up clogged areas in the filter bed and to liberate some debris, before removing part of the water.

ly the same volume of water as the volume of new seawater you prepared. It is sometimes advised that debris in the filter bed should not be removed, because of its high content of filter bacteria. In experiments conducted at the Institute for Aquarium Studies, however, we found that bacteriological filtration was not impaired

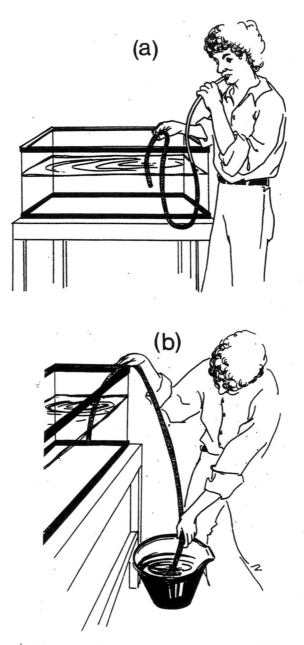

Figure 43. How to siphon water out of an aquarium. (a) Place one end of the hose in the aquarium, and raise the other end well above the water level. The hose should form a "U" shape with its lowest part *below* the water surface. Apply strong suction to the outer end of the hose with your mouth to fill the hose with water, then cover the opening tightly with your thumb. (b) Quickly lower the covered end of the hose to a bucket, remove your thumb from the opening, and allow the water to drain out. The flow of water can be stopped by covering either end of the hose, by removing the hose from the aquarium, or by returning the outflow end to a position above the water level.

even after the gravel was stirred thoroughly and nearly all the debris was siphoned out.[5]

8. *Do not remove or wash the aquarium gravel.* It is, unfortunately, a fairly common practice to remove a portion of the gravel, wash it under tap water, and then reinstall it, or to discard some gravel and replace it with new gravel periodically.[6] I do not recommend either practice. Gravel washing is undesirable because the process may kill or dislodge filter bacteria, thereby decreasing the rate of bacteriological filtration. Gravel replacement has been advocated as a way to maintain aquarium water at an appropriately alkaline pH, a recommendation based on the assumption that carbonate filtrants acquire a coating of insoluble substances that isolate them from contact with the seawater and prevent them from dissolving. As discussed in Chapter 3, however, it is now known that no commonly available carbonate filtrant is ever capable of maintaining pH values in the range of 8.1 to 8.3, mainly because they are not soluble in seawater at pH values above 8. It is therefore pointless to replace aquarium gravel periodically; new gravel is no more effective than old gravel for maintaining the proper pH.

9. *Replace the activated carbon.* There is no simple method of determining when activated carbon has become exhausted. Because it adsorbs organic substances that can be broken down by bacteria and released as soluble inorganic substances into the water, it is best to replace the carbon frequently. Remove the filter box from the aquarium, discard its contents, and refill it as described in Chapter 4.

Some aquarists are under the mistaken impression that "spent" activated carbon (carbon that is incapable of removing any more dissolved substances) can be reactivated by washing, boiling, baking in a oven, or soaking in bleach. None of these methods is effective. On an industrial scale reactivation is usually accomplished by subjecting the carbon to steam under pressure at exceedingly high temperatures (over 1,600°F or 900°C), conditions that obviously cannot be duplicated by the average aquarist. Because activated carbon is reasonably priced and comparatively small amounts of it are required for aquarium water purification, it constitutes a small but very important part of an aquarist's expenses.

10. *Refill the aquarium with new seawater.* Carefully pour the newly prepared artificial seawater into the aquarium, until the appropriate level has been reached. Alternatively, elevate the container of sea-

water to a height above the aquarium water level, and siphon it into the tank.

11. *Make the finishing touches.* Smooth the gravel surface, and reposition any "uprooted" decor. Replace the aquarium cover, and plug in the heater and light. Wet newspaper works miraculously for removing smudges and salt streaks from the outside glass. Commercial glass-cleaning sprays should be used with caution. In experiments conducted at the Institute for Aquarium Studies, it was determined that the use of glass cleaners with ammonia does not increase the concentration of ammonia in aquaium water, even when the cleaners are sprayed directly into the aquarium.[7] Thus, ammonia fumes from glass cleaners apparently are not troublesome. Because the detergents and other cleaning agents they contain may be toxic, however, care should be taken to avoid introducing them into aquarium water. The safest way to use a glass cleaner is to spray it onto a cloth or paper towel, and then use the dampened towel to clean the glass.

12. *Feed the fishes.* The process of cleaning an aquarium and changing part of the water undoubtedly is frightening to the fishes and may stress them. It has been shown that the stress reaction to physical manipulation can be eliminated by teaching the fishes to associate the unpleasant experience with a pleasant reward at its conclusion.[8,9] It therefore may be helpful to feed the fishes one of their favorite foods immediately after the aquarium is cleaned, so they become accustomed to the process and will be less disturbed by it in the future.

SEMIANNUAL CARE

Maintaining the Heater

The contact points in a thermostatically controlled aquarium heater are the parts that are most likely to malfunction. After prolonged use, the points lose their ability to make the direct contact that completes the electrical circuit and turns on the heater. The result is "arcing," or sparking, between the points that causes corrosion and, in the extreme, fuses the points together. Once the points fuse together, the electrical circuit cannot be broken; the heater does not shut off, and the water overheats.

As an important preventive measure, the contact points in a heater should be cleaned or replaced every six months. This procedure involves removing the glass heater tube and rubbing the contact points with emery cloth (very fine sandpaper) to remove the corrosion or unscrewing the contact-point assembly and installing a new one. Most aquarium dealers will perform either service.

Chapter 7

COMMON MAINTENANCE PROBLEMS: THEIR CAUSES AND SOLUTIONS

Turbidity of the water of an aquarium may be caused by . . . the presence of an immense multitude of animalcules belonging to the tribe of infusoria . . . .

Reginald A.R. Bennett
Marine Aquaria, 1889

The first signs of unpleasant effluvia rising from the tank must . . . be carefully attended to; and, in such cases, the Aquarium ought to be immediately searched for the cause; which, when discovered, should be immediately removed.

H. Noel Humphreys
Ocean Gardens, 1857

CLOUDY WATER

Causes

A GRAY clouding of aquarium water can occur under three conditions:

1. Clouding is normal in water containing artificial sea salts that have not dissolved completely.

2. The water in a new aquarium will become temporarily cloudy if the filtrant has not been rinsed thoroughly before being installed. Persistent cloudiness of this nature may indicate that the filtrant grains are too large to trap suspended particles.

3. Cloudy water in a new or established aquarium that is stocked with animals might indicate a sudden bloom of bacteria or yeasts. The growth of bacteria is promoted by inadequate aeration and by excessive amounts of organic matter that are symptomatic of incomplete conditioning, overfeeding, or overcrowding. Clouding of

bacterial or fungal origin also occurs in aquariums that have been medicated with drugs such as chloramphenicol.

Solutions

1 and 2. The cloudiness in new aquariums that is attributable to undissolved salts or fine particles of filtrant usually disappears within 24 hours or less. If cloudiness occurs because the filtrant grains are too large, the entire filter bed should be replaced with filtrant of the proper grain size (see Chapter 2).

3. When clouding of bacterial origin is suspected (i.e., when clear water suddenly becomes cloudy), check all the pumping and aeration equipment to make sure it is functioning properly. In aquariums having filters with more than one airlift tube, *all* the tubes should be discharging at equal rates. If one airlift tube is not discharging air and water, none of the other tubes will function properly. As illustrated in Figure 44, water flow will follow the path of

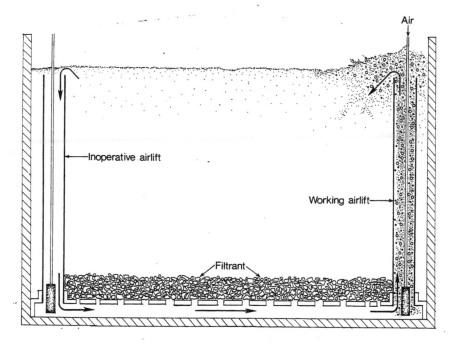

Figure 44. The pattern of water circulation in an aquarium with one inoperative airlift tube. See text for explanation.

least resistance down the inoperative tube, under the filter plate, and up the other tube(s), thus bypassing the filter bed. You can see this for yourself by disconnecting the supply of air from one airlift tube and dropping a bit of food into the water. The food will be sucked into the inoperative tube and discharged at the mouth of the other tube.

If the air pump and air diffusers are operating properly, check the aquarium bottom for decaying organic matter, such as large pieces of uneaten food or dead animals, and remove them promptly. If the aquarium appears to be overcrowded, transfer some of the fishes to another tank. Bacterial or fungal clouding that is initiated by drug treatment will disappear some time after activated carbon filtration is resumed or after a partial water change. (Filtration with activated carbon is usually discontinued during drug therapy, because it removes most medications from the water.)

YELLOW WATER

Causes

Yellow water signifies the presence of pigmented organic substances that are dissolved in the water. These substances, some of which are resistant to breakdown by filter bacteria, accumulate most rapidly in aquariums containing dense growths of algae or in which vegetable matter and flake foods are major constituents of the fishes' diets. Organic matter that turns the water yellow also is released from some types of carbonate filtrants.

Solutions

Pigmented organic compounds are removed from seawater by activated carbon. If the water becomes yellow in an aquarium *with* activated carbon filtration, it means that the carbon is exhausted and should be replaced. In aquariums *without* activated carbon filtration, yellow color can be controlled by frequent water changes or by the installation of activated carbon in a box filter.

SURFACE FOAMING AND SCUM FORMATION

Causes

Persistent foam on the surface of aquarium water, accompanied by a build-up of scum around the tank rim, indicates the presence of excessive amounts of certain organic substances in the water. High concentrations of these organic compounds are typical of aquariums that are overcrowded, overfed, or that have had insufficient water changes.

Solutions

The organic compounds that form foam and scum can be removed by using activated carbon or by changing the aquarium water frequently. Foaming and scum formation in tanks with activated carbon filtration indicate that the carbon needs replacement. When foam and scum occur in a properly equipped and maintained aquarium, a reduction of the animal population or a decrease in the input of food is advisable.

EXCESSIVE DEBRIS ON THE BOTTOM

Causes

Debris formation is a natural result of biological, chemical, and physical processes that occur normally in an aquarium. Most of the pale brown or orange debris on the tank bottom is *not* composed of solid animal wastes and uneaten food. Rather, it consists chiefly of aggregates of organic and inorganic substances; they form, in part, as a result of the activities of the filter bacteria and, in part, by the same physical processes that are responsible for the formation of surface foam and scum.[1] These aggregates are not harmful to fishes, and are not subject to further breakdown by the filter bacteria.

Under normal conditions, debris is drawn into the filter bed, where it remains until it is stirred into suspension and siphoned off as part of a water change. Excessive amounts of debris rarely, if ever, accumulate in an aquarium that is not overcrowded or overfed. I have found that excessive debris is a greater problem when fishes are fed large quantities of flake foods than when they are fed a variety of fresh and frozen foods with little or no flake food supplements. In aquariums having filter beds composed of very small grains of filtrant or sand, the debris cannot be pulled into the beds and forms unsightly deposits on the filtrant surface.

Solutions

Regular partial water changes and the use of activated carbon filtration will remove much of the dissolved organic matter that eventually can end up as debris. If the filtrant grains are too small to allow the entry of the debris into the filter bed, the entire bed should be replaced with suitable filtrant (see Chapter 2). The formation of excessive debris that results from overcrowded conditions or overfeeding can be corrected by decreasing the animal population or the food input.

LOW pH

Causes

The pH of aquarium water tends to decline continuously, as a result of the release of respiratory carbon dioxide and acids into the water by the fishes and filter bacteria. Some factors that can increase the rate of acidification follow:

1. the use of noncarbonate (silica or glass) filtrants;
2. insufficient quantities of carbonate filtrants;
3. overcrowding;
4. overfeeding;
5. failure to add baking soda to the water periodically.

Solutions

If you are using a noncarbonate filtrant, replace it with dolomitic limestone, crushed oyster shell, limestone, "crushed coral," or other appropriate gravel. If the filter bed is too shallow, add more filtrant. If the tank is overcrowded or overfed, remove some of the fishes or decrease the amount of food they are given. Be sure to measure the pH of the water each week, and to add baking soda regularly if the pH reaches values of 8.1 or lower.

"U.F.O.s"

Causes

Hobbyists with older, established aquariums often complain about the presence of U.F.O.s (Unidentified Foreign Organisms) in the filter beds and on the decor and walls of their tanks. Some of these organisms resemble fleas, some look like worms, and others form fuzzy, fungus-like colonies. Among the most commonly observed of these creatures are amphipods, which are crustacean invertebrates related to shrimps and crabs, a variety of segmented and unsegmented worms, and branched colonies of hydroids, animals that resemble and are related to jellyfish, sea anemones, and corals. These organisms, along with copepods, water mites, and other tiny animals that cannot be seen without a microscope, are typical marine aquarium microfauna. The way in which these creatures are introduced into an aquarium is unknown, but it is likely that they are carried in on food, on the surfaces of untreated natural decorations (beach rocks, etc.), and on the bodies of fishes, crabs, snails, and other aquarium inhabitants. Some common invertebrate organisms are shown in Figure 45.

Solutions

Should an aquarist be disturbed by the presence of tiny invertebrates in the aquarium, and should attempts be made to eradicate them? The answer, under most circumstances, is no. Although a few species of marine invertebrates are parasitic on fishes, those that populate aquariums generally are not. Tiny crustaceans and worms benefit an aquarium in a few important ways. In much the same way that earthworms plough garden soil, crusta-

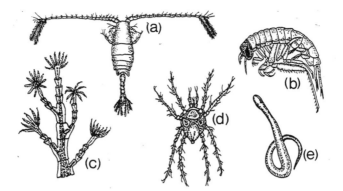

Figure 45. Some invertebrate animals that often appear in established aquariums: (a) copepod; (b) amphipod; (c) colonial hydroid; (d) water mite; (e) nematode worm. All drawings greatly enlarged. Redrawn from various sources.

ceans and marine worms help prevent the filter bed from becoming clogged with debris. Because they are scavengers, they help keep the aquarium clean by feeding on solid fish wastes and uneaten food. They also can constitute important natural foods for captive fishes that feed on small invertebrates in the wild.

The only organisms that might be considered pests in an aquarium are colonial hydroids. Hydroids occur most commonly in aquariums to which newly hatched brine shrimp are added regularly as food for small fishes and filter-feeding tubeworms and anemones. It is thought that they are a contaminant of brine shrimp eggs.[2] The problems caused by colonial hydroids are (1) they form unsightly brownish mats on the aquarium walls and decor and (2) they feed on baby brine shrimp. It is possible to eradicate hydroids from aquariums, but the procedure is complex and requires that the aquarium be treated with formalin and then torn down and chlorinated. The growth of hydroids can also be controlled by stocking aquariums with hermit crabs or with nudibranchs, both of which feed on hydroids. In most aquariums, however, hydroids can be ignored, since they are not harmful to fishes, and they can be cropped from decor and removed from the aquarium glass each time the tank is cleaned.

ALGAE

Some aquarists become concerned when algae begin to grow in their aquariums, while others become worried when they do not. Whether algal growth is a bane or boon to a marine aquarist depends largely on attitude and personal preference; an aquarium can be maintained successfully with or without algae.

Many hobbyists deliberately discourage the growth of algae in their tanks by providing too little illumination for too few hours, and by periodically removing and chlorinating all decor to eliminate whatever sparse growth has occurred. These aquarists, it seems, have never seen a living reef, even if only in a photograph, for their conception of a "natural" aquarium is one that contains bright, white (dead) corals and spotless plastic plants.

The coral reef is far from a random aggregation of bleached, shining, inanimate objects. It is, rather, a most remarkable association of life forms, encrusted upon one another and woven into intricate patterns of colors and textures. Although it is difficult to cultivate most encrusting organisms (chiefly sponges) in an aquarium, the growth of red, green, and brown algae on aquarium decorations gives a natural appearance to otherwise artificial-looking corals, rocks, and plastic plants.

In addition to improving the appearance of an aquarium, algae have other beneficial effects. They use ammonia and other nitrogenous substances for growth, and thus reduce the concentrations of these compounds in aquarium water (see Fig. 19 in Chapter 3). They also constitute a valuable food for many species of fishes and invertebrates.

The conditions recommended in this book for fish keeping (no direct sunlight, low concentrations of carbon dioxide, nitrate, phosphate, etc.) are not optimal for the growth of algae. Most aquariums maintained in this way seldom develop more than patches of green and brown algae on the glass and decor, even after several months. If the growth of filamentous green algae is desired, conditions can be improved by increasing the intensity of the artificial lighting and by replacing the activated carbon more often to prevent the accumulation of dissolved organic substances that may inhibit algal growth. The use of additives that promote the growth of algae is not necessarily helpful; most of their components are substances that are present in adequate concentrations in water harboring fishes or other animals. Just as the establishment of filter bacteria in a new aquarium can be accelerated by "seeding" with filtrant from a conditioned aquarium (Chapter 5), the establishment of filamentous green algae in a new tank may be promoted by seeding with the proper type of algae from an established aquarium.

Unwanted algae (those which grow on the front glass or form dense mats on the surface of the filter bed) should be removed as described in Chapter 6. The practice of removing and bleaching decor periodically is not recommended, because it undoubtedly disrupts established territories and may therefore cause undue stress to the fishes.

"BLACK SLIME"

Causes

Under certain conditions, a blackish, slimy coating may develop on the walls, decor, and filtrant surface in a marine aquarium. Soon after this growth appears, beneficial green, red, and brown algae die-off rapidly, and some fish deaths may also occur.

The organisms responsible for the above events are *blue-green algae*, an opportunistic variety, the growth of which is favored by conditions such as insufficient illumination and high concentrations of dissolved organic matter, ammonia, nitrate, and phosphate. These conditions occur in aquariums that are not maintained properly. Blue-green algae secrete substances that kill other species of algae, and they also may be toxic to algae-eating animals.

Solutions

Once blue-green algae have become established in an aquarium, they are extremely difficult to eradicate. Merely improving water quality will not guarantee their demise. When sudden fish and algal die-offs occur in a previously healthy established tank, and these problems coincide with the appearance of blue-green algae, any surviving fishes should be transferred to another aquarium immediately. The contaminated aquarium and all its contents must then be sterilized with chlorine bleach, rinsed thoroughly and dechlorinated, and set up anew, as described in Chapters 4 and 5. Care should then be taken to avoid the condtions that favor the growth of blue-green algae.

POWER FAILURE

Every aquarist lives in fear of electrical power failures, and with good reason. All aquarium pumps and filters run on electricity, and the interruption of filtration could have disastrous consequences. In geographical regions with cold winters, prolonged power failures result in cooling of the aquarium water, because the heater stops working.

To determine the effects of power failures on established marine aquariums, the following study was conducted at the Institute for Aquarium Studies.[3] Undergravel filtration was interrupted in pairs of 10-gallon (38-liter) aquariums by unplugging the air pumps for 3, 6, 12, or 24 hours. Each tank contained three fish (total weight about 14.5 grams per tank, and total length about 6 inches or 15 centimeters per tank). Because the experiment was conducted during the summer, water temperatures were maintained at 77°F (25°C) in all the aquariums.

As shown in Figure 46, the concentration of ammonia in the water increased slightly after only 3 hours without pumping, and progressively greater increases accompanied interruptions of longer duration. Only in the case of 24-hour interruption, however, did the ammonia approach toxic levels. There was no substantial increase in nitrite until filtration had been stopped for 24 hours. The pH values in the control tanks (in which the pumps were not unplugged) and in the 3-hour tanks were about 8.16. In the tanks that had been without filtration for 6, 12, and 24 hours, the pH decreased to 8.12, 8.10, and 8.00, respectively. Concentrations of ammonia and nitrite fell to normal low values within 24 hours after pumping and filtration were

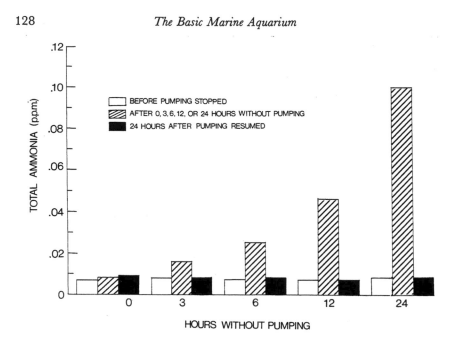

Figure 46. Changes in the concentrations of ammonia in aquariums subjected to power failures of various durations. Prepared from data in Bower and Turner (1981).[3]

resumed in all the aquariums.

These findings suggest that power failures are of little consequence for periods up to about 12 hours, but that harmful changes in water quality can occur after longer intervals without filtration. These changes, however, are not permanent. The aquariums used in this study were newly established (they had been seeded with conditioned gravel and operated for only one week before the experiment was begun), and they contained a fairly small load of fish. A more substantial deterioration in water quality might be expected to occur under the same circumstances in older or overcrowded aquariums.

Several years ago, when I was working at the Childrens' Museum of Hartford, one of our exhibits was a 200-gallon aquarium displaying a sargassumweed community. The tank contained a dense mass of sargassumweed, a seaweed that floats, and various fishes and invertebrates commonly associated with this algae. Because we could not provide enough light to cultivate the sargassumweed, we had fresh shipments flown to Connecticut from Florida twice a month. Even so, the water in the exhibit was usually brown, and always contained decomposing seaweed.

The sargassum animals hid among the fronds of the weed, so at feeding times we found it necessary to disconnect the air pumps to quiet the water surface, and then to locate and hand-feed each animal. One night the aquarist responsible for the last feeding neglected to reconnect the pumps. The next morning the mistake was discovered, but too late. The water in the tank resembled, to put it mildly, cabbage soup; the concentration of ammonia had soared, the pH had plunged, and judging by the foul odor, it was obvious that the dissolved oxygen had been severely depleted. Every animal in the tank was dead.

A useful device to have on hand in the event of a power failure is a portable air pump. Portable air pumps, which are available at most bait and tackle shops and at some aquarium stores, operate on flashlight batteries and retail for about $10 each.

Although the effects of interrupted heating were not studied, it is known that filter bacteria are less active at lower temperatures, and that rapid decreases in temperature are stressful to fishes. To my knowledge there are no battery-operated aquarium heaters, nor are converters available. Glass is a poor insulator, so any decrease in room temperature is followed closely by a decrease in water temperature.

The only practical way to keep aquarium water from becoming too cold during a long-term power failure is to insulate the tank to minimize heat loss. Styrofoam is an excellent insulator that is inexpensive and commonly available. Sheets of plastic foam called Fome-Cor® can be purchased at most stores that sell artist and drafting supplies. Fome-Cor sheets are ¼ inch (6 millimeters) thick, and measure 32 × 40 inches or 4 × 8 feet (81 × 102 centimeters or 1.2 × 2.4 meters) in size. The Fome-Cor should be cut to fit the tank dimensions with a utility knife, and then taped to the outer glass walls of the aquarium. In cases of extreme cold, more than one thickness of Fome-Cor should be used. If Fome-Cor or other Styrofoam products cannot be obtained, heat loss can also be reduced by wrapping the tank with blankets, and by floating leak-proof plastic bags filled with warm water in the aquarium.

PART TWO

THE BASICS OF FISH CARE

Chapter 8

PROVIDING A STRESS-FREE ENVIRONMENT

Although fishes are beautiful objects to be kept in an Aquarium, some of them are difficult . . . because from their delicate organization they are peculiarly susceptible of injury from any impurities in the water . . . .

George B. Sowerby
Popular History of the Aquarium, 1857

. . . it is the height of cruelty to keep the tank in sunlight, for the fishes, having no eyelids, and therefore not being able to close their eyes, are blinded by the glare of the sun.

Reginald A.R. Benett
Marine Aquaria, 1889

THE IMPORTANCE OF AVOIDING STRESS

TROPICAL marine fishes come from one of the most stable habitats on earth. Because their natural environment is so constant, reef fishes in general are ill-equipped to adjust to environmental variations, and their ability to tolerate most changes is comparatively low.

A fish, when subjected to an environmental change or condition that is harmful to its health and well-being, experiences disturbances in its normal body processes. Some workers use the term "stress" to indicate the adverse environmental condition (e.g. temperature stress, handling stress, social stress, etc.), whereas others regard stress as the physiological responses or disturbances that result from exposure to the hostile environment. In this discussion and throughout this book, the latter definition of stress is used.

A fish that is undergoing stress exhibits three levels of physiological responses, which are outlined in Table 13. The *primary response* is an increase in the blood of hormones called corticosteriods and catecholamines, which are secreted by the adrenal glands. The

133

Table 13

TYPICAL PHYSIOLOGICAL STRESS RESPONSES IN MARINE FISHES

Primary Response
  Adrenal glands secrete "stress hormones"
Secondary Responses
  GENERAL
    Heart rate increases
    Breathing rate increases
    Paling (loss of color)
  BLOOD CHARACTERISTICS
    Blood sugar increases
    Lactic acid increases
    Number of white blood cells decreases
    Number of red blood cells increases
    Immunological responses are suppressed:
      Gamma globulin formation is impaired
      Interferon production decreases
  SALT-WATER BALANCE
    Urine excretion increases
    Body water decreases
    Drinking rate increases
    Sodium and chloride retention increases
    Potassium excretion increases
Tertiary Responses
  Increased susceptibility to disease
  Changes in mucus production

From Wedemeyer (1970)[1] and Mazeaud et al. (1977)[2]

secondary responses, which are brought about by these hormones, include a great variety of metabolic disturbances. From an aquarist's point of view, the most significant of these responses are decreases in the production of white blood cells and antiviral and antibacterial substances. The *tertiary response,* which results from the secondary responses, is that the fish loses part or all of its ability to resist disease.

The aquarium can be a highly unstable environment for a captive fish, and potential inducers of stress are present everywhere. Any extreme environmental change or prolonged exposure to an unfavorable condition can cause a fish to become stressed, thereby increasing its susceptibility to disease. These changes or conditions may be physical, chemical, psychological, or nutritional. It is not yet understood specifically how much of what kinds of environmental changes reef fishes can and cannot tolerate, though stress in freshwater fishes has been studied extensively. Until the tolerance limits for tropical marine species have been established, it is wise to try to eliminate all possible initiators of stress from the aquarium environment; it is better to be safe than sorry.

THE ELEMENTS OF A STRESS-FREE AQUARIUM

Chemical Aspects

Salinity

It has been demonstrated that exposure to extreme changes in salinity (e.g. from 30 to 60 parts per thousand or from 32 to 10 parts per thousand) can cause acute stress to a marine fish,[3] but the effects of slight or gradual changes have not been studied. In the light of the delicate salt and water balance between a fish and its surrounding water, however, it is obvious that most changes are undesirable (see Chapter 1). A marine fish in full-strength seawater fights a constant battle against dehydration. It has been observed at a fish hatchery that tropcial marine fishes seem to grow faster and are generally healthier when maintained in water that is somewhat less salty than natural seawater,[4] and this opinion is also shared by many professional aquarists. The salinity of marine aquarium should be maintained at values of 30 to 32 parts per thousand, and not allowed to fluctuate outside this range. This corresponds to a specific gravity value of about 1.0205 at 77°F (25°C).

pH

No studies have been conducted to determine if changes in pH are stressful to marine fishes, or even if the natural pH range of the ocean is optimal for captive reef fishes. Until there is reason to believe otherwise, however, the pH of aquarium seawater should be maintained at values of 8.1 to 8.3.

Dissolved Oxygen

The primary stress response is elicited by exposure of fishes to low concentrations of dissolved oxygen.[5] Although no direct relationship has been demonstrated, it has been reported that outbreaks of disease often follow the subjection of fishes to chronically low oxygen levels.[6,7] Concentrations of dissolved oxygen at or near saturation values should always be maintained in aquariums by means of vigorous aeration.

Ammonia and Nitrite

Exposure to ammonia and nitrite is stressful to freshwater fishes,[8] and ammonia also has been related to increased susceptibility to bacterial disease.[9,10] Concentrations of ammonia and nitrite should be maintained at barely detectable values by bacteriological filtration.

Excessive Nitrate, Dissolved Organics, and Minerals

High concentrations of nitrate, dissolved organics, and certain minerals that accumulate in aquarium water have not yet been related to stress and outbreaks of disease. It has been shown, however, that exposure to high nitrate levels increases the mortalities of larvae of a tropical marine fish, *Amphiprion ocellaris,* and also adversely affects the growth and coloration of juveniles of the same species.[11] The accumulation of nonbiodegradable organic and inorganic substances should be minimized by replacing part of the aquarium water regularly.

Foreign Pollutants

Various foreign pollutants, such as the chemicals present in glass cleaners, insecticides, hair sprays, tobacco smoke, etc., are toxic to fishes, so care should be taken to avoid their introduction into aquarium water. The presence of certain pollutants, such as metals, pesticides, and PCBs, also has been associated with the occurrence of certain diseases of fishes,[7] and they may stress fishes indirectly by killing or by inhibiting the growth or metabolism of filter bacteria, which results in elevated concentrations of ammonia.[12,13] Nicotine, a component of tobacco and tobacco smoke, can react with nitrite in water to form nitrosamines, substances which have been shown to cause cancer.[14] The most simple way to prevent the contamination of aquarium water is never to use sprays or volatile chemicals in the vicinity of the tank (Fig. 47). Activated carbon will remove most foreign pollutants that inadvertently enter the water.

Figure 47. Household sprays that contain toxic chemicals should not be used on or near an aquarium.

An additional category of foreign pollutants that should be mentioned here is the one that includes all the drugs and chemicals used for the treatment of fish diseases. Some of the most commonly used medications — copper and formalin — are capable of stressing fishes,[15-17] and exposure to concentrations of copper well below those used to treat diseases also has been shown to *increase* the susceptibility of fishes to other diseases,[18-20] presumably by suppressing the immune response.[21,22] Some drugs and chemicals also are capable of interrupting bacteriological filtration, which can lead to the accumulation of stressful or toxic concentrations of ammonia. Medications should therefore be chosen with extreme care. This subject is discussed further in Chapters 11 and 13.

Physical Aspects

Temperature

It is well known that fishes exposed to rapid and severe increases or decreases in temperature become stressed.[23-25] Changes in temperature also have been related to the occurrence of diseases of captive fishes.[6,7,26,27] It is therefore important that the temperature of aquarium water remains stable and that it does not vary by more than a few degrees throughout the year.

Few studies have been conducted on the temperature tolerance of tropical marine fishes, but it appears that some species can survive a range of temperatures between the lethal limits of about 46°F (8°C) and 104°F (40°C).[28,29] Experiments concerning the temperature preferences of Hawaiian reef fishes, however, indicate that when given a choice, various fishes select temperatures ranging from about 66 to 86°F (19 to 30°C), with values depending on the size and species of fish and the time of day.[30-32] The temperature range recommended here for captive reef fishes is 75 to 79°F (24 to 26°C).

Light

Little is known about the effects of light on fishes or the lighting preferences of captive fishes. Fishes exhibit noticable signs of distress when light comes from any direction other than above,[33] however, and they also become extremely frightened and presumably stressed when subjected to sudden changes in light intensity. There is also some evidence that some types of fluorescent lamps, particularly "cool white," are detrimental to the reproduction of some fish species.[34-36] The length of the photoperiod (the hours of daily illumination) does not appear to be of great importance to captive fishes but is definitely related to the reproductive cycles of many species.

To avoid stressing or shocking aquarium fishes with sudden changes in light intensity, always turn the room lights on *before* turning on the aquarium light, and always turn the room lights off *after* turning off the aquarium light. In other words, change the light intensity *gradually* every morning and night. Because fishes seem to be most disturbed by a change from total darkness to some light, if the aquarium is located in a room that receives no natural daylight, a low-wattage night light (7 to 25 watts) should be kept in the room. The aquarium should be fully lighted for approximately 12 hours daily throughout the year.

Handling

Capture and handling are extremely stressful to fishes,[37-43] and physical injury from handling also has been associated with deaths and diseases of fishes.[44,45] This subject will be discussed in greater detail in Chapter 10. To avoid stressing fishes when moving them from one tank to another, try to handle them as little as possible, and never remove them from water with nets.

Psychological Aspects

Stocking Density

It has been shown that crowding too many fishes into too small a volume of water causes stress,[43,46-48] and overcrowding also may predispose fishes to certain diseases.[7,49] To avoid overcrowding a tropical marine aquarium, use the following rule of thumb: *the final stocking density should be one fish (adult length or height 5 inches or 13 centimeters) for each 10 gallons (38 liters) of water.* The rationale for this recommendation is given in Chapter 9.

Species Compatibility

Most reef fishes are highly territorial. Although it has not been demonstrated experimentally, it is likely that aggressive behavior within the confines of an aquarium is stressful to fishes. The selection of compatible individuals and species is therefore an important consideration in providing a stress-free environment. Care should also be taken to avoid predatory fishes that might feed on smaller fishes (see Chapter 9).

Shelter and Refuge

Most reef fishes retreat to cracks and crevices within the coral formations for shelter and refuge when they are threatened or become frightened. A fish that is deprived of such refuge undoubtedly becomes stressed. The aquarium should therefore be decorated with many large objects that provide the fishes with safe hiding places (see Chapters 1, 2, and 9).

Frightening Stimuli

Any stimulus that frightens a fish probably also stresses it. Experiments have demonstrated that shrimp grow faster and are less aggressive when cultivated in a comparatively quiet environment[50]; conversely, shrimp grown under noisy conditions exhibit metabolic disturbances characteristic of stress.[51] Although no analogous studies have been conducted, it seems likely that loud noises also may be stressful to fishes. In addition to loud noises, other stimuli that frighten fishes, such as tapping on the glass, sudden movements, prodding, and chasing, should be avoided.

Nutritional Aspects

Types of Food

Little is known about the nutritional requirements of tropical marine fishes, but there is reason to believe that a lack of proper nutrients weakens fishes and decreases their ability to resist disease. It has been reported that fish fed diets deficient in the amino acid lysine develop "fin rot,"[52] and many other diseases of fishes are known to be nutritionally mediated.[53,54] In the absence of specific information about the nutritional needs of fishes, their diets should be varied to include as many different kinds of foods as possible (see Chapter 12).

Frequency of Feedings

Except for some predatory fishes, most reef species feed constantly throughout the day. It is therefore unnatural and possibly stressful for captive reef fishes to be fed only once or twice a day. A more natural feeding regimen is to offer the fishes small amounts of food as many times a day as possible (see Chapter 12).

Chapter 9

STOCKING THE AQUARIUM

Don't be tempted into overstocking the tank. A small number of creatures in good health is far more interesting than a large number of weak and sickly specimens, some of which are daily found in a defunct state at the bottom of the tank.

Reginald A.R. Bennett
Marine Aquaria, 1889

There is one sure rule of guidance to a beginner in these matters — have too few animals rather than too many. They will compensate for numbers in the sense of health they seem to enjoy, in their vivacious gambols, and sprightly habits.

J.E. Taylor
The Aquarium, 1881

. . . the next danger is the association of animals that were never intended by nature to agree . . . . In stocking the tank bear in mind the necessity of a proper method of grouping, and proportion the number of animals to the bulk of water and the extent of surface exposed to the atmosphere.

Shirley Hibberd
The Book of the Marine Aquarium, 1860

ONE must consider many factors when trying to decide which kinds of fishes to keep in a single aquarium. The most important of these considerations is what species are amenable to life in captivity. How long will they live? How large will they grow? Will they be able to adapt to captive conditions? Will they get along well with one another? Another consideration is how many fishes of a given size can be kept successfully in an aquarium of a given size. In addition, it is also helpful to think about what kinds of animals, other than fishes, might contribute to the beauty and well-being of the aquarium. Finally, having decided how many of what species will be suitable for your particular aquarium, you must be able to choose the healthiest of all the specimens that are available from your marine fish retailer.

THE LONGEVITY OF REEF FISHES

One question asked frequently by aquarists is, "How long will the fishes live?" Although there are dozens of technical papers about the age and growth of commercially important freshwater species, comparatively little is known about reef fishes, except for the generalization that they grow faster than and do not live as long as species that inhabit temperate and arctic waters. Fortunately, curators of public aquariums have kept records on the longevity of their captive specimens. In 1962 a compilation of data collected by public aquarists on species that survived five or more years in captivity was published.[1] Some examples from this paper are given in Table 14. In addition to the species listed, I have personal knowledge of other species, including the blue devil (*Pomacentrus coeruleus*), the false clown anemonefish (*Amphiprion ocellaris*), and the domino damselfish (*Dascyllus trimaculatus*) that have survived in aquairums for five years or longer. Although not all species of reef fishes may have such long life spans (the neon goby, *Gobiosoma oceanops*, for example, lives for only about two years[2]), under optimal conditions the average longevity of most species should be at least three years, and often longer.

WHICH SPECIES TO KEEP

There are three important questions to answer before selecting different fishes for a given aquarium: (1) How large does the species grow? (2) Will the species adapt well to life in captivity? (3) Will the species be compatible with other fishes in the aquarium?

Adult Size

The majority of fishes sold at aquarium stores are juveniles with considerable potential for growth. The adult size of a particular

Table 14

LIFE SPANS IN CAPTIVITY
OF SOME TROPICAL MARINE FISHES

Scientific name	Common name(s)	No. years
ANGELFISHES:		
Holacanthus isabelita	Blue angelfish	5
DAMSELFISHES:		
Amphiprion ephippium	Red saddleback anemonefish	16½
Chromis chromis	Damselfish	6½
Dascyllus aruanus	White-tailed damselfish	6
Premnas biaculeatus	Spine-cheek anemonefish	7
PARROTFISHES:		
Scarus cretensis	?	7
SCORPIONFISHES:		
Pterois volitans	Turkeyfish, lionfish	10
SPADEFISHES:		
Platax orbicularis	Orbiculate batfish	7
TRIGGERFISHES:		
Balistes capriscus	Gray triggerfish	9
Balistes vetula	Queen triggerfish	5
WRASSES:		
Coris julis	Mediterranean wrasse	7
Labrus bergylta	Ballan wrasse	5

From Hinton (1962)

species is therefore of considerable importance, especially in the context of the size of the aquarium, assuming that the fish will survive to adulthood.

I do not recommend that any species that grows to lengths or heights of more than 5 inches (13 centimeters) be kept in aquariums of 100 gallons (380 liters) or less. This recommendation definitely narrows the variety of fishes from which one may choose, but is firmly based on experience.

Two of the most commonly available species in the eastern United States, for example, are the queen angelfish (*Holacanthus ciliaris*) and the French angelfish (*Pomacanthus paru*). Aquarium-store specimens rarely are larger than a few inches in length, and are particularly attractive to hobbyists because of their brilliant colors. These little gemstones of the sea, however, have been known to reach adult lengths in excess of 16 inches (41 centimeters), so unless you are willing and able to accommodate them in progressively larger (and more expensive) aquariums or to donate them to the nearest public aquarium, they should be avoided.

Several years ago, I purchased a 2-inch (6-centimeter) queen angelfish for a 30-gallon (114-liter) tank. After only 18 months, it had tripled in size and had to be transferred to a larger aquarium, and upon its untimely death (due to the failure of an aquarium heater) less than one year later, it was 9 inches (23 centimeters) long and weighed just over 1 pound (0.5 kilogram). Similarly, as the curator of a public aquarium, I received an endless stream of telephone calls asking if I would like a triggerfish, batfish, surgeonfish, or grouper that had outgrown its present quarters. With the intention of sparing the reader the experience of having to give up a treasured but overgrown specimen, Table 15, which lists some species that do not attain unmanageable proportions, is provided.

Adaptability

Many species of reef fishes, particularly certain butterflyfishes, angelfishes, and surgeonfishes, are difficult or impossible to keep in aquariums. The major problem is their feeding habits, which are so highly specialized that appropriate foods cannot be provided by even the most conscientious aquarist. Sponges, for example constitute 97 percent of the food of adult rock beauty angelfish (*Holacanthus tricolor*).[3]

The feeding habits of many reef fishes become increasingly specialized with age; young fishes generally are less choosey about foods than older fishes, and therefore are the best candidates for aquarium life. For this reason, if you have the option to buy a small or large individual of the same species, *always choose the smaller specimen.*

Another reason why some fishes are difficult to keep alive in captivity is their sensitivity to the unavoidable trauma of capture and handling. Whether these species are more susceptible to physical in-

Table 15

SOME TROPICAL MARINE FISHES WITH ADULT LENGTHS THAT USUALLY DO NOT EXCEED 5 INCHES (13 CENTIMETERS)[a]

Scientific name	Common name(s)
ANEMONEFISHES	
All *Amphiprion* species	Various
Premnas biaculeatus	Spine-cheek anemonefish
ANGELFISHES	
Centropyge acanthops	African flameback angelfish
Centropyge argi	Cherubfish
Centropyge bispinosus	Dusky angelfish, coral beauty
Centropyge loriculus	Flame angelfish
Centropyge vroliki	Pearl-scaled angelfish
BUTTERFLYFISHES	
Chaetodon argentatus	Black and white butterflyfish
Chaetodon chrysurus	Pearlscale butterflyfish
Chaetodon citrinellus	Speckled butterflyfish
Chaetodon larvatus	Red Sea butterflyfish
Chaetodon plebius	Coral butterflyfish
Chaetodon sedentarius	Reef butterflyfish
Forcipiger flavissimus	Longnose butterflyfish
Forcipiger longirostris	Longnose butterflyfish
Prognathodes aculeatus	Longsnout butterflyfish
CARDINALFISHES	
Apogon binotatus	Barred cardinalfiish
Apogon maculatus	Flamefish
Apogon orbicularis	Orbiculate cardinalfish
DAMSELFISHES	
Most *Abudefduf* species	Various
Chromis species	Various
Dascyllus species	Various
Eupomacentrus (formerly *Pomacentrus*) species	Various
FILEFISHES	
Monacanthus ciliatus	Fringed filefish
Monacanthus tuckeri	Slender filefish

Scientific name	Common name(s)

GOBIES AND BLENNIES
  Most species — Various
PARROTFISHES
  None or rare
SEABASSES AND BASSLETS

Scientific name	Common name(s)
Anthias squamipinnis	Wreckfish, lyretail coralfish
Gramma loreto	Royal gramma, fairy basslet
Hypoplectrus aberrans	Yellowbellied hamlet
Hypoplectrus chlorurus	Yellowtail hamlet
Hypoplectrus indigo	Indigo hamlet
Hypoplectrus unicolor	Butter hamlet
Liopropoma carmabi	Candy basslet
Lipogramma klayi	Bicolor basslet
Lipogramma trilineata	Threeline basslet
Pseudochromis paccagnellae	Royal dottyback, two-colored basslet
Serranus annularis	Orangeback bass
Serranus baldwini	Lantern bass
Serranus tigrinus	Harlequin bass

SQUIRRELFISHES

Scientific name	Common name(s)
Adioryx vexillarius	Dusky squirrelfish
Plectrypops retrospinis	Cardinal soldierfish

SURGEONFISHES AND TANGS

Scientific name	Common name(s)
Acanthurus glaucopareius	Golden-rimmed surgeonfish
Paracanthurus hepatus	Regal tang, hippo tang, hypo tang, flagtail surgeonfish
Zebrasoma flavescens	Yellow (sailfin) tang

TRIGGERFISHES

Scientific name	Common name(s)
Amanses pardalis	Variegated triggerfish

WRASSES

Scientific name	Common name(s)
Halichoeres argus	Argus wrasse
Halichoeres maculipinna	Clown wrasse
Halichoeres margaritaceus	Pearly wrasse

Scientific name	Common name(s)
WRASSES (continued)	
Halichoeres pictus	Painted wrasse
Hemipteronotus martinicensis	Straight-tail razorfish
Hemipteronotus splendens	Green razorfish
Labroides dimidiatus	Cleaner wrasse
Thalassoma bifasciatum	Bluehead
MISCELLANEOUS FISHES	
Amblycirrhitus pinos	Redspotted hawkfish
Opistognathus aurifrons	Yellowhead jawfish
Oxycirrhites typus	Longnose hawkfish

ªMany other species that do not grow very large are not included in this table, because they are difficult to keep alive in captivity (see Table 16).

jury than others or are simply more "high-strung" and "nervous" is not known. The fact remains, however, that the process of getting some fishes from the ocean to an aquarium, no matter how carefully it is carried out, is so stressful that they never recover.

It is often tempting to buy an uncommon species that you have rarely or never seen offered for sale before. It should be remembered, however, that the relative unavailability of many species is related to the difficulty of maintaining them in captivity. It is wisest and safest to choose familiar species, which are available widely and have long histories of successful maintenance in aquariums. A listing of some species that should be avoided because, for one reason or another, they do not adapt well to life in captivity, is given in Table 16.

Compatibility

Compatibility, the ability to exist in harmony with others, is the third important consideration in selecting fishes for an aquarium. Some species, such as groupers and anglerfishes, are not desirable residents in most aquariums, because they are predators that feed on other fishes. Scorpionfishes, including the lionfish (*Pterois volitans*)

Table 16

SOME SPECIES OF REEF FISHES
THAT USUALLY DO NOT SURVIVE IN CAPTIVITY

Scientific name	Common name(s)	Notes[a]
ANGELFISHES		
Centropyge bicolor	Two-colored angelfish	A
Centropyge flavissimus	Lemonpeel angelfish	A
Centropyge heraldi	Golden angelfish	A
Centropyge potteri	Russet angelfish, Potter's angelfish	A
Euxiphipops navarchus	Majestic angelfish	C
Holacanthus tricolor	Rock beauty angelfish	A,D
Pomacanthus arcuatus	Gray angelfish	A,D
Pomacanthus paru	French angelfish	A,D
Pygoplites diacanthus	Royal empress angelfish, regal angelfish	B
BUTTERFLYFISHES		
Chaetodon capistratus	Foureye butterflyfish	B
Chaetodon collaris	Pakistani butterflyfish	C,E
Chaetodon ephippium	Saddleback butterflyfish black-blotched butterflyfish	B,E
Chaetodon fremblii	Blue-striped butterflyfish	A,E
Chaetodon ornatissimus	Orange-striped butterflyfish	B,E
Chaetodon reticulatus	Reticulated butterflyfish	B,E
Chaetodon trifasciatus	Redfin butterflyfish, rainbow butterflyfish, three-banded butterflyfish	B,E
Chelmon rostratus	Copperband butterflyfish	C,E
WRASSES		
Anampses cuvieri	Cuvier's wrasse, speckled wrasse	A
Anampses rubrocaudatus	Red-tailed wrasse	B

Scientific name	Common name(s)	Notes[a]
Coris gaimard	Clown wrasse, red labrid	A,E
Labroides phthirophagus	Hawaiian cleaner wrasse	B

PORCUPINEFISHES
Chilomycterus schoepfi	Striped burrfish	A
Diodon hystrix	Porcupinefish	C

MISCELLANEOUS FISHES
Dunckerocampus dactyliophorus	Zebra pipefish	B
Equetus lanceolatus	Jackknife fish	B
Heniochus intermedius	Red Sea bannerfish	A
Hippocampus species	Seahorses	C
Lactoria cornuta	Long-horned cowfish	A,E
Mirolabrichthys tuka	Purple queen sea bass	C
Monocentrus japonicus	Pinecone fish	C
Naso lituratus	Smoothhead unicornfish, red-lipped tang	C,E
Ostracion meleagris	Spotted boxfish	C
Oxymonacanthus longirostris	Long-nosed filefish	B
Platax pinnatus	Long-finned batfish	A
Plectorhynchus chaetodonoides	Clown sweetlips	C
Synchiropus splendidus	Mandarin fish	A
Zanclus canescens	Moorish idol	A

[a]A 50/50 likelihood for survival, dependent on the degree to which an individual has been stressed. These species usually die of starvation or disease.

B Rarely, if ever, survives long in captivity.

C Fair likelihood for survival, if the individual is healthy and feeding well in the retailer's aquarium.

D The smaller the individual the greater the likelihood for survival in captivity.

E The larger the individual the greater the likelihood for survival in captivity. Specimens should be at least 2 inches (5 centimeters) in length.

and its relatives, are not recommended for amateur aquarists, because they have venomous spines and can inflict extremely painful wounds. The same is true of the coral catfish, *Plotosus anguillaris*. Although it is often said that *Pterois* species never use their spines as offensive weapons and will not attack unless provoked, at least one incident has been reported in which a lionfish raced across a large aquarium and stung the arm of a careless aquarist.[4] A lionfish in its characteristic defensive position — head down and venomous dorsal spines pointed toward the intruding animal or object — is shown attacking the handle of a screwdriver in Figure 48. Trunkfishes and pufferfishes also should not be kept in most aquariums, because the former species, when stressed in any manner, secrete a powerful toxin that can kill every living creature in an aquarium within a few hours, and the latter species contain a toxin which, upon the death of the fish, might be released and poison the other aquarium inhabitants.

The aggressive behavior that is a manifestation of the territoriality of most reef fishes is the major compatability problem that aquarists encounter. In a highly competitive habitat such as the coral reef, a fish guarantees itself a constant food supply and a safe place in which to hide and reproduce by establishing a territory from which other fishes are excluded. Most of the commonly imported species of reef fishes (anemonefishes, damselfishes, angelfishes, butterflyfishes, etc.) are highly territorial. Once they have staked out a part of the aquarium as their home ground, they defend it aggressively against intrusion by others. Scuba divers often report being nipped repeatedly by tiny fishes whose territorial boundaries they have transgressed, and I have been "attacked" on many occasions by a variety of territorial fishes while cleaning their aquariums. Many individuals will attack their mirror images or photographs of other fishes, and some will even make aggressive displays toward new shells or other new decorations that are added to their tanks.

Try as you may, there is no way to convince a territorial fish that it need not bully its tankmates into corners to protect its home and food supply. Its "instincts," fixed behavior patterns imprinted deeply within its brain circuitry, make it a poor subject for behavior modification.

In reality, few aquariums are large enough to satisfy the spatial requirements of even the smallest territorial fish. Wild reef

Figure 48. Some captive lionfish (*Pterois volitans*) are highly aggressive and will attack even inanimate objects, such as the handle of a screwdriver, with their venomous dorsal spines. From Animal Kingdom 65(2):37, 1962, courtesy of New York Zoological Society.

fishes have been observed to attack some intruders at distances up to 4 meters (4.4 yards) from their own residences.[5,6] This represents a territory of more than 100 cubic meters, whereas the total available territory in a 100-gallon (380-liter) aquarium is only about two-fifths of a cubic meter.

The aggressive behavior of wild reef fishes has received considerable study, and much of the information can be applied to the management of aquarium fishes. Although there are exceptions, brightly colored fishes tend to be more aggressive than drab colored species. Behavioral scientist Konrad Lorenz noted the relationship between "poster" coloration and territoriality as follows: "In the poster-colored species, the young . . . are not only more colorful and fiercer but also more firmly attached to their territories than the adults are . . . there is a connection between coloring, aggressiveness, and sedentary territorial habits."[7]

Researchers at the University of Miami in Florida[5,8,9] have found that territorial fishes do not treat all intruders equally; in fact, "like avoids like" appears to be the rule. The defenses, from strongest to weakest, are directed against (1) individuals of their own species, (2) individuals with shapes similar to their own, and (3) individuals with coloration similar to their own. Thus, species that bear the least resemblance to the resident fish usually elicit the least aggressive behavior.

In a study on the territorial behavior of the dusky damselfish, *Eupomacentrus dorsopunicans*, dietary preferences also were found to be related to aggressiveness; species with diets similar to that of the resident fish evoked the fiercest aggressive responses.[10]

Although the territorial behavior of reef fishes is extremely complex, a general rule for reducing the potential for aggression when stocking an aquarium is: *an aquarium should contain only one individual of a particular species, of a particular body shape, and of a particular color or pattern of colors.* In other words, choose species that bear the least imaginable resemblance to one another. Based on this criterion, an example of a relatively compatible combination of fishes for a 40-gallon (142-liter) aquarium would be: one blue damselfish, one yellow tang, one orange anemonefish, and one striped cleaner wrasse or neon goby.

There are, of course, exceptions to the rule. Not all reef fishes are territorial, and many not only are compatible with members of their own species but also seem to prefer their company. The most notable of such peaceful fishes are the false clown anemonefish, *Amphiprion ocellaris*, and various species that normally swim in schools.

The territorial nature of reef fishes leads to a point that cannot be overemphasized: the aquarium must contain enough decor to enable the establishment of a territory by each fish and to provide shelter and refuge for territorial and nonterritorial species alike. Generally speaking, young territorial fishes confine themselves to a small area, the center of which is their residence; they rarely stray more than a few yards from their lairs, except to feed or to chase away an intruder. In a study on habitat selection and territorial behavior, it was found that juvenile Cortez angelfish (*Pomacanthus zonipectus*) spent three times as much time in rocky areas of an aquarium than in undecorated sand-bottomed areas.[11] In the wild, they were observed to defend specific rock crevices against intrusion by other fishes, and to wedge themselves into these crevices at night and when threatened or pursued.

In the sea, a fish can escape from a territorial-defensive attack simply by swimming out of the territorial range, or by retreating to protective cover. Within a sparsely decorated aquarium, however, there is no escape. In the extreme, the "winner" kills the "loser," but more commonly the most aggressive individual attacks the others and intimidates them into corners, where they may eventually succumb to disease or starvation.

The fishes in a well-decorated aquarium adjust their territorial requirements to what is available, one claiming a conch shell, one a cluster of rocks or corals, and so on. Once territories have been divided up among a given population of captive fishes, the fishes seem to learn quickly to honor one another's boundary lines, and only minor squabbles occur.

The matter of aggressiveness among young reef fishes and their need for the security of decor presents a problem to sellers of tropical marine fishes. By economic necessity their tanks are usually overcrowded, often with aggressive and incompatible species. Moreover, the quantity of decor needed to make the fishes happy leaves the dealer extremely unhappy, because it makes the capture of a particular specimen inconvenient, if not impossible.

Experiments with young territorial angelfish have shown that the removal of decor from an aquarium produces a drastic reduction in territorial aggression, apparently because territories are centered around specific solid objects, and, in the absence of these objects, the fishes simply have no territories to defend.[11] This observation may provide a solution to the problem of the fish seller: an undecorated holding tank, or one that provides no shelter at all, may be superior to a well-decorated tank in terms of reducing the aggressive behavior of its inhabitants. It still remains to be demonstrated, however, whether territorial deprivation is, in itself, stressful, and if so, if it is more or less stressful than aggression. I do not recommend that reef fishes be kept in undecorated aquariums by hobbyists under any circumstances.

The Importance of "Cleaner Fishes"

All fishes occasionally develop mild infections or skin abrasions, and they also are susceptible to infestation with skin and gill parasites. At such times, the affected individuals seek out the services of "cleaner fishes," fishes that remove external parasites, dead tissue, and other annoying matter from the bodies of other fishes.[12] More than two dozen species of fishes are known to be "professional" cleaners. Some like the neon goby, *Gobiosoma oceanops*, (Fig. 49) and the Pacific cleaner wrasse, *Labroides dimidiatus*, are cleaners

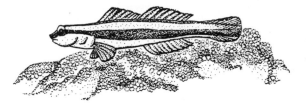

Figure 49. The neon goby, *Gobiosoma oceanops*, is a specialized "cleaner fish." It removes parasites, dead scales, and other irritating material from the skin and gills of other fishes.

throughout their postlarval lives. Certain wrasses, angelfishes, and butterflyfishes perform cleaning services only during the juvenile stages of their lives.

Cleaner fishes have characteristic coloration, usually bright blue and black stripes, that seem to be recognized universally throughout the sea. Despite their small sizes, they rarely are eaten by large predators. In the wild many fishes have their bodies cleaned regularly, and some visit the residence or cleaning station of a particular cleaner fish once or several times daily. Few animal interactions are as astonishing to observe as a tiny neon goby swimming into the mouth and gills of a huge grouper, and then swimming out, unharmed.

Most cleaners can survive without customers, and most fishes can survive without cleaners. I have noticed, in fact, that some species, such as the false clown anemonefish (*Amphiprion ocellaris*) and the yellowhead jawfish (*Opistognathus aurifrons*) seem to avoid the services of cleaner fishes and become upset when a cleaner fish tries to perform its service for them. Nevertheless, it is a good idea to include one cleaner fish in every aquarium that houses reef fishes.

When purchasing a cleaner fish, take care to avoid the sharp-toothed blenny, *Aspidontus taeniatus*. This fish, which is also known as the "false cleaner wrasse" resembles the Pacific cleaner wrasse closely in both appearance and behavior. Unlike the wrasse, however, *Aspidontus* is not a cleaner; instead of removing unwanted materials from the bodies of other fishes, it feeds on the fishes themselves, nipping the scales and fins of the unsuspecting customers, then darting away before its victims have time to react. *Aspidontus taeniatus* and *Labroides dimidiatus* can be distinguished easily by the trained observer who is alert to the anatomical differences between the two. These differences are illustrated in Figure 50.

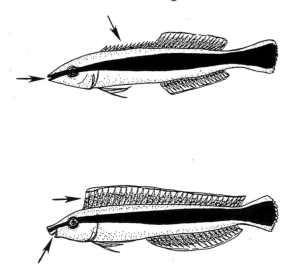

Figure 50. Some conspicuous differences between the cleaner wrasse, *Labroides dimidiatus* (top) and the saw-toothed blenny or "false cleaner wrasse," *Aspidontus taeniatus* (bottom). The wrasse's mouth is located at the tip of its snout, in the middle of the black band, whereas the blenny's mouth is situated on the underside of its snout, below the black band. The dorsal fin of the wrasse is tapered toward the head, whereas the blenny's dorsal fin is the same height throughout its length.

Animals Without Backbones

In the preceding discussion about appropriate species for aquariums, there has been no mention of *invertebrates,* animals without backbones. This omission was made because recommendations for invertebrates differ greatly from those for fishes. The types of invertebrates sold at most aquarium stores fall into two broad categories: (1) relatively immobile filter feeders; and (2) relatively mobile, carnivorous (flesh-eating) bottom scavengers.

Filter Feeders

The invertebrates in this category include live corals, tube worms, mollusks (clams, oysters, scallops, etc.), sponges, some sea anemones, and "living rock." With few exceptions, the sizes and numbers of these animals and their compatibility with one another usually do not present stocking problems, because these creatures have no eyes or legs and are therefore incapable of establishing territories or behaving aggressively toward one another or to fishes.

The major limiting factor in maintaining filter-feeding invertebrates is the aquarist's ability to keep them properly nourished. In nature, these creatures consume a wide variety of planktonic organisms, for which substitutes are not easily obtained. In the aquarium, they can be fed such delicacies as newly hatched brine shrimp, puréed or minced shellfish, or fresh blood. The latter foods can pollute aquarium water rapidly, and their presence in the water also may be unhealthy to fishes that reside in the same tank.

Because they are so difficult to keep alive, even in an aquarium that contains no fishes, I do not advise that filter-feeding invertebrates be kept in a community aquarium. Their death from starvation after a few weeks or months in captivity is inevitable, so to purchase them with this foreknowledge is not only senseless but also cruel.

Some filter-feeding sea anemones can be acclimated to accept diets of chopped fish, shrimp, clams, and brine shrimp. These species, which include the members of the genera *Anthopleura, Condylactis, Stoichactis, Radianthus, and Tealia,* can be distinguished from strict filter feeders by their stout, tubular tentacles. An aquarium with an established bacteriological filter can accommodate many sea anemones, but for practical purposes, only one anemone for each square foot (929 square centimeters) of bottom surface area is desirable. (See Table 2 in Chapter 2 for bottom surface areas of various standard aquariums.) Many tropical marine anemones are found in association with various species of anemonefishes. An anemone can survive, however, without an anemonefish, and anemonefishes can be kept successfully without anemones. Because sea anemones do not have gills and therefore cannot "pump" water over their respiratory surfaces, they seem to thrive best in aquariums in which a rapid flow of water (e.g. from a water pump) is directed over their bodies.

Scavengers

Scavengers include such animals as shrimps, crabs, and lobsters. Unlike the filter-feeding invertebrates, these crustacean animals have excellent vision and can move rapidly around an aquarium. They all are carnivores which, in addition to feeding on bottom debris, consume small invertebrates and fishes in nature, and can be maintained on chopped seafoods in captivity.

Crabs and other crustaceans are notorious for their unpleasant dispositions, and for their combative behavior. An aquarium that is stocked initially with several crabs and shrimps generally becomes an aquarium containing only one or two *fat* crabs after a short time. Because they are so aggressive and are cannibalistic as well, few crustaceans should be kept in the same saltwater tank. Only one or two small crabs or shrips are compatible in even the largest aquarium. The banded coral shrimp, *Stenopus hispidus*, is a particularly attractive species, and is not aggressive toward fishes. It is, however, territorial. Like reef fishes, crustaceans require adequate decor for shelter and refuge. Also, no crustacean should be kept in an aquarium that houses a triggerfish, because they are a favorite food of this type of fish.

Bottom feeders or *scavengers* play an important role in aquarium management. Regardless of how carefully one tries to avoid overfeeding, some uneaten food always seems to end up on the bottom of the aquarium, and it often escapes detection during tank checks. Uneaten foods decompose rapidly in a conditioned aquarium, and they are capable of fouling the water. Scavengers consume uneaten food, thus keeping the tank bottom clean. Hermit crabs (Fig. 51), particularly varieties that do not grow very large, are

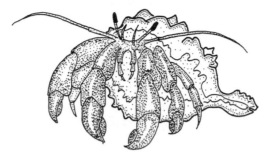

Figure 51. Every aquarium should be stocked with a scavenger, such as a hermit crab.

excellent invertebrates to add to an aquarium for scavenging purposes. In addition to their contribution to housekeeping, they are delightful creatures with a most comical array of behaviors. It is important to point out that hermit crabs do not manufacture their own shells; rather, they occupy the empty shells of dead snails. When keeping hermit crabs, it is therefore necessary to provide them with several empty snail shells of various sizes, into which they may move as they grow.

HOW MANY FISHES TO KEEP

From a strictly technical standpoint, an aquarium can accommodate as many fishes as its bacteriological filter can support. A tank with efficient bacteriological filtration probably could maintain low levels of ammonia even if it were packed wall to wall with fishes; indeed stocking densities are nearly this high at some laboratories and fish farms. The efficiency of the bacteriological filter is not, however, the only consideration in determining how many fishes to keep in a tropical marine aquarium. A second and perhaps more important criterion is based on the spatial needs of reef fishes, and on the adverse effects of crowding on fish behavior and physiology. From a psychological standpoint, a marine aquarium can become dangerously overcrowded long before its filtration capacity is reached.

Fishes held under crowded conditions develop changes in their blood compositon that are symptomatic of stress,[13-15] and crowding may also inhibit their growth and decrease their resistance to disease.[16] Moreover, aggressive behavior from a tankmate from which a captive fish cannot escape causes a variety of physiological disturbances that are characteristic of stress and can have unfavorable consequences.[13]

Most recommendations about stocking fishes in marine aquariums are based on the efficiency of filtration. The variety of recommendations is as diverse as the authors who write them, and include such suggestions as, "one inch of fish for every two gallons of water,"[17] "six to eight fishes not bigger than three or four inches for every 27 gallons of water,"[18] "1 to 2 gallons per medium-sized [2- to 3-inch] fish,"[19] and "three inches of animal (fish or invertebrate) per square foot of filter bed surface area."[20]

My recommendation for stocking an aquarium, which is based simply on behavioral considerations, is *one fish per 10 gallons (38 liters) of water*. As discussed previously in this chapter, the only fishes appropriate for an aquarium of 100 gallons (380 liters) or less are those whose adult sizes are 5 inches (13 centimeters) or less. Thus, a 30-gallon aquarium should contain three fishes, a 40-gallon aquarium four fishes, and so on.

Because the fishes you obtain will be juveniles, the aquarium will seem empty at first. But only at first. Under favorable conditions most reef fishes grow rapidly, and your tank will be filled more than adequately in less time than you imagine. In one of the few published studies on the growth of reef fishes, for example, it was reported that the filefish, *Navodon modestus*, was 13 centimeters (5.1 inches) long at age 4 months, 15 centimeters (5.9 inches) at age 5 months, 18 centimeters (7.1 inches) at age 1 year, and 25 to 26 centimeters (10 inches) at age 3 years.[21] A smaller, more suitable aquarium fish, the false clown anemonefish (*Amphiprion ocellaris*), is about ¾ to 1 inch (1.9 to 2.5 centimeters) long at age 4 months, 1.5 inches (3.8 centimeters) at age 6 months, 2 to 2.5 inches (5.1 to 6.4 centimeters) at age 1 year, and 3 inches (7.6 centimeters) at age 2 years.[22]

STOCKING ORDER

Even the most aggressive animal usually becomes timid after being transferred to new, unfamiliar surroundings. The aquarist can take advantage of this fact when gradually increasing the population of a newly conditioned aquarium.

The general rule to follow when stocking a new aquarium with fishes is to *introduce the LEAST aggressive species FIRST, and the MOST aggressive species LAST.*

The first additions to the aquarium should be relatively nonaggressive species, such as the false clown anemonefish (*Amphiprion ocellaris*), *Centropyge* species of angelfishes, and gobies and blennies. Slightly more aggressive species, such as small wrasses, butterflyfishes, and surgeonfishes should be added next. Fishes that are notorious bullies (various damselfishes, most anemonefishes, and triggerfishes) should be added last.

In this way, no aggressive fish is given the chance to establish all or most of the tank as its territory before the more timid species are introduced. As noted in Chapter 5, after a new fish has been added, always allow about a week for the filter bacteria to adjust before further increasing the aquarium's population. It should be pointed out that nearly every newly introduced fish is frightened and timid, and spends most of its time in hiding for a few weeks to one month, so territoriality-related problems are not immediately apparent to. the aquarist.

It is also necessary to mention again that the above recommendations pertain only to the small fishes listed in Table 15. Many juveniles of species that exceed 5 inches in length as adults are highly aggressive and territorial even when newly captured, and for reasons other than size restrictions, they are undesirable additions to most tanks.

HOW TO CHOOSE HEALTHY FISHES

The high cost of tropical marine fishes reflects the fact that, with few exceptions, they are not "farmed" commercially. Rather, they must be collected individually from their native habitats and then processed and shipped by various exporters, importers, and distributors, before reaching a retailer's tanks. The care and handling of reef fishes, from the time they are collected until the time you purchase them, generally are far from ideal, and fishes undoubtedly suffer considerable stress at each step along the way. Regardless of how rare or beautiful a newly arrived fish may be, it is worthless if it is not in good health. Some suggestions for selecting healthy individuals from a dealer's aquarium follow.

1. Buy fishes only from reputable suppliers. Avoid the tropical fish departments of discount stores, because their personnel are often less experienced and knowledgable about marine species and their care.

2. Examine the retailer's aquariums carefully. They should be clean and properly equipped, and should contain no dead animals or excessive debris. The quality of a dealer's own tanks is a good indication of the quality of his fishes and of the care they receive.

3. A healthy fish can be recognized in two ways: by its behavior and by its appearance. If you are interested in a particular species, try to learn as much as you can about its normal behavior before trying to select a healthy specimen. It is perfectly normal, for example, for a goby to rest on the bottom, or for a royal gramma (*Gramma loreto*) to swim upside down along the contours of a rock, whereas these behaviors are, to say the least, signs of poor health in many other species. Excellent discussions of the behavior of many Caribbean fishes are given in *Reef Fish: Behavior and Ecology on the Reef and in the Aquarium,* by Ronald E. Thresher (Palmetto Publishing Co., St. Petersburg), and the nature and habits of many other tropical species can be found in a variety of fish catalogues.[18,19,23-25] Part of the normal behavior of almost every healthy fish is to feed aggressively. Do not buy a fish until you have seen it accept food in the dealer's aquarium.

4. The physical appearance of a fish is the second major indicator of its health. The appearance of a healthy fish is characterized by the absence of all signs of stress and disease. Symptoms of stress and disease are given in Tables 20 and 21 in Chapter 13. If the specimen that interests you or, for that matter, any of its tankmates, exhibits one or a number of these symptoms, pass it up and choose a healthier fish from another aquarium.

5. Whenever possible, avoid buying a fish that has just arrived at a retail store. Instead, choose one that has been in the dealer's tank for at least one week. The majority of newly imported fishes are severely stressed, and it is also likely that they have been fed inadequately, if at all, from the time of their capture. Stressed fishes usually refuse to feed, and they develop overt signs of disease soon after they are introduced into an aquarium. It is to your advantage

to let the fishes go through the critical period of transition at the retailer's store; if a fish cannot adjust to life in captivity, better that it should die in his tank than in yours.

Chapter 10

CAPTURING, HANDLING, AND TRANSPORTING FISHES

It is as well not to handle the fish more than is absolutely necessary when tranferring them to another vessel. . . .

Reginald A.R. Bennett
Marine Aquaria, 1889

The transportation of live fish has always been a laborious business to me, and hazardous to the fish, until I hit upon the plan of conveying them in water, made very cold by the addition of ice . . . Young fish are much more easily transported than older ones [because] they do not exhaust the water so rapidly. . . .

Theodatus Garlick
Artificial Propagation, 1857

HAVING selected an apparently healthy fish in a retailer's aquarium, the aquarist is faced with the task of capturing it and then transporting it to its final destination. Because traditional methods of capturing and transporting fishes can be stressful, new methods have been developed that should reduce the trauma of these procedures.

CAPTURING FISHES IN AN AQUARIUM

Of all aquarium accessories, the net probably is the most dangerous and the most abused — by amateurs and professionals alike. Consider the plight of the netted fish. Contact with even the softest fabric can tear off its scales, scrape protective mucus from its skin, and scratch its lidless eyes, leaving it vulnerable to invasion by disease-causing bacteria and fungi. When the fish is lifted from the water in a net, it panics and struggles; in addition to the physical injury it incurs from contact with the net, its gills collapse, and it is soon deprived of dissolved oxygen.

After netting, a fish experiences severe physiological stress, and it may take several days to several weeks for full recovery.[1-9] During this time, a fish's ability to resist disease is lower than normal, making it an ideal candidate for attack by any pathogenic organism that happens to be present in the water.[10-12]

It has been demonstrated experimentally that fewer fishes die after handling if they are not removed from water, and that mortalities increase after removal from water in nets.[13] One procedure that has been recommended for capturing a fish in an aquarium requires that a transparent plastic bag be used in place of a net.[14] The rationale is that the plastic cannot abrade the fish's skin and eyes, that a new bag is less likely than an old net to harbor disease organisms, and that fishes are less frightened by capture in a transparent bag, because it is not as visible as is a net.

Although the above water-transfer method is certainly superior to netting, it, too, has drawbacks. The first is that it is extremely difficult to capture a fish in a plastic bag, particularly if the aquarium is filled with decor; the bag collapses from the water pressure, and is difficult to navigate around rocks and corals. Second, when one considers that manipulating a plastic bag underwater requires two hands, it seems unlikely that capture by this method is any less frightening than netting. In fact, even if a fish were blind, its lateral-line sense (see Chapter 1) would keep it aware of every movement of the bag, thus enabling it to avoid capture.

One further point must be made about the capture of a fish in an aquarium. Fishes become stressed by being chased and then confined in a small area, and the longer the capture procedure and confinement, the more severe the stress response.[3,4,15] A fish that has been subjected to excessive exercise from being chased may die of sheer exhaustion, even though it has not been touched.

Regardless of the procedure used for capturing a fish, it is crucial that capture and transfer to a transport container be carried out as quickly and efficiently as possible to avoid exhausting the fish. This often requires that a strategy for capturing a particular fish be devised ahead of time. It may be necessary to remove some decor from the tank, or it may be helpful to have another person available to assist you. The less agitated and frightened a fish becomes during capture, the less it is stressed, and the greater are its chances to survive.

Procedure for Capturing a Fish

The following procedure employs a net for capturing a fish in an aquarium, but avoids the stress and injury incurred by removing a fish from water.

1. The net used for capturing a fish should be as large as can easily be manipulated in the aquarium. A fish can be captured more quickly in a large net than in a small one, and it is also less likely to panic after being captured, because it will have more swimming room.

2. When netting a fish, move as slowly as possible. The rapid movement of a net in an aquarium may be more frightening to the fish than the mere presence of the net.

3. Capture the fish, and then turn the net upright, so the fish cannot escape (Fig. 52a). Move the net slowly toward the surface.

4. Keeping the net (and the fish) fully submerged, transfer the fish to a drinking glass, a glass or plastic jar, or any other suitable container (Fig. 52b).

5. Pour some tank water into a suitably sized polyethylene bag and gently transfer the fish to the bag. This may be carried out by submerging the capture vessel in the water in the bag, and allowing the fish to swim out.

6. Inflate the bag with air (from a small air pump) or with oxygen gas, if available. Twist the top of the bag, and seal it tightly

(a)

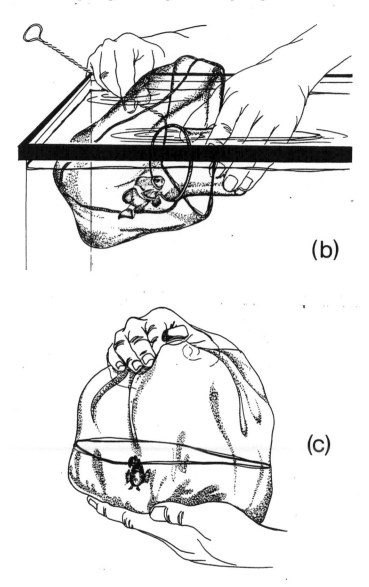

Figure 52. Procedure for capturing and "bagging" a fish without removing it from the water. (a) Trap the fish in a large, soft net, and move it gently toward the water surface. (b) Keeping the net and fish submerged, allow the fish to swim into a glass jar or any other suitable container. (c) Carefully transfer the fish and water to a clear plastic bag. Add enough water to cover the fish comfortably. Inflate the bag with air from an air pump or with compressed oxygen, then twist the top of the bag and seal it tightly with an elastic band.

with an elastic band. The bag should contain approximately 1/5 water and 4/5 air or oxygen (Fig. 52c).

This procedure is somewhat more time-consuming than capturing a fish in a net, removing the net from water, and dropping the fish into a water-filled bag. Despite the common sense behind this method, many retailers may be reluctant to adopt it, even though it is to their advantage in terms of fish survival and customer satisfaction. If your dealer refuses to capture and handle a fish according to the recommended procedure, do it yourself or take your business elsewhere.

TRANSPORTING FISHES

Harmful environmental changes can occur during the transportation of fishes in sealed plastic bags. These are: (1) changes in temperature; (2) a decrease in the concentration of dissolved oxygen; (3) an increase in the concentration of free carbon dioxide, and an accompanying decrease in pH; and (4) an increase in the concentration of ammonia in the water. All of these changes are stressful to fishes (Chapter 8) and therefore should be avoided.

Most tropical fish dealers displace the air in transport bags with oxygen gas before sealing them, so depletion of dissolved oxygen generally is not a problem during transportation. Temperature, however, can be a critical factor, especially if fishes are transported during the winter months, because the small volume of water in a transport bag can lose heat rapidly.

To avoid subjecting fishes to a change in temperature, the bag(s) should be placed in an insulated container. A Styrofoam ice bucket is ideal for carrying one or two small bags; several bags or one large bag should be carried in a Styrofoam chest. Harmful changes in pH and in the concentrations of carbon dioxide and ammonia should be of little concern if the fishes will be in transit for one hour or less. If the fishes are to be transported for longer intervals, however, provisions must be made to prevent such changes from taking place.

Preventing Changes in pH and Carbon Dioxide

Fishes consume oxygen and excrete carbon dioxide. When the

water in which they are held is not aerated, increased concentrations of carbon dioxide can cause the fishes to suffocate, even though adequate concentrations of dissolved oxygen are still present. The accumulation of carbon dioxide also lowers the pH of the water.

Decreases in pH and increases in the concentration of carbon dioxide during the transportation of marine fishes can be prevented by adding an organic buffer called *tris* to the water. Tris buffer can increase the acid-absorbing capacity of seawater by as much as 50 times without harming fishes, and its use has been shown to reduce shipping mortalities substantially.[16]

A form of tris buffer that was formulated for shipping marine fishes is called Trizma®-8.3 (Sigma Chemical Co., St. Louis, Missouri). Its recommended usage is 6.77 grams per liter (about 25 grams per gallon) of seawater. At the Institute for Aquarium Studies, we found that this concentration of the buffer, when used in sealed shipping bags stocked with fish, resulted in pH decreases of less than 0.2 pH unit after 24 hours of simulated transportation; in contrast, the pH had decreased by about 1.0 pH unit during the same period in bags containing unbuffered seawater.[17]

Preventing the Accumulation of Ammonia

A shipping bag is similar to an unconditioned aquarium, because ammonia begins to accumulate in the water soon after a fish has been introduced into it. Ammonia is thought to be the second important factor that contributes to the mortalities of fishes during and after transportation. Two approaches are commonly taken to prevent the build-up of ammonia in shipping water. The first is to reduce the quantity of ammonia excreted by decreasing the metabolic rate of the captive fishes. This can be accomplished by lowering the water temperature, adding anesthetics to the water, or starving the fishes before they are transported. The major drawback of these methods is that they are all capable of stressing fishes.

The second approach is to remove ammonia from the water after it has been excreted. Ion exchangers such as clinoptilolite (a naturally occurring mineral) and various synthetic resins are marketed for hobbyists as "ammonia absorbers." Although they work well in freshwater, they are ineffective in seawater, because of salt interference. Ammonia can be removed from seawater in shipping bags, however, by the same method that prevents its accumulation in marine aquariums — bacteriological filtration (see Chapters 3 and 5).

Studies conducted in our laboratory have shown that the addition to shipping bags of small amounts of bottom filtrant (crushed oyster shell, dolomitic limestone, etc.) from a conditioned aquarium significantly reduces the build-up of ammonia during the simulated transportation of marine fishes.[17] The efficiency of ammonia removal might be expected to vary with each transportation situation, and would depend on such factors as the weight of the fishes, the concentration of dissolved oxygen, and the initial capacity of the bacteria on the filtrant to consume ammonia. Generally speaking, however, enough filtrant should be added to each shipping bag to form a thin layer across the entire bottom.

Regardless of whether the seawater in shipping bags is buffered or unbuffered, conditioned filtrant will control the accumulation of ammonia. Ammonia removal by this method is therefore recommended, even if the transport water does not contain Trizma-8.3 for pH control. *Under no circumstances, however, should the water be buffered in the absence of conditioned filtrant during shipping.* The toxicity of ammonia to fishes depends chiefly on pH, and the higher the pH, the greater its toxicity. Thus, the concentration of ammonia that accumulates in a shipping bag *without* conditioned filtrant might be harmless in unbuffered seawater, whereas the same concentration in buffered seawater might be deadly.

SUMMARY

To reduce the chances of stressing a fish during capture, handling, and transportation, the following procedure is recommended.

1. Capture the fish in a large aquarium net, but do not remove the net or the fish from the water.

2. Keeping the fish submerged at all times, transfer it from the net to any suitable glass or plastic container.

3. Carefully transfer the fish to a heavy polyethylene shipping bag that contains some aquarium water. The volume of seawater required will vary with the size of the fish and the size of the bag, but it

should be enough to cover the fish completely and to allow it room to swim.

4. If the fish will be in transit for one hour or less, proceed directly to Step 6.

5. If the fish will be in transit for more than one hour, the bottom of the shipping bag should be covered with a thin layer of filtrant from a conditioned aquarium, to reduce the accumulation of ammonia. To prevent a decrease in pH and the accumulation of carbon dioxide, the seawater in the bag should be buffered with 6.77 grams per liter (25 grams per gallon) of Trizma-8.3.

6. Inflate the bag with compressed oxygen, if available, and seal it tightly. The ratio of water to oxygen in the bag should be about 1:4 by volume.

7. Place the bag in a Styrofoam container to insulate it against a change in temperature.

No formal studies have been carried out to determine whether the use of the above procedure reduces stress and fish deaths related to capture, handling, and transportation. I have found, though, that fishes handled and transported as described seemed to arrive in better condition, were less prone to disease, and adapted to aquarium conditions more rapidly than fishes that were not.

Recently, for example, our laboratory in Connecticut received an air shipment of approximately 350 juvenile anemonefish from a hatchery in Florida. The fish had been captured, transferred to shipping bags, and transported according to the recommendations given in this chapter. Although the fish had been in transit for more than 12 hours, not a single one was dead on arrival. At the time of this writing (40 days after the shipment arrived), only one fish has died, and the others are in excellent health.

Chapter 11

ACCLIMATION AND SPECIAL CARE OF NEW FISHES

Of course, it is always best to transfer any captured aquatic objects to their new habitats as quickly as possible. Keeping them in unnatural conditions is cruel, and no true naturalist will inflict pain on the humblest creature if he can possibly avoid it.

J.E. Taylor
The Aquarium, 1881

[The owner] must not . . . be dismayed if he find a good many of his stock do not survive the ordeal of domestication; some will be sure to die in the first twenty-four hours . . . some in the course of the first week; but those which live over the first ten days or a fortnight may be considered acclimatised, and will probably continue to exist happily in the tank for years.

Reginald A.R. Bennett
Marine Aquaria,1889

ACCLIMATION

B ECAUSE tropical marine fishes may be stressed by slight changes in temperature, pH, salt concentration, and other factors, it is important to allow a new specimen ample time to adjust or become *acclimated* to the conditions in your aquarium, which almost always will be different from those in a retailer's tanks.

Before you purchase your first fish, it is always a good idea to measure the temperature and salt concentration of the water in the retailer's aquarium *with your own thermometer and hydrometer* (readings obtained with different instruments often vary greatly). Then, before bringing the fish home, you can adjust the temperature and specific gravity of the water in your aquarium to those of the retailer's tank (see Chapter 6). Do not be overly concerned if the values are higher or lower than those recommended in this book.

They can be readjusted to appropriate values after the initial acclimation is carried out, as described later in this section.

Procedure for Acclimating a New Fish

1. If the fish has been transported in a light-proof container, it is important to avoid stressing it with sudden exposure to bright light. Turn off the aquarium light, and dim the room lights.

2. Remove the shipping bag from its container, open the bag, and pour off and discard all but enough water to cover the fish comfortably.

3. Roll down the top of the bag to form an air-filled cuff, and lower the bag into the aquarium. If the cuff has been formed properly, the bag will remain open and will float freely at the water surface (Fig. 53).

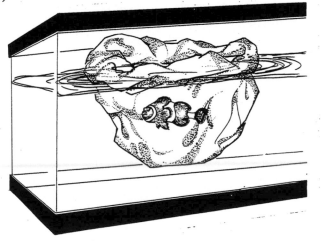

Figure 53. An air-filled cuff around the edge of a plastic bag keeps the bag open and afloat during the acclimation of a fish to the water in a different aquarium.

4. Pour a small volume of tank water (approximately 1/5 the volume already in the bag) into the floating bag. Repeat every five minutes for at least 45 minutes, or until the volume of water in the bag has been tripled.

5. As an alternative to Steps 3 and 4 (the "flotation" method of acclimation) you may wish to carry out acclimation by the "drip"

method as described below.

a. After opening the shipping bag, place it in an appropriately sized
   container (e.g. a small bucket) and set it on the floor, or on a
   table or chair beside the aquarium.
b. Cut a length of airline tubing long enough to be used as a
   miniature siphon hose from the aquarium to the bag. Tie a loose
   knot near the center of the tubing. The knot will act as a valve to
   control the flow of water.
c. Begin siphoning water through the tubing from the aquarium into the bag (see Chapter 6). Tighten or loosen the knot as
   necessary to produce a steady, drop-by-drop flow rate. Continue
   to drip water into the bag for at least 45 minutes, or until the
   volume of water in the bag has been tripled or quadrupled.

6. Pour off and discard all but enough water to cover the fish
comfortably.

7. Lower the bag into the aquarium, tip it, and allow the fish to
swim out. If the fish refuses to leave the bag, elevate the bottom of
the bag, keeping its open end in the water, and pour the fish gently
out of the bag.

8. Do not turn on the aquarium light for at least one hour to
allow the fish to calm down, and do not try to feed it or disturb it in
any way. The best cure for the harmful effects of stress is complete
rest.

Acclimating Fishes to a Different Temperature

Before introducing a new fish into a new aquarium, it is sometimes
necessary to adjust the temperature of the water to a value that is
outside the range recommended in this book, to make it the same as
the temperature in the retailer's tank and to prevent stressing the fish
with a change in temperature. A temperature adjustment of this
nature should *not* be made if your tank already contains fishes; instead, the adjustment and the entire acclimation process should be
carried out in an auxiliary aquarium.

If such an adjustment has to be made, the fish subsequently must
be acclimated slowly to a temperature within the recommended
range of 75 to 79°F (24 to 26°C). Starting the day after you bring
the fish home, make slight adjustments on the thermostat control

dial of your aquarium heater, thereby increasing or decreasing the temperature by no more than 2°F (1°C) every 24 hours, until the desired temperature has been reached. If, for example, the initial temperature were 86°F (30°C) and the desired temperature were 77°F (25°C), the change-over should take about 5 days.

Acclimating Fishes to a Different Salt Concentration

The specific gravity of your aquarium water also may have to be adjusted to a value that is higher or lower than the recommended values. *Acclimation of the fish to the proper specific gravity should not begin until temperature acclimation has been completed.* At that time, the specific gravity should be increased or decreased by no more than 0.001 units every 24 hours, until the desired value is reached. Procedures for adjusting the specific gravity are given in Chapter 6. Although the specific gravity values in retailers' aquariums usually are too high, requiring that the value in your tank be lowered gradually by adding fresh water, occasionally it is necessary to raise the specific gravity of your tank water by adding more artificial sea salts. In this event, I must repeat that *dry sea salts must never be poured directly into an aquarium that contains fishes.* Rather, they should be dissolved in water and then added to the tank.

SPECIAL CARE OF NEW FISHES

The first month in captivity is a critical period for any fish. Without doubt, it has suffered considerable abuse from subjection to indelicate handling and transportation, and from confinement in various aquariums under stressful environmental conditions. As a result, the odds are high that the new fish is experiencing some degree of physiological stress that may impair its ability to defend itself against competing fishes and against disease-causing microorganisms.

The Case Against Quarantine with Drugs

Most authors recommend that newly acquired fishes be held in quarantine for at least two weeks. The word "quarantine" connotes isolation from others to prevent the spread of infectious diseases. Traditionally, quarantined fishes are treated with one or more medicinal baths to rid them of the disease organisms they carry. Such treatment is thought to protect resident fishes in the aquarium from the diseases afflicting the new specimen. This line of thought, in my estimation, shows a lack of understanding of the disease process and of the value of drug treatment for fish diseases. I strongly disagree with it for several reasons.

First, there is never any justification for administering drugs to any animal that is not clinically diseased. Assuming that the aquarist has selected an apparently healthy fish, there is no reason to regard it as otherwise. Treating a newly acquired fish with drugs and chemicals before introducing it into an aquarium is as senseless and illogical as administering antibiotics and other drugs to a child before he enters a new school to prevent him from contaminating his classmates with disease organisms.

Second, there is no known way to disinfect a fish and the water in which it was transported that will not kill the fish itself. This statement applies to physical as well as chemical methods of disinfection. Through the use of an elaborate computer model, for example, it has been found that it would take infinite time to disinfect a stocked aquarium with ultraviolet radiation, even if the disinfection unit were 100 percent effective.[1] Aquarium water always contains tremendous numbers and varieties of microorganisms, some with the potential to cause disease,[2] and it can be said without qualification that every fish always carries some of these microorganisms, regardless of whether it has been treated with drugs or not.

Third, it has been demonstrated experimentally that many medications sold for aquarium use are not effective at the recommended dosages.[3,4] The administration of subclinical dosages of antibiotics and other drugs can breed drug-resistant microorganisms that are difficult or impossible to kill when drug treatment actually becomes necessary.

Fourth, "bath" administration of drugs (adding them to the water) is an imprecise and ineffective method of treating diseases of fishes, as compared with methods such as topical applications, oral administration, and injections; with the exception of one or two antibiotics, there is no evidence that drugs administered in baths are absorbed in adequate concentrations to be effective against internal disease organisms.[5] Nevertheless, nearly every drug available to hobbyists is designed simply to be added to the water.

Fifth, there is increasing evidence that drug treatment, in itself, is capable of stressing fishes. Among the compounds that have been found to be stressful are copper, malachite green, and formalin.[6-10] Moreover, the physiological stress resulting from drug administration may actually increase the susceptibility of fishes to certain diseases. Copper compounds, which have been studied more extensively than other medications, will be used to illustrate this point.

Copper is a metal which, when present in sufficient concentrations, is toxic to all forms of life. It is used widely treat certain parasitic infestations of fishes (see Chapter 13). According to an estimate by the owner of a large retail aquarium store in Hartford, medications containing copper may constitute 50 percent or more of the disease-related products available to saltwater aquarium hobbyists.[11]

The chemistry of copper in water is extremely complicated, and the toxicity of a given concentration of "total" copper depends largely on various chemical characteristics of the water; in hard water containing high concentrations of dissolved organics, for example, a given dosage of copper usually is less toxic than the same dosage in soft water of low organic content. In addition, the copper that is added to an aquarium can be removed from solution rapidly by adsorption on solid substrates, including glass, carbonate filtrants, and activated carbon.[12]

It has been shown through careful experimentation that fishes can be stressed by exposure to concentrations of copper well below the dosages recommended for disease treatment and prevention (0.1 to 0.3 parts per million) and that exposure to very low concentrations of copper can also increase the fishes' susceptibility to bacterial and viral infections. Some of these findings are summarized below.

- Yearling coho salmon were exposed to water containing 0, 0.015, 0.060, and 0.090 parts per million of copper for intervals of two hours to one week. All the copper-exposed fish developed high concentrations of cortisol, a hormone that indicates stress, in their blood. Moreover, the fish that were exposed to the highest level of copper for the longest time died about 12 to 15 hours after being captured and transferred to buckets of copper-free water, whereas the control fish (those which were not exposed to copper) survived the same handling procedure.[7]

- Eels were taken from brackish water and divided into two groups. The first group was transferred to fresh water that contained no copper, and the second group was transferred to fresh water containing as little as 0.03 parts per million of copper. The eels in the first group survived for more than one year, but those in the second group developed vibriosis, a bacterial disease, and died within two to four months.[13]

- Fingerling rainbow trout were bathed for one week in water containing 0.002 to 0.010 parts per million of copper, and then were exposed to IHN virus (a major pathogen of trout) and transferred to copper-free water. The control fish were exposed only to copper or only to the virus. It was found that pre-exposure to even the lowest concentration of copper increased the number of deaths of fish exposed to the virus, and that the greatest number of deaths occurred after exposure to the highest level of copper.[14]

- Steelhead trout were exposed to 0.007 to 0.010 parts per million of copper for four days and then infected with bacteria known to cause redmouth disease. Significantly more fish died in the test groups than in the control groups, which were exposed to only copper or only the bacteria.[15]

Although no comparable studies have been conducted with marine fishes or with tropical freshwater fishes, the results of the above experiments have important implications that should be of concern to any aquarist who considers using copper for disease prevention or treatment. First, concentrations of copper *ten times lower than the recommended therapeutic dosage* can stress fishes. Second, the stress caused by exposure to copper can decrease a fish's ability to survive subsequent stressful procedures or environmental conditions. Third, stress from copper can increase a fish's susceptibility to certain bacterial and viral diseases; these diseases have the potential to be more deadly than the parasistic infestations that copper is used to prevent or eradicate.

The sixth and final reason I do not recommend quarantining new fishes in drug baths is that the addition of medications to aquarium water can kill or inhibit the growth and metabolism of filter bacteria. When bacteriological filtration is impaired, the aquarium is reverted to an unconditioned state, one in which ammonia accumulates in the water. Terramycin®, chloramphenicol, erythromycin, methylene blue, chlortetracycline, potassium permanganate, sulfadiazine, and sulfanilamide can inhibit bacteriological filtration substantially in 'fresh water.[16-19] Research conducted at the Institute for Aquarium Studies showed that bacteriological filtration in seawater aquariums was inhibited to various degrees by methylene blue, neomycin sulfate, chloramphenicol, and copper sulfate.[20] Therapeutic dosages of each of these compounds resulted in increased concentrations of ammonia in the water, whereas treatment with gentamycin sulfate, nifurpirinol (Furanace®), and quinacrine hydrochloride did not. Because fishes may become stressed, and their disease resistance lowered by exposure to ammonia (Chapters 5 and 8), medications that inhibit the activities of filter bacteria should not be used for disease prevention.

The "Intensive Care Unit"

The last thing that a stressed fish needs is to be subjected to additional stressful conditions. The one thing it does need is time to recuperate from the trauma of capture and handling and to adjust to captivity in an aquarium that is completely free of stressful environmental conditions. The "Intensive Care Unit" (ICU) is the aquarium in which a newly acquired fish spends its first two weeks. During this period of intensive care, which is, in many respects, analogous to the treatment given to critically ill people in hospitals, all efforts should be made to help the fish regain its strength and its natural defenses against disease.

The ICU is any aquarium that contains no established aggressive fishes. If your aquarium has just been set up, it can serve as an ICU for the first fishes you introduce into it. If the aquarium is more than a few months old and is inhabited by one or more territorial species, the intensive care of a new arrival should be carried out in an auxiliary aquarium (see Chapter 2).

If the auxiliary aquarium is to be used as an ICU, it should be set up and maintained exactly the same way as the main tank. Adequate decor for concealment is particularly important, because the newest fishes usually are the least secure and spend much of their time in hiding. If no extra plastic plants or large pieces of rocks or coral are available, an arrangement of broken clay flowerpots can be set up to provide suitable shelter in the form of an "artificial reef."

When you arrive home with a new specimen, acclimate it to the aquarium water as described previously in this chapter, and release it into the ICU. After a few hours have passed, turn on the aquarium light, and offer the fish a little food. Live foods, such as newly hatched or adult brine shrimp, are accepted more readily than prepared foods by most "undomesticated" fishes (see Chapter 12). If the fish does not eat, *leave it alone* and try again later.

During its first several days in the ICU a new fish may be extremely timid and may keep out of sight for long periods. Do not make the mistake of trying to prod it out of its refuge, which would only frighten it more. Instead, try to encourage it out of hiding with food. Experiment with several different foods to learn what kinds the fish prefers.

It is particularly important to spend a lot of time around the ICU, to enable the fish to become accustomed to your presence and to give yourself the opportunity to observe the fish closely, so you can become familiar with its behavior and habits. Watch the fish carefully for any obvious signs of stress and disease (see Chapter 13). The appearance of small white nodules on the body and fins of a fish during its first week in captivity is not uncommon. These spots are tiny parasites called *Cryptocaryon irritans,* which attach to the skin and gills of marine fishes (Chapter 13). The occurrence of a mild infestation with this microorganism is often an indicator that a fish is stressed. If your fish develops a few white spots, *do not add medications to the water* to kill the parasites. Rather, try to let the infestation run its course naturally. If your aquarium is one from which all stressors are absent, the spots will disappear without drug treatment 99 percent of the time.

If after two weeks in the ICU your new fish appears healthy and active and is eating well, it can then be transferred to the main aquarium by the procedure described below. If the main aquarium was used as the ICU, continue to care for the fish as usual.

Transferring a New Fish into the Main Aquarium

A newly introduced fish will always be at a disadvantage in an aquarium that contains an established population of fishes. The surroundings are unfamiliar to it, and it has no territory of its own. For this reason, special steps should be taken to avoid psychological stress when any fish is transferred from the ICU to the main aquarium.

1. Plan to transfer the fish to the main aquarium at night, just before you intend to shut off the lights and go to sleep. Most fishes are relatively inactive and nonaggresive at night, so the likelihood of immediate attacks against the newly introduced fish will be reduced considerably.

2. Before introducing the new fish, feed the residents in the main aquarium. Many kinds of fishes are less aggressive when their bellies are full than when they are hungry.

3. Rearrange some of the decor in the main aquarium, especially the favorite shelters of the most aggressive resident fishes, to partially disrupt established territories. The resident fishes will feel a little insecure and will behave less aggressively when their own territories are not clearly defined.

4. Acclimate the new fish to the water in the main aquarium by the procedure described earlier in this chapter, and then release it. Observe it carefully for several minutes. Depending on the fish, it either will find a hiding place immediately or will begin to investigate its new home. Once you have been convinced that the new fish is safe and secure, turn off the lights.

5. On some occasions, the new fish or established resident fishes in the main aquarium may develop signs of stress or disease a few days after the population of the aquarium is increased. If the water quality is good, however, and if the fishes are compatible with one another according to the general criteria given in Chapter 9, such symptoms should be no cause for great concern. After the newly introduced fish adjusts to its new surroundings and the established resident fishes adjust to the presence of the newcomer, the symptoms usually disappear spontaneously.

THE CARE AND HANDLING OF INVERTEBRATES

The invertebrates recommended for a marine aquarium (some types of anemones, small crabs, and shrimps) undoubtedly suffer some degree of stress from capture, handling, and transportation. Nevertheless, they do not seem to require a period of "intensive care" before being introduced into an aquarium with or without established residents. The following guidelines are suggested for the care and handling of invertebrates.

Sea Anemones

Handling and Transportation

Because sea anemones have soft bodies, they should not be removed from water in nets. To dislodge an anemone from its attachment site in a retailer's tank, insert your fingers between the bottom of the anemone's "foot" and the surface to which it is attached. Push gently and slowly until the anemone releases its grip.

Lift the anemone out of the water with your hand, and transfer it to a plastic bag containing enough tank water to cover it. Transport it by the same procedure described in Chapter 10 for transporting fishes.

Acclimation and Special Care

Acclimate the anemone to the water in your aquarium by the procedure given in Chapter 10 for fishes. After acclimation, do not pour the anemone out of the bag and into the tank, but remove it from the bag by hand and set it, "foot" side down, on the tank bottom or on a flat, smooth rock. Do not try to feed an anemone until its tentacles have become fully expanded and its "foot" is firmly attached to a solid surface.

The excessive mucus and solid wastes excreted by some anemones should be removed periodically by suction with a plastic gravy baster.

Crabs and Shrimps

Handling and Transportation

Crabs and shrimps, being hard-shelled animals, may be moved with nets or by hand. Special care should be taken however, when handling fragile animals, such as the banded coral shrimp, to avoid breaking off their legs or claws; this is most likely to occur when they become entangled in the meshes of a net. Transport crabs and shrimps in plastic bags containing aquarium water (see Chapter 10).

Acclimation and Special Care

Crabs and shrimps should be acclimated to the water in your aquarium by the standard procedure for fishes (Chapter 10). After acclimation, lift the animal from the bag, and set it gently on the tank bottom.

The shell of a crab or shrimp actually is its skeleton. An animal with an *exoskeleton* grows in an unusual way. Its inner, soft tissues grow until they can no longer fit inside the shell. At this time, the crab or shrimp *molts*. Its skeleton splits open, and the animal wiggles out, covered with a new, soft skeleton. After a few days, the new shell hardens, but until hardening is complete, the animal is extremely vulnerable to predation. It usually stops eating, and stays in a safe hiding place.

Only the head and claws of a hermit crab have a hard covering; its hindparts are relatively soft and unprotected. To protect its soft body parts, a hermit crab lives inside an empty snail shell. When it molts, its sheds its old skeleton and grows a new one, but it also must move to a larger snail shell. For this reason, a tank that houses a hermit crab should contain a good supply of empty snail shells of various sizes.

The old exoskeleton of a crab or shrimp is difficult to distinguish from a dead crab or shrimp. If you think one of your crustaceans has died, remove its remains from the aquarium, and examine them carefully. If it is only a cast-off exoskeleton, it will be very light in weight and will not have an offensive odor, because it contains no decaying tissue.

Chapter 12

FOODS AND FEEDING

On no account get into the habit of feeding fish . . . with pieces of raw beef, or even pieces of earth worms. Whether they will accept them or not depends on their capricious humour, and if they are not eaten they only accumulate on the bottom and foul the water.

J.E. Taylor
The Aquarium, 1881

The only principle on which the feeding of . . . animals should be based is that the food must be as natural as possible. This applies not only to quantity and quality but also to the method and time of feeding . . . . Monotony in any form is unnatural because life for animals in the wild is full of variety and change, especially in regard to food.

Heini Hediger
Man and Animal in the Zoo: Zoo Biology, 1969

GENERAL CONSIDERATIONS

NOTHING is known about the nutritional requirements of tropical marine fishes. Although it may be assumed that all fishes need various amounts of certain proteins, carbohydrates, fats, vitamins, and minerals in their diets, the optimal nutritional constituents have not yet been established for a single species, whether freshwater or marine.

Because of the diversity of life and the resulting competitive nature of the tropical marine environment, the dietary preferences of reef fishes vary greatly among different species and are often highly specific (Chapter 9). Although the fact that some species consume only one type of food organism in the wild severely limits an aquarist's ability to keep them in captivity, most of the commonly available fishes eventually adapt to substitutes for the foods they consumed in their natural habitats.

We do not know what foodstuffs marine fishes *need*; what they *eat* in the wild, however, has been determined for many species. Based on the types of foods they eat, fishes are categorized as *carnivores* or flesh-eaters, *herbivores* or vegetarians, and *omnivores,* which eat both animal and vegetable matter. Knowing to which category a particular species belongs is only a starting point in deciding exactly what to feed a captive marine fish, because, like other animals, fishes have distinct preferences and dislikes. Various individuals of the same species may choose entirely different foods in captivity, and an individual's tastes may change dramatically with time.

Two wild-captured anemonefish (*Amphiprion ocellaris*) have been held in our laboratory for three years. During the first several months in captivity, they consumed only newly hatched brine shrimp. Later, they began to accept small amounts of minced shrimp and spinach, but still ignored all flake, freeze-dried, and frozen commercial fish foods that were offered to them. One day we noticed that some brackish-water fish in another tank had spawned. Because we already had an overabundance of that particular species and had no need or desire to rear any more, we collected the eggs and a few larvae and offered them to the anemonefish. Much to our suprise the two fish, normally placid, nonaggressive feeders, went wild, darting around excitedly and snapping up the eggs with great enthusiasm. From that time on, the finicky pair have refused to eat anything but smelt eggs and an occasional live adult brine shrimp, provided that the shrimp is not too large or too small. In contrast, in another aquarium that houses tank-reared anemonefish of the same species, every food offered — from oatmeal to turnip greens — is devoured ravenously.

I have found that three factors seem to determine what foods reef fishes will accept in captivity. The first is individual prejudice. Some fishes will reject certain foods simply because they are unfamiliar. A food that is ignored with disdain one week may become the individual's favorite at some later date. Second, owing to the well-developed chemosensory perception of fishes, the food must taste good. Time and time again, I have seen fishes reject commercial foods, such as trout pellets and flake foods, that should be nutritious and appear to be appetizing. Although such diets may be well-balanced and loaded with vitamins, they seem to lack the essential ingredients that stimulate the taste buds, and this appears to be the only explanation for their rejection. The same foods, when camouflaged with a flavoring agent such as clam juice, often are consumed as if they were gourmet delights. The importance of flavoring agents as feeding stimulants and taste attractants also has been demonstrated experimentally.[1]

The third factor that can determine the acceptance or rejection of a food is its freshness. In their natural habitats, tropical marine fishes eat only the freshest of foods, because their diets consist almost exclusively of live organisms. Captive fishes learn quickly to accept fresh or frozen seafoods and vegetables, but they are likely to refuse stale or spoiled foods. Although an aquarist's tastes may not coincide with those of his or her fishes (I know of no one who has ventured to sample live brine shrimp or freeze-dried plankton), it makes good sense to avoid offering captive fishes anything that is not fit for human consumption.

HOW OFTEN AND HOW MUCH TO FEED

Most tropical marine fishes feed continually throughout the daylight hours. It is therefore a good policy to feed captive fishes frequently — three or four times a day, and more often whenever possible. Sea anemones should be fed once a day, and scavengers such as crabs and shrimps eat any leftover food that falls to the bottom.

Unlike freshwater fishes, some of which may gorge themselves with food until their bellies burst, most reef fishes stop eating when their appetites have been satisfied. For this reason, several light feedings daily are preferable to one or two heavy ones. Drop a small amount of food into the water; after it has been eaten, add a little more. Continue to feed the fishes until they lose interest and swim away. Aggressive fishes usually are the first to feed, whereas timid species feed last, so be sure to add enough food so that even the most shy individuals receive some.

If no one is available to feed fishes during most of the day, it is sometimes desirable to add a little extra food to the aquarium before leaving for school or work. The only foods appropriate for this purpose are *live* organisms, such as adult or baby brine shrimp, and fresh vegetables, such as a leaf of spinach or romaine lettuce or a sprig of parsley. Excessive amounts of prepared commercial foods should never be introduced into the aquarium, because most of these foods fall to the bottom and decay rapidly. Always remove visible pieces of uneaten food from the bottom at the end of each day.

THE IMPORTANCE OF VARIETY

Although hungry fishes will eat almost anything, it is to their advantage that they be offered a variety of foods. Variety is important for two reasons. First, all foods do not contain the same nutrients; by providing several different foods, the likelihood that the fishes will receive all the nutrients they need is increased. Second, fishes seem capable of becoming tired of too much of the same food. Anyone who has ever eaten a multiple-course meal knows that it is common to reach a point at which one simply cannot swallow another bite of meat or potato, but still has room for a bit of dessert. Fishes are similar, in that they may lose interest in one type of food after a few minutes, but will eagerly devour a different food that is offered immediately after the first.

At each feeding, it is therefore desirable to offer the fishes two or more different foods in sequence. In our laboratory, we usually begin a feeding with "Omnivore Diet" (a home-made food described below), followed by fish eggs and then frozen brine shrimp. Between regular feedings, we often drop a few morsels of freeze-dried brine shrimp into the tanks, if the fishes seem hungry. I have found it desirable to save their favorite food for last, to keep the fishes from avoiding the less tasty but more nutritious items on the menu.

SUITABLE FOODS: PREPARATION AND
FEEDING TECHNIQUES

In the absence of information about the nutritional requirements of reef fishes, fish nutrition remains more an art than a science. Meeting the dietary requirements of captive fishes is a matter of trial and error, but the odds for success can be improved substantially by using only foods that are wholesome and nutritious by human standards. Techniques for preparing various foods and dispensing them to aquarium animals are described below.

Raw Seafoods

Raw fish fillets and roe (eggs), shrimp, scallops, squid, and clams are excellent staples in the diets of most captive marine fishes and invertebrates (Table 17). A single jumbo shrimp or sea scallop will keep for several months in a freezer, and will go a long way as food for the residents of the average aquarium.

To prevent spoilage, seafood should not be left at room temperature, nor should it be stored in a refrigerator for more than two days. Fresh seafood should be sliced or chopped (never mashed) into pieces appropriate to the mouth sizes of the animals. The chopped food should then be rinsed briefly under cool water in an aquarium net to remove excess juices, and dropped into the aquarium from the tip of a paring knife. Frozen seafoods can be thawed and prepared as above, or alternatively, small bits can be scraped from the frozen material and dropped directly into the aquarium water.

Sea anemones should receive a small piece of shrimp, fish, scallop, or clam once a day. Place the food gently on the anemone's tentacles near its mouth, which is located at the center of its ring of tentacles. If the food is accepted, the anemone will fold in its tentacles, forcing the food into its mouth. If a particular type of food is rejected (it will be transferred to the tips of the tentacles and dropped off), remove the uneaten matter and offer something different.

Raw Vegetables

Parsley, spinach, broccoli, green peas, carrots, and beet, collard, dandelion, mustard, and turnip greens are the most nutritious food substitutes for fishes that require algae in their diets. Vegetables contain relatively little protein when compared with seafoods, but they constitute a major source of many vitamins and minerals (Table 18). The pigments present in raw vegetables may also prevent the colors of captive fishes from becoming less brilliant, although this has not yet been demonstrated experimentally.

Many leafy vegetables are treated with chemical insecticides and molluscicides, so be sure to wash all fresh vegetables thoroughly before introducing them into an aquarium. Bean sprouts are not

Table 17

THE NUTRIENTS CONTAINED IN 100 GRAMS OF VARIOUS RAW SEAFOODS
AND IN UNFLAVORED GELATIN

Nutrient[a]	Clams	Flounder or sole	Haddock	Shrimp	Fish roe	Oysters	Scallops	Smelt	Squid	Gelatin
Protein (g)	14	14.9	18.3	18.8	24.4	8.4	15.3	18.6	16.4	85.6
Carbohydrate (g)	1.3	0	0	1.5	1.5	3.4	3.3	0	1.5	0
Fat (g)	1.9	0.5	0.1	0.8	2.3	1.8	0.2	2.1	0.9	0.1
Minerals										
Sodium (mg)	36	56	61	140	-	73	255	-	-	-
Calcium (mg)	-	61	23	63	-	94	26	-	12	-
Phosphorus (mg)	183	195	197	166	-	143	208	272	119	-
Potassium (mg)	235	366	304	220	-	121	396	-	-	-
Magnesium (mg)	-	30	24	42	-	32	-	-	-	-
Iron (mg)	3.4	0.8	0.7	1.6	0.6	5.5	1.8	0.4	0.5	-
Vitamins										
Thiamine (mcg)	-	60	40	20	100	140	-	10	20	-
Niacin (mg)	-	1.7	3.0	3.2	1.4	2.5	1.3	1.4	-	-
A (i.u.)	-	-	-	-	-	310	-	-	-	-
Riboflavin (mcg)	-	50	70	30	760	180	60	120	120	-
C (mg)	-	-	-	-	14	-	-	-	-	-
D (i.u.)	-	-	-	-	-	-	-	-	-	-

[a]Quantities are grams (g), milligrams (mg), micrograms (mcg), and international units (i.u.)

From Church and Church (1970)

Table 18

THE NUTRIENTS CONTAINED IN 100 GRAMS OF VARIOUS RAW VEGETABLES
AND BREWER'S YEAST

Nutrient[a]	Beet greens	Broccoli	Carrots	Collard greens	Dandelion greens	Mustard greens
Protein (g)	2.2	3.6	1.1	3.6	2.7	3.0
Carbohydrate (g)	4.6	5.9	9.7	7.2	9.2	5.6
Fat (g)	0.3	0.3	0.2	0.7	0.7	0.5
Minerals						
Sodium (mg)	130	15	47	43	76	32
Calcium (mg)	119	103	37	203	187	183
Phosphorus (mg)	40	78	36	63	66	50
Potassium (mg)	570	382	341	401	397	377
Magnesium (mg)	106	24	23	57	36	27
Iron (mg)	3.3	1.1	0.7	1.0	3.1	3.0
Vitamins						
Thiamine (mcg)	100	100	60	200	190	110
Niacin (mg)	0.4	9	0.6	1.7	–	0.8
A (i.u.)	6,100	2,500	11,000	6,500	14,000	7,000
Riboflavin (mcg)	220	230	50	310	260	220
C (mg)	30	113	8	92	35	97
D (i.u.)	–	–	–	–	–	–

Nutrient[a]	Parsley	Green peas	Spinach	Turnip greens	Brewer's yeast
Protein (g)	3.6	6.3	3.2	3.0	38.8
Carbohydrate (g)	8.5	14.4	4.3	5.0	38.4
Fat (g)	0.6	0.4	0.3	0.3	1.0
Minerals					
Sodium (mg)	45	2	71	—	121
Calcium (mg)	203	26	93	246	210
Phosphorus (mg)	63	116	51	58	1,753
Potassium (mg)	727	316	470	—	1,894
Magnesium (mg)	41	35	88	58	231
Iron (mg)	6.2	1.9	3.1	1.8	17.3
Vitamins					
Thiamine (mcg)	120	350	100	210	15,610
Niacin (mg)	1.2	2.9	0.6	0.8	37.9
A (i.u.)	8,500	640	8,100	7,600	trace
Riboflavin (mcg)	260	140	200	390	4,280
C (mg)	172	27	51	139	trace
D (i.u.)	—	—	—	—	—

[a]Quantities are grams (g), milligrams (mg), micrograms (mcg), and international units (i.u.)
From Church and Church (1970)

recommended, because they may be toxic to some species. It was observed, for example, that a yellow tang (*Zebrasoma flavescens*) lost all nervous control and died within one minute after consuming raw alfalfa sprouts, whereas other species in the same tank ate the sprouts and did not become ill.[3]

Fresh or frozen vegetables should be chopped or shredded into edible-sized pieces, rinsed with tap water, and then dropped into the aquarium from the tip of a paring knife. To keep a constant supply of vegetable matter available for grazing fishes (e.g. angelfishes, butterflyfishes, surgeonfishes, and tangs), attach a sprig of parsley or a leaf of spinach to a small rock with an elastic band, and place the rock at the bottom of the aquarium. Remove the greens from the water before they begin to decay.

"Omnivore Diet": Home-made Fish Food

Various foodstuffs, puréed and bound together with gelatin or other binders, are used extensively to maintain freshwater and marine animals at many hatcheries, research centers, and public aquariums.[4-7] Such artificial diets usually contain substantial quantities of trout meal or pellets (complex formulations designed to meet the dietary needs of trout), blended with small amounts of flavoring agents (natural seafoods) and held together with animal gelatin. Gelatin-based artificial diets have four advantages over other processed foods: (1) they are nutritious; (2) their composition can be varied as desired; (3) they are easy to store and convenient to dispense; and (4) they are stable in water; that is, they disintegrate quite slowly as long as the water temperature remains below 83°F (28.3°C), the temperature at which gelatin melts.

The gelatin-bound food described below, "Omnivore Diet," is used almost exclusively for fishes at the Institute for Aquarium Studies. It differs from other artificial diets in that it consists mostly of natural seafoods and vegetables, instead of trout meal or pellets. Several years ago, I found that aquarium water seemed to foul more rapidly if trout meal was included in the diet, so I eliminated it from the recipe. Also, I believe that in fish nutrition as well as human nutrition, wholesome natural foods are more desirable than their highly processed artificial equivalents.

Omnivore Diet may be used instead of chopped seafoods and vegetables as the major food for all fishes and invertebrates that require both animal and vegetable matter. It is a particularly convenient form of food for use by aquarists who maintain several aquariums and wish to save time on food preparation. With the exception of the two anemonefish mentioned earlier in this chapter, I have not yet encountered any omnivorous fish, whether freshwater or marine, that will not accept Omnivore Diet. All of the ingredients needed to prepare the diet (Table 19) are available at supermarkets or health-food stores. Directions for preparing and dispensing the food are given below.

Preparing Omnivore Diet

1. Rinse the fresh or thawed seafood and vegetables with cool tap water. Drain, weigh, and chop into small pieces.

2. Transfer the seafood and vegetables to a food blender, add about 5 ounces (150 millileters) of water, and blend at medium speed until well minced.

3. Pour the mixture into a large bowl. Stir in the oatmeal cereal, brewer's yeast, paprika, and vitamins.

4. Bring the remaining water to a boil; dissolve the gelatin in the boiling water and let it cool to about 100°F (38°C). Pour the dissolved gelatin into the food mixture, and stir until well mixed.

5. Transfer the contents of the bowl back into the blender, and blend at high speed until puréed to a very fine consistency. The longer the mixture is blended, the more air will be incorporated into it. Thus, if you would like the finished product to float, blend until it is light and foamy.

6. Line a large cookie sheet or baking pan with plastic wrap. Pour the puréed food into the pan, and refrigerate until it hardens into a rubbery mass (about 2 to 4 hours).

7. Remove the hardened gel from its container, and cut it into conveniently sized pieces (e.g. 2-inch squares). Wrap each piece separately in plastic wrap or aluminum foil, and store in a freezer. Frozen Omnivore Diet can be stored for several months, if tightly wrapped.

Table 19

INGREDIENTS (ALL RAW) OF "OMNIVORE DIET"
A Food for Marine Fishes that Require
Both Animal and Vegetable Matter in Their Diets

Yield is approximately 1.75 pounds (0.8 kilograms).

Ingredient	Amount	
Fish fillets[a]	3 ounces	(90 grams)
Whole shrimp	3 ounces	(90 grams)
Green vegetables[b]	2 ounces	(60 grams)
Fresh parsley leaves	½ cup	(10 grams)
Grated carrots	1 ounce	(30 grams)
Oatmeal cereal[c]	3 Tbsp.	(10 grams)
Brewer's yeast[d]	2½ tsp.	(5 grams)
Paprika[e]	1 tsp.	(5 grams)
Liquid baby vitamins[f]	½ tsp.	(2 milliliters)
Unflavored gelatin	2 ounces	(60 grams)
Water	15 ounces	(450 milliliters)

[a]Whole smelts, with heads, skins, and guts removed, may be substituted for fillets.
[b]Use 1 ounce (30 grams) of fresh or frozen leaf spinach, and an equal quantity of collard, turnip, or mustard greens.
[c]Beech-Nut® or Gerber® dry cereal for babies, or an equivalent.
[d]Available at most health-food stores.
[e]Paprika contains pigments that may enhance the colors of fishes.
[f]Poly-Vi-Sol® multivitamin supplement, or equivalent.

Dispensing Omnivore Diet

1. Each morning, thaw as much of the gel as you intend to use in one day. Slice or chop it into bite-sized pieces (Fig. 54). If used to feed small fishes or fishes with small mouths, the gel may be mashed

Figure 54. "Omnivore Diet" is home-made fish food containing natural seafoods and vegetables bound together with gelatin. Frozen blocks of the food can be thawed and then sliced or chopped into pieces of any size.

lightly with the blade of a knife.

2. Drop small quantities of the food into the aquarium, from the tip of a paring-knife blade.

3. Wrap unused food and store in a refrigerator for no more than 24 hours. Do not refreeze.

4. As an alternative procedure for dispensing Omnivore Diet, cut or scrape tiny pieces from a frozen block of gel, and drop them directly into the aquarium. This method is most convenient for aquarists who keep few fishes and do not use large quantities of food each day.

Figure 55. Freeze-dried plankton constitutes a nutritious food for aquarium fishes.

Freeze-dried Foods

A variety of natural seafoods (shrimps, squid, plankton, brine shrimp, etc.) are available in freeze-dried form (Fig. 55). Freeze-dried brine shrimp (Jungle Laboratories Corp., Comfort, Texas) are readily accepted by most fishes, whereas the acceptability of other freeze-dried foods varies with individual preferences of the fishes. Freeze-dried foods should be rehydrated by mixing with a little tap water, and then introduced without delay into the aquarium from an eyedropper or gravy baster. "Unwetted" freeze-dried foods float on the water surface, which makes it easy to remove any uneaten pieces. Many reef fishes, however, will not feed at the surface.

Figure 56. Flake foods are convenient to dispense, but most reef fishes refuse to eat them.

Flake Foods

Dry flakes (Fig. 56), consisting of fish meal, flour, insect eggs or larvae, and a variety of other dry substances, are favored by aquarists because they are so convenient to use; but they are not accepted by many species of reef fishes. In my estimation, flake foods are a poor substitute for the diverse live foods that fishes eat in their natural habitats, and it iş my experience that fishes fed only flake foods develop dull coloration and do not grow as rapidly as those fed fresh seafoods and vegetables. I do not recommend flake foods for the maintenance of tropical marine fishes.

Brine Shrimp

Both live and frozen brine shrimp (*Artemia salina*) are the preferred foods of nearly all captive reef fishes. Live brine shrimp are often the first food a newly acquired fish will accept, since they resemble the natural foods of reef fishes more closely than any other commonly available food substitute. Newly hatched brine shrimp larvae are indispensible for feeding very young fishes, and they also are eaten by some juvenile and adult fishes and by filter-feeding invertebrates.

Frozen Brine Shrimp

Adult brine shrimp can be purchased in frozen blocks of various weights. Some brands contain mostly stringy or clumpy material (suggesting that the shrimp had died before they were frozen) that fishes have difficulty swallowing, but I have encountered this problem only rarely with Living World, San Francisco Bay Brand® (Metaframe Corp., Elmwood Park, New Jersey).

To feed frozen brine shrimp to fishes, cut a small piece from the large block, and drop it into the aquarium. As the frozen mass melts, the shrimp are released into the water (Fig. 57). As an alternative method, you may prewash the shrimp to remove debris as follows. Drop a small chunk of frozen brine shrimp into a cup of warm water. After it thaws, the shrimp will sink to the bottom. Swirl the water in the cup, then wait for the shrimp to settle again, and pour off most of the water. Introduce the shrimp into the aquarium with an eyedropper or gravy baster. Any thawed, unused shrimp should be discarded at at the conclusion of each feeding.

It should be pointed out that frozen and freeze-dried foods lose their nutritional value rapidly upon their introduction into water. This happens because freezing ruptures the cells of food organisms, and soluble nutrients begin to leach out of the cells the moment they thaw. It has been shown, for example, that about 70 to 75 percent of the activities of certain enzymes, and even higher percentages of amino acids, are lost from frozen and freeze-dried plankton after only 10 minutes in water, and that the lost substances can be recovered in soluble form from the water.[8]

Figure 57. Adult brine shrimp, such as the frozen ones illustrated, are a preferred food of most fishes.

Live Adult Brine Shrimp

Live adult brine shrimp are available from most large aquarium retail stores. Shipments usually arrive once a week. Try to buy live shrimp soon after they are delivered to the store, to ensure that they are in the best possible condition. (Retailers usually keep live brine shrimp in aquariums without food or filtration, so their quality and nutritional value decline rapidly.)

When you arrive home with the shrimp, pour them into a net and discard the water in which they were transported; the transport water invariably is loaded with ammonia and other wastes. Transfer the shrimp to a shallow glass bowl containing new seawater or some aquarium water, and store them in a refrigerator. When kept refrigerated, brine shrimp may survive for a week or longer, depending on their original condition. If the water in the bowl becomes foul, replace it with new seawater that has been chilled before use. Large quantities of shrimp may be stored in a gallon jug in a refrigerator, provided that the water is aerated with compressed air from a small air pump kept *inside* the refrigerator. Alternatively, they may be kept at room temperature in a small aquarium that is aerated gently. Adults held at room temperature should be fed a pinch or two of brewer's yeast every other day.

To feed live adult brine shrimp to fishes, scoop some out of their holding container into a net, and transfer them to a cup containing a little aquarium water. Introduce them into the aquarium with an eyedropper or gravy baster.

Larval Brine Shrimp

Larval brine shrimp, called *nauplii*, can be hatched readily from dried *Artemia* cysts or "eggs." Low hatching yields are common with some brands of brine shrimp eggs, but I have had consistent success with Living World, San Francisco Bay Brand, which are packaged in vacuum-sealed cans. Eggs are killed by humidity, so once a can has been opened it is important to keep the unused eggs dry. They will remain viable for a year or longer if stored in a tightly sealed glass jar containing a desiccant (moisture absorber) such as silica gel, activated alumina, calcium sulfate, or magnesium perchlorate. Desiccants that change color when saturated with moisture and that can be reactivated by heating in an oven can be obtained from most laboratory supply companies. A reliable procedure for hatching brine shrimp eggs is described below.

1. Add about ½ teaspoon of eggs to a clean gallon jug, and fill the jug with aquarium seawater to a level just below the shoulder. A combination of un-iodized table salt and epsom salts may be substituted for seawater, but better yields are obtained with seawater. The eggs will float on the surface.

2. Drop an air diffuser into the water, and aerate vigorously to

keep the eggs in motion. If some eggs accumulate at the top, swirl the jug to put them back into suspension.

3. The higher the temperature, the more rapidly the eggs will hatch. An easy way to raise the water temperature is by placing a lamp containing a 40-watt incandescent bulb a few inches away from the jug (Fig. 58).

Figure 58. To promote the hatching of brine shrimp eggs, increase the temperature of the water by placing a low-wattage incandescent lamp a few inches away from the hatching jar.

4. After 24 hours most of the eggs will have hatched. Remove the air diffuser and set the jug *at an angle* on an elevated support beside a sink (an inverted paint bucket is an ideal support). Wait about 10 minutes to allow the eggshells and nauplii to separate. The nauplii

(orange-colored) will sink to the bottom, and the empty shells (brown) will float at the surface.

5. To remove the larval brine shrimp from the jar, you will need a fine-mesh net and a miniature siphon hose. If you are unable to purchase a suitable net, you can make one by sewing a square of nylon cloth (such as fabric cut from a pair of lady's panties) to the frame of a small aquarium net. A glass eyedropper tube, inserted into one end of a 2½-foot (75-centimeter) length of flexible airline tubing, makes a perfect siphon hose. A homemade net and siphon are shown in Figure 59.

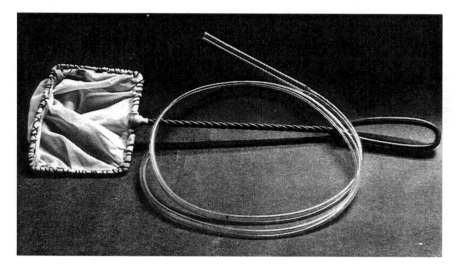

Figure 59. A miniature siphon hose and homemade net for collecting brine shrimp nauplii.

6. Set the net on the edge of the sink, and anchor it firmly in place. Lower the glass end of the siphon hose into the jar, taking care not to disturb the eggshells, until the dropper tip rests on the bottom. Start the siphon flowing (see Chapter 6), and position the hose so that it empties into the net (Fig. 60). The nauplii will be retained in the net, and the water will drain into the sink. Do not try to save this water; it is usually foul and teeming with bacteria.

7. Break the siphon when about 1 inch (2.5 centimeters) of water remains in the jug, to avoid sucking up unhatched eggs and shells. Allow the net to drain completely; its bottom should be filled with thousands of nauplii (Fig. 61).

Figure 60. Apparatus for transferring brine shrimp nauplii from the hatching jar to the net. By propping the jar at an angle on an inverted paint bucket, the possibility of siphoning out empty shells or unhatched eggs is reduced.

8. Dip the net into a shallow glass or plastic bowl containing a few inches of seawater to release the nauplii. Store the open bowl in a refrigerator. The nauplii will live for about a week if kept

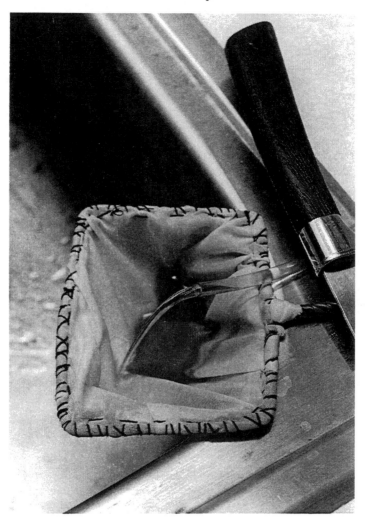

Figure 61. Net filled with brine shrimp nauplii.

refrigerated, during which time a water change should not be necessary.

To introduce brine shrimp nauplii into an aquarium, transfer them to the tank with a glass eyedropper or gravy baster. Take care to avoid adding too many nauplii to the aquarium at one time, because they can be extremely irritating to the gills of some fishes. (If the fishes "twitch" and "shake their heads," you will know you have added too many nauplii to the tank.)

Rearing Brine Shrimp

Aquarists who keep fishes that will accept only live foods may find it desirable to rear larval brine shrimp to maturity at home. Rearing one's own brine shrimp has two advantages over purchasing live adults from an aquarium retail store. First, it is less expensive, since adult brine shrimp are exceedingly costly as compared with other foods. Second, it gives an aquarist the opportunity to offer live food of appropriate sizes as his or her fishes grow. There is great disparity between the size of brine shrimp nauplii and adults: the former are about 1/125 inch (0.2 millimeters) long, and the latter are 40 times larger or about ⅓ inch (8 millimeters) in length. Nauplii often are too small to be eaten by certain fishes, whereas adults may be too large. Brine shrimp of small, intermediate, and large sizes all are available when reared at home.

Many methods have been recommended for rearing brine shrimp. The major problem is providing them with a suitable food. The best food for brine shrimp is probably live, single-celled algae, *Dunaliella salina,* which must be cultured separately. Other, more convenient foods, such as dog vitamins, rice flour, and yeast, have also been used. I have tried them all, and have had the most, albeit inconsistent, success with the method described below, which is a modification of a procedure used at the Mystic Marinelife Aquarium.

1. Hatch about ¼ to ½ teaspoon of eggs by the method given in the previous section.

2. Harvest the nauplii and release them into a *bare*, 5½-gallon (21-liter) aquarium filled with newly mixed artificial seawater. Keep the water temperature at about 80°F (27°C) with an immersion

heater to promote rapid growth of the nauplii. The salinity of the water should be maintained at 30 to 32 parts per thousand (see Table 8 in Chapter 6 for corresponding specific gravity values).

3. Connect an air diffuser to an air pump. A small, inefficient pump is preferable, because very little air is required. Adjust the air flow to produce a weak stream of bubbles, bleeding off excess air through an extra gang valve, if necessary. The bubbling should be just strong enough to keep the water and the nauplii in motion; vigorous aeration may damage the nauplii or impair their ability to feed.

4. Dissolve a pinch or two of brewer's yeast in some tap water, and mix thoroughly. Let the larger flakes of yeast settle, then pour the suspension containing the smaller particles into the tank. The water will become slightly cloudy. Some of the yeast will settle to the bottom. When this happens, get it back into suspension by stirring the water with the air diffuser. Add a small amount of yeast to the water, as described above, every other day, or more frequently if the water becomes clear.

5. Keep the aquarium covered to prevent evaporation. After about one week, the nauplii will have transformed into "miniature adults" that are suitable food for juvenile or small-mouthed fishes. The brine shrimp reach maturity in one month or less, depending on the water temperature.

6. Brine shrimp at any stage of development may be removed from the culture tank with a net, transferred to small container of seawater from the fish tank, and then introduced directly into the aquarium. Brine shrimp of any size also may be collected in a net, transferred to a container of clean seawater, and stored in a refrigerator, if no further growth is desired.

Chapter 13

DISEASE PREVENTION AND CONTROL

Unfortunately, people who commence keeping aquaria are usually too anxious to have as many . . . animals as possible . . . . The aquarium becomes a painful scene of misery, disease and death — a too vivid picture of similar conditions among humanity when the latter is horded in fetid and over-populated alleys . . . .

J.E. Taylor
The Aquarium, 1881

Violet most amiably knitted a small woollen frock for several of the fishes, and Slingsby administered some opium drops to them, through which kindness they became quite warm and slept soundly.

Edward Lear

When fish appear dull and stupid from no apparent cause, I have found that it often enlivens them to put them in a pail, and setting it under a croton-water tap, allow the water to run on them for about a quarter of an hour.

Arthur M. Edwards
Life Beneath the Waters, 1858

TOO many aquarists regard disease as an inevitable consequence of maintaining fishes in captivity. As a result, there probably exist as many amateur "fish doctors" as there are hobbyists and retailers. In truth, extremely little is known about the diseases of fishes, and few controlled experiments have been conducted on methods of preventing or eradicating diseases of captive marine fishes. Thus, the treatment of a sick fish is essentially a process of trial and error. There is increasing evidence, however, that most *infectious* diseases of captive fishes — those that are transmitted from one fish to another — can be avoided, chiefly through environmental manipulation. It is my contention that under most circumstances, disease in the aquarium should be regarded as an entity

207

to be prevented, not treated.

BASIC APPROACHES TO DISEASE PREVENTION

There are two general approaches to the prevention of infectious diseases of captive marine fishes: (1) the eliminaton of pathogenic (disease-causing) organisms from the aquarium; and (2) the elimination of stressful environmental conditions that might increase the susceptibility of fishes to disease.

Elimination of Pathogens

Certain disease organisms, such as *Cryptocaryon irritans* (a parasite that causes "saltwater Ich"), *Oodinium ocellatum* (a parasite causing "velvet disease" or "coral fish disease"), and *Vibrio anguillarum* (the bacterial agent of vibriosis, "red pest," "red sore," or "ulcer" disease), are frequently responsible for disease outbreakes in aquariums but are not known to cause mass mortalities in wild populations of fishes.[1] The frequency with which these diseases occur often has been attributed to the restricted volume of water in an aquarium. It is thought that within the confines of an aquarium, the transmission of an infectious disease from one fish to another is unavoidable. Accordingly, disease prevention is attempted by exposing newly acquired fishes to various medications, and by disinfecting the aquarium water with ultraviolet (UV) radiation or ozone.

The argument against quarantining newly acquired fishes in drug baths was presented in Chapter 11, in which it was pointed out that exposure to certain drugs may be harmful to fishes and to beneficial filter bacteria.

The application of ozone or UV radiation to aquarium water can decrease the numbers of microorganisms in the water, but neither method seems to be of much value in preventing the spread of disease in recirculating aquariums. Moreover, both processes have severe limitations and drawbacks.[2] The efficiency of UV and ozone disinfection, for example, is reduced when the water contains high concentrations of dissolved and particulate organic substances, and the exact levels of exposure needed to kill pathogens are different for different microorganisms.

When one considers that UV and ozone generators can sterilize only the water with which they are directly in contact, it becomes obvious that it is highly improbable that an aquarium can be completely sterilized. Both processes are effective against free-floating pathogens, but do not necessarily affect bacteria, fungi, or parasites that live in or on the bodies of fishes, or in parts of the aquarium that are remote from the disinfection unit.[3] UV radiation leaves no residuals in the water and is therefore effective only at the site of contact. Ozone, to the contrary, may react with dissolved salts in the water, to form residuals such as hypochlorite (the active ingredient in chlorine bleach) and hypobromite.[2] There is increasing evidence that these residuals, along with ozone itself, are toxic to marine animals.[4,5]

Using computer projections, it has been shown that in a closed aquarium (one in which the same water is recirculated continuously) containing diseased fishes, *it is impossible to achieve even 90 percent disinfection of the water with UV radiation.*[6] There are two major reasons why total disinfection cannot be attained. First, if the UV sterilizer kills less than 100 percent of the pathogens passing through it, the fishes might become reinfected by the microorganisms reintroduced into the aquarium from the sterilizer. Even if 99.99 percent of the pathogens were killed at the contact site, the remaining 0.01 percent might be sufficient to allow the continued spread of disease.[7] Second, disease organisms may be transmitted directly from one fish to another, bypassing the sterilizer completely.[6] It is therefore not surprising that the mortalities of captive fishes are not reduced even when the numbers of microorganisms in the water have been decreased by 98 percent or more following UV disinfection.[3,8] The authors of one study comparing the survival of fishes in aquariums with and without UV irradiation concluded, "Fishes in good health in an uncrowded aquarium with proper aeration and filtration can, and do, live satisfactorily without the use of UV water sterilizers."[3] The same can undoubtedly be said about the usefulness of ozone for preventing or controlling fish diseases.

Elimination of Stressful Environmental Conditions

The Relationship Between Stress and Disease

Under natural conditions, fishes harbor a variety of microorganisms that are capable of causing disease, yet most wild fishes are disease-free.[1] Similarly, it has been demonstrated that many species of potentially pathogenic bacteria exist in most aquariums,[9] and that captive fishes that are apparently healthy may actually have a high incidence of asymptomatic bacterial infections.[10]

These phenomena are not surprising for two reasons. First, it has long been recognized that the most successful pathogen is the one that causes the least damage to its animal host; after all, the survival of the host is essential to the survival of the pathogen that lives in or on it. Second, vertebrate animals, including fishes, have a remarkable immunological defense system that enables them to resist disease. The immunological "fitness" of an animal is closely related to its overall physiological condition, which, in turn, is determined chiefly by environmental conditions. A healthy environment breeds healthy animals, and healthy animals usually are able to resist most diseases.

Contrary to the opinions of those who consider disinfection of the water essential to aquarium management, the mere exposure of a fish to a pathogenic microorganism does not always produce disease. The relationship is somewhat more complex. Infectious diseases are most likely to occur when a *susceptible host fish* is exposed to a *virulent pathogen* under the proper *environmental conditions*[11](Fig. 62).

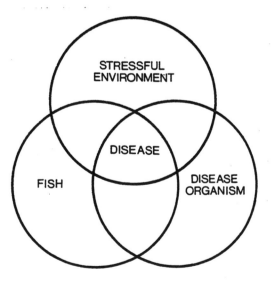

Figure 62. For disease to occur, a susceptible fish must be exposed to a virulent disease-causing organism under stressful environmental conditions. Redrawn and modified from Snieszko (1974).[11]

A *susceptible host fish* is one that is capable of providing a pathogenic organism with suitable nutrients and growth conditions. Many pathogens are *species specific;* that is, they can live in or on only certain species, other species being innately unsuitable hosts. The factors that determine the suitability of a host are poorly understood.

A *virulent pathogen* is a microorganisms that is capable of invading a host, becoming established and multiplying within the host, and causing damage to the host. In other words, a virulent pathogen is capable of producing disease.

Proper *environmental conditions* are also necessary for the occurrence of most diseases. The relationship between environmental stress and the onset of disease is well established, and a number of the environmental factors that predispose fishes to certain diseases have been determined. They include crowding, rough handling, improper diet, exposure to low levels of dissolved oxygen, ammonia, insecticides, or heavy metals such as copper, and changes in temperature.[12] There are additional chemical, physical, psychological, and nutritional factors (discussed in Chapter 8) that might also be stressful, and therefore have the potential to decrease the ability of fishes to resist disease.

Although it cannot be disputed that a fish is more apt to encounter a pathogen in the small volume of water in an aquarium than in the immensity of the ocean, every *latent infection* (in which pathogens are present in or on a fish, but do not produce clinical symptoms of disease) of captive fishes does not always become an overt disease. The transformation from infection to disease occurs most frequently when the physiological condition of a susceptible fish is "ripe" for disease, that is, when the fish's natural resistance or normal immune responses have been weakened by environmental stress. This process is illustrated in Figure 63.

Cumulative Effects of Stress

The effects of stress are often cumulative. Fishes can and do tolerate some stressful environmental conditions without developing disease, but only to a point. Invariably, when fishes are maintained for long periods in a stressful environment, the delicate balance between the fishes' natural resistance and a pathogenic organism's virulence is tipped, and the result is a sudden outbreak of disease.

Consider, for example, two aquariums that are stocked with

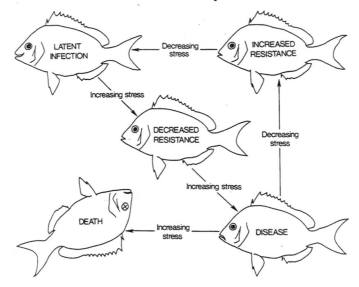

Figure 63. The influence of stress on the transformation of a latent infection to a disease. The greater the stress, the more a fish's resistance is lowered, and the greater the likelihood for disease to occur. Conversely, if stress is reduced, the fish's resistance increases, and the infection remains latent. Modified from Spotte (1979).[13]

identical numbers and species of fishes. In the first aquarium, which is poorly maintained, there is inefficient bacteriological filtration, resulting in elevated but sublethal concentrations of ammonia in the water, the salinity is too high, the pH is too low, and the water has not been replaced for several months. In the second tank, which is well-maintained and has had periodic water changes, the salinity and pH of the water are within the recommended range of values, and no ammonia has accumulated. Now, imagine that the heaters in both aquariums malfunction, and the water temperatures suddenly increase by several degrees. In which tank would an outbreak of disease most likely occur? In the first, of course, for the fishes in this aquarium, already subjected to stressful environmental conditions, would be less able to cope with the additional stress resulting from a rapid temperature change.

It is clear that the best approach to disease prevention in aquariums is to eliminate all environmental conditions that can induce stress. Compatible, well-fed fishes in an aquarium that is free of toxic pollutants and is chemically and physically stable are fishes that are the best equipped to combat disease, even after exposure to a sudden, unavoidable environmental change.

HOW TO RECOGNIZE STRESSED FISHES

Characteristic indicators of physiological stress in fishes, such as changes in the concentrations of various substances in the blood (see Chapter 8, Table 13), are impossible for an aquarist to detect. There are, however, some visible, behavioral signs of stress that can be recognized easily (Table 20). The aquarist should always be on the

Table 20

BEHAVIORAL SYMPTOMS OF STRESS IN FISHES

Symptom
Rapid breathing
Fading or darkening of color
Abnormal swimming behavior (darting, shaking, etc.)
Loss of appetite
Listlessness or hyperactivity
Fins folded close to body

lookout for any changes in the behavior of his or her fishes, because such changes may indicate that the fishes are undergoing stress.

In many instances, behavioral signs of stress are the only clues the aquarist may have that something in the aquarium environment is not quite right. Some causes of stress, such as a rapid change in temperature or excessive aggression among the fishes, are easy to identify and eliminate, but most of them are less obvious. Whenever fishes exhibit symptoms of stress, the aquarist should consult the listing of "The Elements of a Stress-free Aquarium" in Chapter 8, and then try to determine whether any environmental conditions might be unhealthy. The aquarist should then correct any irregularities as soon as possible.

DISEASE SYMPTOMS AND TREATMENT: OVERVIEW

Symptoms of Disease

Some general symptoms of infectious diseases are listed in Table 21. Any fish that exhibits two or more of these symptoms is likely to be in serious trouble.

Table 21

SOME GENERAL SYMPTOMS
OF INFECTIOUS DISEASES IN FISHES

Physical symptoms
  Cloudy or bulging eyes
  Ragged fins with cloudy edges
  Small white, yellow, or gray spots, nodules, or blotches on body or fins
  Bloody lines, spots, or patches on body or fins
  Open sores on body or fins
  Cotton-like growths on body or fins
  Swelling or redness around anus
  Protrusion of gill covers

Behavioral symptoms
  Persistent scratching against gravel, decor, or tank walls
  Erratic swimming behavior
  Loss of balance
  Cessation of feeding

Captive fishes most frequently exhibit signs of disease during their stay in the "Intensive Care Unit" (see Chapter 11) or soon after a new fish is introduced into an aquarium that has long-established residents. There is no reason for an aquarist to panic and begin pouring drugs into an aquarium upon the first occasion of "scratching," or the moment a few white spots are noticed on a fish's body or fins. Provided that all environmental conditions are well-controlled and are not stressful, such symptoms commonly disappear spontaneously, as soon as the new fish has adjusted to its new environment, or the resident fishes have adjusted to the presence of the newcomer.

Environmental Therapy *versus* Chemical Therapy

Although most disease symptoms that are associated with the introduction of a new fish into an aquarium usually clear up without the administration of drugs, some do not. As is the case with diseases of humans and other animals, nearly every fish disease has a "point of no return," beyond which recovery is improbable without the aid of chemical therapy.

A fish that has been netted, handled roughly, starved, exposed to anesthetics and temperature extremes, and held in shipping bags and aquariums containing foul water may be stressed so severely that even dramatic improvements in its living conditions cannot enable it to regain its natural defenses quickly enough to survive invasion by the multitude of pathogenic microorganisms that are always present in aquarium water.

The relationships among severity of stress, natural resistance to disease, pathogenicity of infection, and proper kind of treatment are depicted in Figure 64. As stress increases, a fish's resistance to disease decreases. At the same time, the damage to the fish by the invading pathogen increases, and a latent, nondestructive infection transforms into a disease of increasing severity. When stress is absent or mild and the disease resistance of a fish is moderate to strong, *environmental therapy,* that is, improving the environment to eliminate the stressful conditions, will usually serve as effective disease treatment. When a fish is under moderate stress and its resistance is very weak, *chemical (drug) therapy* becomes necessary for disease treatment. When a fish is severely diseased and under severe environmental stress, its resistance may be lost entirely, and even drug treatment may be ineffective.

It is, unfortunately, no simple matter for an aquarist to evaluate the severity of disease in a fish, so it is difficult to determine when treatment with drugs has become imperative. It is my experience that captive reef fishes rarely, if ever, become even moderately diseased when they are maintained under nonstressful environmental conditions. In fact, the only times that I have found drug treatment necessary were when the fishes had been overcrowded deliber-

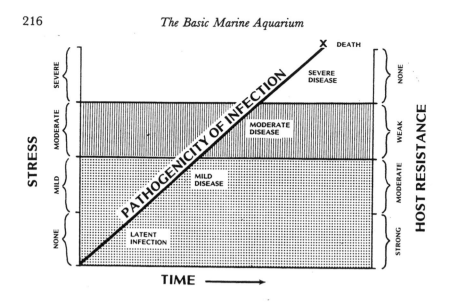

Figure 64. The relationships among severity of stress, degree of disease resistance, and severity of infection or disease. Effective treatments under the various conditions are depicted as follows (from bottom to top): stippled area = treatment by improving the environment; shaded area = treatment with drugs; white area = no effective treatment. See text for explanation. From Bower (1975).[14]

ately and the water quality had been allowed to decline. Because the fishes were being used in experiments, it was not possible either to alleviate the crowding or to improve the quality of the water. On the contrary, most diseased fishes that I have acquired have recovered without drug treatment, and I have found that outbreaks of disease in established aquariums are invariably related to a stressful environmental change; the disease often subsides spontaneously when the source of stress is quickly eliminated.

Chemical Treatment: General Considerations

Drugs and chemicals should be used to treat diseases of fishes *only after environmental therapy has failed.* The effects of environmental improvement are usually apparent after three or four days. Some general recommendations concerning the choice and use of medications are given below.

1. Before you attempt to treat any disease, be certain that it has been diagnosed correctly. Many diseases have similar symptoms,

although the agents that cause them may be very different. It must be remembered that most drugs are active against only one category of pathogenic microorganisms (bacteria, fungi, protozoa, etc.). Diseased fishes, for example, usually exhibit rapid respiration, loss of appetite, and folded fins, regardless of the cause of the disease. A completely reliable key to the diagnosis of diseases of tropical marine fishes does not exist, but those given by Kingsford[15] and de Graaf[16] may be useful to novice aquarists.

2. Some "diseases" are not diseases at all. They are, rather, physical or behavioral symptoms caused by environmental changes or poisoning. Although disease usually occurs after a fish is subjected to severe stress, it is pointless to treat a disease with drugs if the cause of stress is not eliminated concomitantly. Before beginning drug treatment, you should therefore carry out a thorough water analysis (or have your aquarium retailer conduct one for you), to ensure that the aquarium water is chemically safe. It is also helpful to replace 50 percent or more of the water and to replace the activated carbon whenever poisoning is suspected.

3. It is important to realize that there are no known effective treatments for some diseases, particularly those of viral origin such as lymphocystis disease. This is one more reason why a correct diagnosis is essential.

4. Once a disease has been diagnosed with relative certainty, the next step is to determine what drug or chemical, and how much of it, is needed for effective treatment, keeping in mind that the indiscriminate use of drugs may be more harmful than disease to the population of an aquarium. Effective remedies for three of the most frequently encountered diseases of tropical marine fishes are given later in this chapter. Recommendations for the treatment of various other infectious diseases are given by Kingsford,[15] van Duijn,[17] and Dulin.[18]

5. Many medications that are marketed exclusively for use in aquariums are of doubtful value in the treatment of fish diseases; some have been shown to be ineffective against bacteria at the dosages recommended by the manufacturers,[19, 20] and others may contain substances that are highly toxic to fishes.[21]

When drug therapy is required, it is therefore a good practice to obtain medications through a licensed veterinarian, if you can. If you must purchase your medications from an aquarium store, use the following criteria for choosing them.

a. The medication should contain a single substance in its pure form, rather than a combination of drugs. "Miracle cures" containing a combination of compounds that are allegedly effective in treating all fish ailments should be avoided.

b. The composition (by generic name) of the drug and the exact amount of the active ingredient in each tablet, capsule, or volume of liquid should be printed clearly on the package label (Fig. 65).

For Aquarium Use Only/Not for Human Use
KEEP OUT OF REACH OF CHILDREN

Each capsule contains: FURANACE (nifurpirinol) . . . 3.8 mg.

NET CONTENTS: SIX CAPSULES

Figure 65. The composition (by generic name) of a drug and the exact amount of the active ingredient in each tablet, capsule, or volume of liquid should be printed clearly on the package label.

6. When administering medications, do not follow the recommendations of the manufacturer. Instead, follow the recommendations given in this book or in the publications cited in Step 4 (above) concerning proper dosages and durations of treatments.

Limitations and Drawbacks of Drug Baths

There are two common methods of administering drugs to fishes:

external treatment, in which a drug is applied topically or added to the aquarium water; and internal treatment, in which a drug is injected into a fish or incorporated into its feed.[22] The bath treatment (adding a drug to the water) is the easiest and most practical way for most aquarists to medicate diseased fishes. Drug baths do, however, have several limitations and drawbacks.

1. As noted in the discussion of quarantining newly acquired fishes in chemical baths (Chapter 11), the addition of certain antibiotics and other drugs to an aquarium can inhibit or interrupt bacteriological filtration, resulting in an increase in the concentration of ammonia in the water. Under certain circumstances, exposure to high concentrations of ammonia may be more harmful than the actual disease to the fishes. The effects of various medications on bacteriological filtration are listed in Table 22. Only those drugs that are not harmful to filter bacteria are recommended for disease treatment in an established aquarium, unless there is no alternative.

2. The ideal drug bath should contain a medication that is absorbed rapidly by fishes (or external parasites), reaches effective levels in the fishes' tissues, and is then excreted rapidly, without harming the fishes or leaving toxic residues.[27] Unless they are taken up by fishes, drugs that are added to the water treat only the surface tissues. Although some drug baths undoubtedly are effective against some external parasites, their value for treating internal, systemic infections caused by bacteria and other microorganisms is variable.

Fishes can absorb drugs by two routes: directly from the water, through their gills, skin, and mucous membranes; and indirectly through their gastrointestinal tracts, after drinking drug-treated water. Very few studies have been conducted on the uptake of antimicrobial drugs by fishes, but it appears that effective tissue levels rarely are produced by bath treatments with most drugs.[28] It has been found, for example, that erythromycin is absorbed poorly, and chloramphinicol is not absorbed at all by channel catfish.[29] On the contrary, oxytetracycline and nifurpirinol (Furanace) not only are absorbed rapidly but also reach effective tissue levels.[27,29,30] The absorption of bath-administered drugs through the digestive systems of marine fishes, which drink water, has not been studied. It is clear, however, that there is nothing to be gained from administering nonabsorbable drugs as baths for the treatment of systemic diseases,

Table 22

THE EFFECTS OF SOME COMMONLY USED DRUGS AND CHEMICALS ON BACTERIOLOGICAL
FILTRATION IN FRESHWATER (FW) AND SEAWATER (SW) AQUARIUMS
Compounds marked with an asterisk (*) may be used safely in seawater aquariums

Generic (trade) name of compound		Effect(s)	Reference no.
*Chloramphenicol	FW:	None.	23
(Chloromycetin®)	SW:	Slight increase in ammonia, accompanied by clouding of the water.	
			24
*Copper sulfate	FW:	None.	25
	SW:	Slight to moderate increase in ammonia; slight to moderate increase in nitrite. Sometimes accompanied by clouding of the water.	24,26
Erythromycin (Ilosone®)	FW:	Substantial increase in ammonia and nitrite.	23
Formalin	FW:	None.	25
*Gentamycin sulfate			
(Gentocin®)	SW:	None	24
Malachite green	FW:	None	25
Methylene blue	FW:	Substantial increase in ammonia.	25
	SW:	Slight to moderate increase in ammonia.	24
Neomycin sulfate (Biosol®)	SW:	Slight to moderate increase in ammonia; substantial increase in nitrite.	24

Generic (trade) name of compound		Effect(s)	Reference no.
*Nifurpirinol (Furanace)	FW:	None.	23
	SW:	None.	24
Oxytetracycline (Terramycin)	FW:	None.	23
Potassium permanganate	FW:	None.	25
*Quinacrine hydrochloride	SW:	None.	24
Sulfamerazine	FW:	None.	23

except, perhaps, a reduction in the numbers of bacteria in the water.

The amount of a drug that is absorbed by a fish is proportional to the concentration of the drug in the water;[29,30] thus, the higher the initial dosage, the higher the resulting blood and tissue levels. There is, however, variation in the amounts of a drug absorbed by different individuals and species of fishes during the same period of exposure to a single concentration.[30] Moreover, different concentrations of a single drug are needed to inhibit or kill different species of bacteria, and some drugs are effective against some bacteria but not against others.[31] In the light of the many factors that can influence the effectiveness of even a well-absorbed drug, the matter of choosing a dosage appropriate for the treatment of a specific disease in a given species is, at best, guesswork.

3. Many drugs are not stable in aquarium water, and their concentrations decrease with time. The concentration of Furanace, for example, does not decrease by more than 10 percent after five hours, whereas 78 to 100 percent of chloramphenicol disappears from water during the same interval.[29]

4. The efficacy of many drugs is influenced strongly by the physical and chemical characteristics of the water. Some become more or less effective at different temperatures and pH values, and others, such as Furanace, quinine sulfate, and quinine hydrochloride, are inactivated by light. It is also unfortunate that some of the most potentially valuable drugs cannot be administered as baths, because of their low solubility in water.

COMMON DISEASES AND THEIR TREATMENT

There are probably thousands of microorganisms that are capable of causing disease in marine fishes. Fish pathogens include viruses, bacteria, fungi, protozoa, worms, and crustaceans. Many diseases have no known treatments. A complete discussion of the diseases of tropical marine fishes and their treatment is beyond the scope of this book; the following section is therefore limited to the three types of diseases that occur most frequently in captive reef fishes. Before discussing these diseases and their appropriate treatment, I wish to reemphasize three points.

First, an outbreak of infectious disease in an established aquarium should always be regarded as a sign that the fishes have been stressed. In the absence of equipment failure, which could produce a rapid change in water temperature or water quality, over-crowding is undoubtedly the most common cause of stress. Stress from overcrowding may be due to its psychological effects on the fishes, or on a related decline in water quality. Regardless of the cause of stress, *if the responsible stressful environmental condition or conditions are not eliminated, disease can never be eradicated by drug treatment; it can only be kept under control temporarily.*

Second, drug treatment should be administered only to diseased fishes. When only a few of the fishes in an aquarium are affected by disease, they should be treated in a separate tank or other suitable container. If it becomes necessary to medicate an entire aquarium, all invertebrates should be removed from the tank before any drug is added; invertebrates are extremely susceptible to poisoning by many fish medications.

Third, just as nourishing food, quiet, and plenty of rest are important factors in the recovery of humans from illness, these factors are also essential to the recovery of diseased fishes. Unless otherwise specified, treatment should be carried out in an aquarium with established bacteriological filtration. Although it is true that bacteriological filtration might decrease the effectiveness of some drugs by breaking them down, I believe that this is the lesser of two evils as compared with the risk of ammonia intoxication. During drug treatment, activated carbon filtration should be discontinued, because carbon will remove most drugs from the water.

Diseased fishes often refuse to feed, and starvation worsens the effects of disease; the fishes should be encouraged to eat by offering them only their favorite foods, such as live brine shrimp nauplii or adults. Sick fishes also spend much of their time in hiding, so the treatment tank should contain an overabundance of decorations that provide shelter. The fishes should not be prodded out of hiding or disturbed in any way.

Bacterial Diseases

"Fin Rot"

Causes and Symptoms

Bacterial fin rot is often associated with the presence of microorganisms of the genera *Pseudomonas, Aeromanas,* and *Vibrio.* A relationship has been demonstrated between the occurrence of fin rot and environmental stress, such as exposure to low levels of dissolved oxygen and various chemical pollutants.[32] This relationship is so prevalent that fin rot has been proposed as an indicator of environmental quality because "an environment which is conducive to fin rot has the potential for inducing other possibly more consequential fish diseases."[33] It has also been suggested that fin rot may be related to inadequate lysine (an amino acid) in fish diets.[34,35]

Fin rot is characterized by a deterioration of the tail and other fins. The fins take on a ragged appearance with white or cloudy edges. In extreme cases, the entire fin is lost.

Treatment

Because fin rot is so closely associated with a decline in environmental quality, any stressful conditions, such as overcrowding, low pH, high or low salinity, etc., should be eliminated. The activated carbon in the aquarium should be replaced to ensure removal of organic and metal pollutants, and 50 percent of the water should also be replaced, to dilute any nonfilterable or nonbiodegradable organic or inorganic substances that may have accumulated.

If the condition does not improve within one week, drug treatment may be necessary. Using the methods described in Chapter 10, capture the affected fishes and transfer them to a bucket containing 1 milligram per liter of nifurpirinol (Furanace), dissolved in aquarium seawater. No acclimation to this water is necessary. Each tablet or capsule of Furanace contains 3.8 milligrams of nifurpirinol. Thus, to achieve the proper concentration of the drug, dissolve one tablet or capsule in each gallon or 3.8 liters of seawater. Leave the fish in this solution for *ten minutes*; then capture it and return it to the aquarium.

If most or all of the fishes in an aquarium are affected with fin rot, an acceptable alternative procedure is to medicate the whole aquarium for several days with a low dosage of Furanace. As noted in Table 22, this drug does not interfere with bacteriological filtration. Remove the activated-carbon filter from the aquarium, then add enough Furanace to produce a final concentration of 0.1 milligram per liter. To achieve this concentration, use one 3.8 -milligram capsule or tablet of Furanace for every 10 gallons (38 liters) of water in the tank. Dissolve the Furanace in a small volume of tap water before adding it to the aquarium. The usual treatment period is five days. During this period, reduce the level of aquarium light-ing, because the light inactivates Furanace. At the end of the treat-ment period, resume filtration with activated carbon; this will re-move any residuals of the drug from the water.

"Vibrio Disease"

Causes and Symptoms

Vibrio disease or "vibriosis" is thought to be caused by bacteria of the genus *Vibrio*, especially *V. anguillarum*. Like bacterial fin rot, the occurrence of vibriosis is often associated with environmental stress. Some factors that may predispose fishes to the disease are rapid in-creases in temperature, exposure to copper and other pollutants, low levels of dissolved oxygen, changes in salinity, overcrowding, and handling.[32,36,37]

The onset of vibrio disease in fishes in characterized by a darken-ing of the skin, loss of appetite, and reduced activity. As the disease proceeds, hemorrhages or bloody spots or patches appear on the skin and fins, often accompanied by inflammation or redness around the anal area. The hemorrhages on the body may later develop into ulcerations or open sores. Internal manifestations of the disease in-clude hemorrhaging and deterioration of the liver, spleen, and kidney.[36,37] It appears that death from vibriosis is due to a poison secreted by the bacteria.[38]

Treatment

The treatment for vibrio disease is the same as that recommend-ed for fin rot, that is, environmental improvement followed, if necessary, by a long- or short-term bath in Furanace.

Miscellaneous Bacterial Infections

Symptoms of infections with unspecified bacteria include cloudy eyes, erect or bristly scales, and loss of skin (beginning at the head and then spreading along the body). These conditions often occur after fishes have been captured in nets, and result from the invasion of opportunistic bacteria into lesions created by physical injury. Fishes also become vulnerable to "secondary" bacterial infections during or after infestation with external parasites. Fishes displaying any of the above symptoms should be treated with Furanace as described for the treatment of fin rot.

"Velvet Disease" or "Coral Fish Disease"

Causes

Marine "velvet" or "coral fish disease" is caused by the parasite, *Oodinium (= Amyloodinium) ocellatum. Oodinium* is a dinoflagellate, a single-celled protozoan related to the microorganisms responsible for "red tides" in the ocean. Dinoflagellates are characterized by two *flagella,* slender, whip-like projections that are used for locomotion.

Like most other parasites, *Oodinium* has a somewhat complex life cycle.[39-42] Many details concerning its growth and development have not even been described conclusively. As shown in Figure 66, the parasitic stage, the *trophont,* is a pear-shaped or rounded cell. It is attached to a fish's gill tissue, skin, or fins by means of rootlike filaments called *rhizoids.* The trophont is surrounded by a tough, cellulose membrane. It usually grows to a certain size and then detaches from the fish and falls into the water. Within two to five minutes after detachment, the parasite retracts its rhizoids and takes in a large volume of water, sometimes enough to cause it to double in size, through an opening at its base, and then secretes a cellulose "cap" to seal the opening. The detached, completely encysted cell, is called the *tomont* or the *palmella.* Immediately after the opening is sealed, provided that the water temperature and other environmental conditions are right, the tomont begins to divide, forming 2, 4, 8, 16, 32, 64, 128, and finally 256 "daughter" cells, all of which are contained within the "mother" cyst. During this period of division, the tomont is usually lying on and possibly attached to a solid substrate.

The time elapsed from the first division until the last may vary from two to several days, depending chiefly on the temperature and salinity of the water. On the average, however, the tomont matures

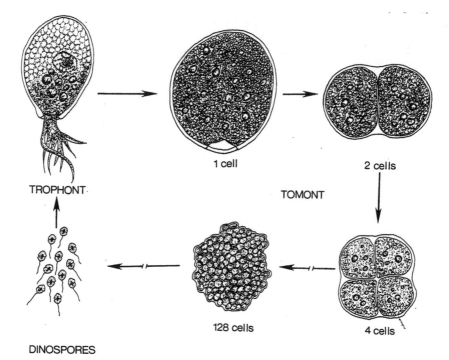

TROPHONT·

TOMONT

1 cell

2 cells

128 cells

4 cells

DINOSPORES

Figure 66. The life cycle of *Oodinium ocellatum*. See text for explanation. Redrawn from various sources.

within three to seven days. The mature tomont, which may contain as few as eight or as many as 256 cells, then appears to rupture, and the daughter cells, called *dinospores,* are liberated into the water. The dinospores consitute the infective stage of the parasite's life cycle. According to one researcher, they are "naked," or unprotected by an outer membrane, and are capable of invading a fish immediately.[40,42] Another researcher, however, believes that the newly liberated dinospore secretes a protective membrane around itself, settles to the bottom, and then undergoes several changes, ultimately transforming into an infective free-swimming cell.[41] In any case, each dinospore, upon location of a suitable host fish, anchors itself to the fish's gill tissue or skin and transforms into a parasitic trophont, thus beginning the life cycle anew. Free-swimming dinospores may survive for periods up to two to four weeks after they are released from tomonts.[15,43]

Although *Oodinium* trophonts have been found on fishes captured in the ocean, mass mortalities caused by the parasite in the wild have never been reported. In aquariums, however, *Oodinium* infestation can be devastating.[39,42,44] The prevalence of the disease in captive fishes frequently is related to overcrowding, because crowded conditions increase the likelihood that dinospores will find and infect a fish. The transformation of latent *Oodinium* infections into the acute disease following physical trauma (capturing fishes before their tanks were cleaned) also has been noted,[44] so outbreaks of disease also can be related to to the subjection of fishes to stressful environmental conditions.

Symptoms

The first noticeable symptom of velvet disease in fishes is a behavior called "flashing"; the fishes exhibit rapid, jerky or spasdic swimming movements, shaking their heads like wet dogs and deliberately brushing their gill covers against the tank walls and decorations. Their breathing is rapid and irregular, with their mouths open. As the disease progresses, the fishes' appetites diminish, and sometimes they stop feeding altogether. In the advanced stages of the disease, the fishes typically secrete excessive amounts of mucus and hover near the bottom or the water surface at a 45-degree angle. When the parasite invades the skin and fins, the trophonts appear as a powdery covering of gray or yellowish spots (Fig. 67). Death can be extremely rapid, often occurring as little as 48 hours after the first symptoms are noted, and fishes have been

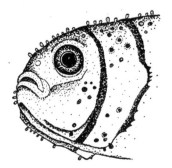

Figure. 67. A false clown anemonefish (*Amphiprion ocellaris*) covered with large trophonts of *Oodinium ocellatum.*

known to die as soon as 12 hours after being introduced into aquariums containing many dinospores.[43] Microscopic examination of the gills of diseased fishes reveals hemorrhages, inflammation, and destruction of gill tissue.

Treatment

Although exposure to various drugs and chemicals causes trophonts of *Oodinium ocellatum* to drop off fishes and encyst, the parasite can never be completely eradicted by any method of treatment, including the administration of drugs. As observed by one early worker, who failed to eliminate *Oodinium* with mercurochrome, potassium permanganate, or chlorine, "The remarkable resistance of the parasite to reagents in the vegetative stage [trophonts] and the stages of sporulation [tomonts] makes it very difficult to eradicate from the Aquarium, it being much easier to kill the host than the parasite."[40]

Such "remarkable resistance" to drug treatment is conferred upon the parasite by its cellulose covering, which apparently is impervious to all chemicals. The immersion of tomonts in fresh water for several days — a treatment that would surely kill most reef fishes — only retards the development of dinospores within the cyst; they multiply slowly when kept in this medium, but resume normal division after being returned to seawater.[40,41] I have found that tomonts immersed in solutions of copper sulfate or quinine hydrochloride develop normally to at least the 32-cell stage. The efficacy of various drugs against *Oodinium ocellatum* is currently being investigated at the Institute for Aquarium Studies.

Copper compounds have been used extensively to control *Oodinium* infestations.[45-47] Despite the severe drawbacks of copper usage (Chapter 11), it is thought that copper is lethal only to the free-swimming dinospores of *Oodinium.* Consequently, the recommended treatment period is lengthy (10 to 14 days) to ensure that all dinospores hatch and are killed. The killing of dinospores by exposure to copper has not been demonstrated experimentally.

I have not found copper to be completely effective against *Oodinium*, regardless of the duration of treatment. In our laboratory, the disease broke out in two severely overcrowded aquariums containing approximately four 1-inch anemonefish per gallon (one fish per liter) of water. All fish in one tank died within 24 hours after they had stopped feeding and the dust-like covering of trophonts had appeared on their bodies. The fish in the other tank, however, were treated with quinine sulfate, which dislodged the trophonts in a few hours, and then with copper sulfate. At the time of this writing, copper treatment has been used continually for seven weeks. Several of the fish still exhibit early signs of *Oodinium* infestation ("flashing," rapid respiration, etc.), but they are feeding well, and no additional deaths have occurred. Each time during treatment that the copper concentration has been lowered by water replacement or activated carbon filtration (which became necessary when the water turned yellow or foamy), the condition of the fish has worsened. As soon as the previous concentration of copper has been restored, however, the disease symptoms have subsided.

Six weeks after copper treatment had commenced, several fish were transferred to a small, unmedicated aquarium with established bacteriological filtration. The stocking density in this tank was eight fish per gallon (two fish per liter). Within one week, these fish had developed severe *Oodinium* infestation, which was relieved upon their return to the copper-treated tank. On the contrary, fish from the original tank that were transferred to an uncrowded, established aquarium did not have a recurrence of the disease, nor did their tankmates become diseased.

From the above, it may be surmised that the usefulness of copper is limited to controlling *Oodinium* in overcrowded aquariums. The mechanism of control is not known, but it seems likely that copper does not kill any stage of the parasite's life cycle; rather, it might either suppress the development of dinospores or prevent their release from the tomonts. This would explain the rapid reinfestation that occurs when copper is removed from a crowded aquarium.

Dislodging any *Oodinium* trophonts that may be present on newly acquired fishes by dipping the fishes in fresh water or quarantining them in drug baths has been recommended for preventing the introduction of the parasite into aquariums. Some trophonts, however, may be retained in the gill mucus even after such treatments;[48] because they can encyst, divide, and form dinospores without ever leaving the fishes' gills, the value of these procedures is questionable.

If the fishes in an aquarium become afflicted with velvet disease to the extent that they lose their appetites and the parasites become visible on their skin and fins, the following treatment should be carried out.

1. Remove the activated carbon from the aquarium.

2. Add quinine hydrochloride to the aquarium water at a dosage of 40 milligrams per gallon (10 milligrams per liter). Dissolve the compound in some tank water before adding it to the aquarium. Quinine hydrochloride will cause the *Oodinium* trophonts to drop off the fishes.

3. Prepare a stock solution of copper sulfate by dissolving 1 gram of copper sulfate in 250 milliliters (8.5 fluid ounces) of distilled water. Store in a clean glass bottle. Each milliliter (20 drops) of this solution contains 1 milligram of copper.

4. Twelve to 24 hours after the quinine hydrochloride was added, replace 50 to 75 percent of the aquarium water with new seawater at the proper temperature and salinity.

5. Add copper sulfate solution to the aquarium water to give a final concentration of 0.15 milligrams of copper per liter (0.57 milligrams per gallon). If, for example, your aquarium contains 30 gallons (114 liters) of seawater, you will need to add 30 × 0.57 (or 114 × 0.15) = 17.1 milligrams of copper (17.1 milliliters or 0.57 ounces of stock solution) to your aquarium. To determine the initial amount of stock solution needed for aquariums of various volumes, refer to Table 23.

Copper is toxic to invertebrates, so be sure to move any anemones, crabs, etc., to another aquarium before adding copper sulfate to the water. Copper will also kill any algae that have grown in the aquarium.

6. All the copper that is added to the aquarium will not stay in solution; most of it will be absorbed on the filtrant and on other solid surfaces.[49] Consequently, it will be necessary to measure the concentration of *total dissolved copper* in the water twice daily throughout the treatment period, and to restore the copper concentration to its initial value after each measurement is made.

a. To measure the concentration of copper, you will need a copper test kit. Accurate and reliable test kits include those manufactured by New Technology Ltd., Hach Chemical Co., and LaMotte Chemical Co.[50] Follow the manufacturer's instructions for measuring the copper.

The Basic Marine Aquarium

Table 23

AMOUNTS OF COPPER SULFATE STOCK SOLUTION NEEDED TO PRODUCE AN INITIAL CONCENTRATION OF 0.57 MILLIGRAMS OF COPPER PER GALLON (0.15 MILLIGRAMS PER LITER) IN AQUARIUMS CONTAINING DIFFERENT VOLUMES OF SEAWATER

Volume of seawater in aquarium		Amount of stock solution	
Gallons	*Liters*	*Milliliters*	*Fluid ounces*
10	38	5.7	0.2
15	57	8.6	0.3
20	76	11.4	0.4
25	95	14.3	0.5
30	114	17.1	0.6
35	133	20.0	0.7
40	152	22.8	0.8
45	171	25.7	0.9
50	190	28.5	1.0
55	209	31.4	1.1
60	228	34.2	1.2
65	247	37.1	1.3
70	266	39.9	1.3
75	285	42.8	1.4
80	304	45.6	1.5
85	323	48.5	1.6
90	342	51.3	1.7
95	361	54.2	1.8
100	380	57.0	1.9

b. After determining the concentration of copper (as milligrams per liter or parts per million) calculate how much additional copper is needed to restore the initial concentration. To do this, subtract the measured concentration from the initial concentration. If, for example, the measured concentration is 0.05 milligrams per liter, you will need to add 0.15 minus 0.05 or 0.10 milligrams per liter.

c. Multiply the number obtained above by the number of liters of seawater in your aquarium (to convert gallons to liters, multiply the number of gallons by 3.8). The resulting number is the amount of copper sulfate stock solution (in milliliters) that you must add to your aquarium. Continuing the example from Steps 5 and 6b (above), if your aquarium contains 30 gallons (114 liters) of seawater, you will need to add 0.10 × 114 or 11.4 milliliters of copper sulfate solution.

7. Continue copper treatment for 14 days. Then replace 50 percent of the aquarium water with new seawater and begin filtration with activated carbon. Be sure to relieve any overcrowding by transferring some of the fishes to another aquarium. *If overcrowding cannot be relieved, do not discontinue copper treatment.* Copper at the recommended dosage may prevent further outbreaks of *Oodinium* indefinitely, provided that 50 percent of the water is replaced every two weeks, and the copper level is maintained.

8. Do not reintroduce invertebrates into a copper-treated aquarium until the water no longer contains detectable amounts of copper.

"White Spot Disease" or "Saltwater Ich"

Causes

This disease is caused by *Cryptocaryon irritans*, a protozoan parasite that is closely related to *Ichthyophthirius multifiliis* or "Ich," the agent of white spot disease in freshwater fishes. *Cryptocaryon* is a ciliated protozoan; that is, its exterior surface is covered with *cilia*, which are short, threadlike structures used for swimming.

Like *Oodinium*, *Cryptocaryon* has three stages in its life cycle[51] (Fig. 68). The parasitic stage, called the *trophont*, lives in the skin, gills, eyes, and mouths of fishes. Trophonts are not anchored to the tissues, but rather, they burrow under the skin and move about freely, feeding upon cellular matter and blood cells. After a time, the trophonts stop feeding, absorb their cilia, and form cycts, which may or may not drop off the fish. The encysted stage, called the *tomont*, then begins to divide, forming 200 or more *tomites*, the number depending on the size of the cyst. The tomites are the free-swimming,

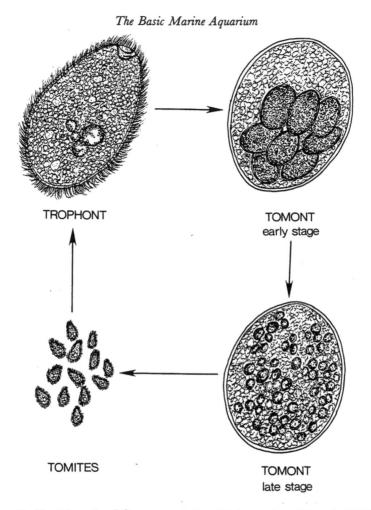

TROPHONT

TOMONT
early stage

TOMITES

TOMONT
late stage

Figure 68. The life cycle of *Cryptocaryon irritans*. Redrawn from Kingsford (1975)[15] and Nigrelli and Ruggieri (1966).[51]

infective stage. They emerge from the tomonts after 6 to 9 days and can swim rapidly; sometimes they form dense swarms around fishes. Tomites appear to be attracted by light. It is not known how long they are infective, but they are said to be free-swimming for less than 24 hours. Upon contacting a suitable host fish, the tomites burrow into the skin and other tissues and become trophonts.

Cryptocaryon is encountered only rarely on wild fishes, and is not regarded as an important pathogen under natural conditions.[1] Outbreaks of white spot disease that result in high mortalities are common, however, in aquariums.[51-53] The factors responsible for initiating the disease are not understood, but they probably include overcrowding and other stressful environmental conditions. It is also possible that the disease is related to inadequate nutrition, because *Cryptocaryon's* freshwater counterpart, *I. multifiliis,* has been controlled effectively in captive fishes by the addition of vitamin A supplements to the fish diets.[54] I have encountered *Cryptocaryon* most frequently on newly imported fishes within a few days of their introduction into an aquarium, so the appearance of the parasite may also be related to stress from capture, handling, and transportation.

Symptoms

Infestation with *Cryptocaryon* is characterized by the appearance of white or grayish spots the size of small pinheads on the fins, bodies, or eyes of fishes. They are considerably larger than the pinpoint-sized spots caused by *Oodinium,* and they do not give the fish a powdery appearance. These spots are large trophonts or tomonts beneath the skin. In severe cases of the disease, the spots may fuse together to form white patches or blotches.

Because the gills are not the major site of infestation, rapid breathing is not usually one of the first signs of disease; breathing does become difficult, however, if the gills become involved. Similarly, fishes with white spot disease may or may not exhibit "flashing" behavior or scratching against solid surfaces, depending on the degree of gill involvement. Some fishes respond to the presence of the parasite by producing excessive amounts of mucus.

In the advanced stage of the disease, the fishes' eyes may become clouded, followed by blindness. There is usually some hemorrhaging beneath the skin, evidenced by the appearance of small bloody spots that are most noticeable on the fins. If bacteria invade the lesions produced by the parasites, "fin rot" may develop. In severe cases, fishes may die as soon as four days after the first spots become visible. It has been suggested that *Cryptocaryon,* itself, is not directly responsible for the deaths of the fishes it infests; rather, mortalities may be attributable to bacterial infections that develop in the open sores produced when mature trophonts break through the skin of the fishes and drop off.[55]

Treatment

Various drugs, including those used against *Oodinium,* have been recommended for the treatment of white spot disease, but there is no evidence that any form of chemotherapy is completely effective. Chemical treatments may be useful under some circumstances for saving the lives of heavily infested fishes, but they do not completely eradicate the parasite from aquariums.

Mild infestations with *Cryptocaryon* often disappear spontaneously, especially when fishes are kept in uncrowded and well-maintained aquariums, and will recur only after the fishes have been stressed in some way. Fishes are probably capable of acquiring some degree of immunity to the parasite. It has been observed, for example, that the survivors of an outbreak of white spot disease do not become sick even when a heavily infested fish is introduced into their aquarium, whereas newly acquired fishes introduced into the same aquarium are quickly attacked by the parasite and usually die.[53] Freshwater fishes can be immunized against *I. multifiliis* by previous exposure to "Ich" and by "vaccination" with ground trophonts or cilia of the parasite,[56] and it seems reasonable that the same should be true of *Cryptocaryon*.

The manipulation of certain environmental conditions may be useful for controlling *Cryptocaryon* infestations. It has been shown, for example, that when trophonts are removed from fishes and held at 98.6°F (37°C), most do not form cysts and eventually die, and that tomonts held at the same temperature die without releasing tomites.[57] Trophonts are destroyed by exposure to low salinity (16 parts per thousand or less),[57] and both trophonts and tomonts are killed by exposure to high salinity (45 to 60 parts per thousand).[58] These conditions can also be lethal to fishes.

Although I have seen *Cryptocaryon* on several occasions on newly acquired fishes and on established fishes that have been unavoidably stressed (e.g. by a rapid increase in temperature resulting from the failure of a heater), I have never lost a fish to this parasite. Moreover, I do not believe that *Cryptocaryon* should be of major concern to aquarists who maintain their fishes in a nonstressful environment, as described throughout this book. Severe infestations resulting in high mortalities can and do occur, but they are most common under intensive culture conditions (i.e. at fish hatcheries and farms, where overcrowding is necessary) and when uncrowded fishes are subjected to suboptimal or fluctuating environmental conditions or psychological stressors.

The parasite undoubtedly can be *controlled* by the use of chemical baths or temperature or salinity manipulation, when it is impossible or unfeasible to reduce the stocking density or improve the water quality. Such measures, however, should not be taken, nor, for that matter, needed by hobbyists. The maintenance of captive fishes in healthful aquariums, together with the immunity that is probably conferred by mild infections, should suffice for the control of *Cryptocaryon,* so I do not recommend any drug treatment.

HOW TO PUT A DYING FISH TO SLEEP

Sometimes it becomes necessary or desirable to kill a fish as humanely and painlessly as possible, because it is sick or diseased beyond all hope for recovery. The choice between sacrificing a fish or allowing it to die a "natural" death is mostly personal; similarly, determining when a fish has become incurably ill and cannot possibly be saved is subjective and equally difficult. It is not known how a fish perceives pain or if it experiences "suffering," but it is hard to avoid anthropomorphism — attributing human traits to non-human animals — when a living creature appears to be in severe distress. In our laboratory we always sacrifice dying fishes to put an end to their misery and ours as well.

Some expedient methods of killing a fish include striking it sharply on the head, "pithing" it (severing its spinal cord with a knife or scissors), dropping it into boiling water, or flushing it down a toilet. With the exception of the latter, these methods are humane because they produce instantaneous death, but they can be exceedingly unpleasant to perform.

An alternative procedure, which is probably less distressing to both fish and aquarist, is to "put a fish to sleep" permanently with a chemical anesthetic or narcotizing agent. The following procedure employs sodium bicarbonate (baking soda), which releases carbon dioxide when it dissolves in water. Exposure to very high concentrations of carbon dioxide causes a fish to lose consciousness quickly, followed by death from oxygen deprivation.

1. Find a plastic container that is large enough to accommodate the dying fish, and fill it with aquarium water.

2. Add several teaspoons of baking soda to the water in the container (use about 10 teaspoons or ¼ cup per quart or liter of water),

and stir vigorously. Wait until the water becomes clear and the excess baking soda settles to the bottom.

3. Capture the fish, and transfer it to the baking soda solution. The fish might struggle briefly before losing consciousness. Do not discard the fish until it is dead, i.e. when it has stopped breathing.

THE AQUARIUM AS A SOURCE OF HUMAN DISEASE

Most methods of filtering aquarium water were originally designed for processing sewage and wastewater. One should not lose sight of the fact that aquarium water is a form of sewage that contains the wastes of the fishes and other animals that live in it. It is neither cleaner nor more healthful that pond, lake, or ocean water. In fact, the numbers of some pathogenic bacteria in aquarium water often exceed the upper limits allowed for swimming and recreational waters in the United States and Canada.[9]

Although no fungal or viral diseases of fishes are known to be transmitted to humans, some bacterial and parasitic diseases might be acquired from aquarium water or infected fishes.[59] Bacteria that cause diarrhea and urinary tract infections in man, for example, have been found in aquarium water,[9] and an ameba that can cause brain and eye infections has also been isolated from aquariums.[60] Despite the presence of these pathogenic microorganisms in aquariums, no specific cases of the diseases they cause have been attributed to contact with or the accidental ingestion of aquarium water.

One human disease syndrome, "fish tank granuloma" (FTG), is known to be transmitted from aquariums to man.[61,62] FTG is caused by the bacterium *Mycobacterium marinum,* which causes tuberculosis in fishes. (Fish tuberculosis was not discussed earlier in this chapter, because it is incurable.)

Fish tank granuloma is a skin infection that is found most frequently on the fingers, hands, and arms of aquarists. The infection usually occurs after the skin has been punctured by a sharp object in or around an aquarium, but cuts acquired elsewhere are also susceptible to infection. A wound that has become infected with *M. marinum* does not heal normally. At the site of the injury, a small lump appears and becomes firm, red, and slightly tender. The lump enlarges slowly for several weeks, and then typically becomes abscessed and discharges pus. In many cases, the infection spreads from the original wound, forming a string of lumps that extend up the hand and arm to the elbow or armpit.

FTG usually disappears without treatment in three months to three years, but infections lasting as long as 45 years have been reported. Several drugs have been used successfully to treat the infection, but none is known to be effective in every case.

The foregoing discussion is not intended to alarm or to frighten aquarists. Rather, it is meant to inform the reader of the potential health hazards posed by the presence of human pathogens in aquariums. These hazards actually are no greater than those presented by associations with cats, dogs, birds, or any other pets. All aquariums do not contain *Mycobacterium marinum* and other pathogens, and every scratch and scrape on an aquarist's hands or arms does not invariably develop into fish tank granuloma. On the contrary, case reports on *M. marinum* infection in humans are few and far between. Nevertheless, a few precautions should be taken to reduce one's chances of acquiring an aquarium-transmitted infection or disease.

1. Do not drink aquarium water. Ridiculous as it may seem, I know of aquarists who swear that they can measure the salinity of seawater by tasting it. Also, take care to avoid swallowing aquarium water when starting a siphon (see procedure for siphoning in Chapter 6).

2. Always rinse your hands after they have been in contact with aquarium water.

3. If you have a fresh cut or open sore on your finger or hand, keep it out of the aquarium or wear rubber gloves until it has healed completely.

4. If an injury on your hand does not heal normally and becomes lumpy and abscessed, there is reason to suspect that it may have become infected with *M. marinum*. Consult a dermatologist, and be sure to inform him of this possibility. Relatively few physicians are familiar with fish tank granuloma, so if contact with aquariums is not mentioned in your case history, improper diagnosis and treatment of the infection may result.

A FINAL NOTE OF OPTIMISM

The fishes that arrive in good condition at aquarium retail stores have, in many respects, been "culled" for survival. By the time a wild fish has grown to a size suitable for capture, it has probably been exposed to and survived several different microbial and parasitic infections. Capture, shipping, and distribution invariably are stressful and traumatic experiences; it is unlikely that more than a small fraction of the fishes collected from the world's tropical seas ever reach a retailer's tanks, but those that do undoubtedly are the hardiest individuals. In most cases, a fish that has survived long enough to reach a retail store should live to ripe old age in a well-managed aquarium.

All aquarists occasionally lose a fish, often through circumstances beyond their control. Cyanide, for example, is used by many Indo-Pacific collectors to "tranquilize" wild fishes during capture. Unfortunately, this poison is extremely slow acting. A fish exposed to cyanide usually appears to be in good health and may even feed aggressively, but then succumbs to the drug's effects suddenly, after a few days or weeks in captivity.

Other factors may also be responsible for the unexplainable deaths of apparently healthy fishes in well-maintained aquariums. Some diseases, such as those caused by certain worms, affect only the muscles or internal organs of a fish, and they have no visible symptoms. Other deaths are completely unrelated to the presence of pathogenic organisms; they are caused by genetic defects of individual fishes, which may develop tumors, misshapen backbones, eye abnormalities, and other internal or external aberrations.

There is little that an aquarist can do to save a fish that is genetically defective or that was exposed to poisons or toxic pollutants before it was purchased. For this reason, one should not be discouraged by an infrequent fish death that cannot be explained.

One bright light has appeared on the horizon. A small number of institutions are now breeding and commercially farming tropical reef fishes. Neon gobies and several species of anemonefishes have been reared successfully in captivity, and the list of tank-reared species is growing longer each year.

The advantages of tank-reared fishes over wild ones are appreciable. From the aquarist's standpoint, a tank-reared fish is preferable because it has known no environment other than the aquarium. From the beginning it has been fed artificial diets, and sometimes has been kept only in artificial seawater. It has been subjected to comparatively little handling trauma, and it is relatively fearless of humans. From an ecological standpoint, the increased availability of tank-reared fishes may contribute to the preservation of the world's coral-reef communities, many of which already have suffered irreversible damage from "over-collecting" — one regrettable consequence of man's desire to keep exotic marine fishes in his home.

REFERENCES

THE books and journals listed below can be found at many government and university libraries. Photocopies of some journal articles can be obtained for a fee through the interlibrary loan service of most private, state, and local libraries.

Chapter 1

1. MACGINITIE, G.E., and N. MACGINITIE. 1968. Natural history of marine animals, 2nd ed. New York, McGraw-Hill Book Co., 523 pp.
2. MILLER, W.J., and M.W. NEATHERY. 1977. Newly recognized trace mineral elements and their role in animal nutrition. BioScience 27: 674-679.
3. WEDEMEYER, G.A., F.P. MEYER, and L. SMITH. 1976. Environmental stress and fish diseases. Diseases of fishes, Book 5, S.F. Snieszko and H.R. Axelrod, eds. Neptune City, NJ, T.F.H. Publications, 192 pp.

Chapter 2

1. COATES, C.W., and J.W. ATZ. 1949. Lighting the tank in a public aquarium. Parks & Recreation 32: 480-485.
2. LANGOWSKA, I. 1980. Effect of activated carbon and brown coal suspensions on growth an development of *Scenedesmus obliquus* (Sc. 449). Pol. Arch. Hydrobiol. 27: 125-136.
3. SALER, A. and J.L. SLABBERT. 1980. A preliminary comparison between various granular active carbons for water reclamation. Water S. Afr. 6: 196-203.
4. LYMAN, J. and R.H. FLEMING. 1940. Composition of sea water. J. Mar. Res. 3: 134-146.
5. KUHNS, J.F., and K. BORGENDALE. 1980. Studies of the relative dechlorinating abilities of aquarium water conditioners. J. Aquariculture 1: 29-34.
6. BOWER, C.E., and T. HOLM-HANSEN. 1979. An evaluation of commercial test kits for saltwater aquariums. Freshwater Mar. Aquarium 2(12): 10-16; 92.

Chapter 3

1. KELLEY, W.E. 1975. The aquarium nitrogen cycle myth. Aquarium Industry (May, 1975), p. 8.

2. KUWATANI, Y., and T. NISHII. 1969. Effects of pH of culture water on the growth of the Japanese pearl oyster. Bull. Jap. Soc. Sci. Fish. 35: 342-350.

3. KUWATANI, Y., T. NISHII, and F. ISOGAI. 1969. Effects of nitrate in culture water on the growth of the Japanese pearl oyster. Bull. Nat. Pearl Res. Lab. 14: 1735-1747.

4. BROWNELL, C.L. 1980. Water quality requirements for first-feeding in marine fish larvae. II. pH, oxygen, and carbon dioxide. J. Exp. Mar. Biol. Ecol. 44: 285-298.

5. SPOTTE, S. 1970. Fish and invertebrate culture: water management in closed systems, 1st ed. New York, John Wiley & Sons, 145 pp.

6. BOWER, C.E., D.T. TURNER, and S. SPOTTE. 1981. pH maintenance in closed seawater culture systems: limitations of calcareous filtrants. Aquaculture 23: 211-217.

7. WICKINS, J.F. 1976. The tolerance of warm-water prawns to recirculated water. Aquaculture 9: 19-37.

8. HIRAYAMA, K. 1966. Influence of nitrate accumulated in culturing water on *Octopus vulgaris*. Bull. Jap. Soc. Sci. Fish. 32: 105-110.

9. BROWNELL, C.L. 1980. Water quality requirements for first-feeding in marine fish larvae. I. Ammonia, nitrite, and nitrate. J. Exp. Mar. Biol. Ecol. 44: 269-283.

10. FRAKES, T.A., and F. HOFF. 1981. Effects of high nitrate on the growth and survival of juvenile and larval clownfish, *Amphiprion ocellaris. Presented at*: 12th Ann. Conf. & Workshop, Int. Assoc. Aquat. Anim. Med., Mystic, CT, May 3-6, 1981.

11. KINNE, O. 1976. Cultivation of marine organisms: water-quality management and technology. Pages 19-300 *in*: Marine ecology. vol. III, part 1, O. Kinne, ed. New York, John Wiley & Sons.

Chapter 5

1. EUROPEAN INLAND FISHERIES ADVISORY COMMISSION. 1973. Water quality criteria for European freshwater fish. Report on ammonia and inland fisheries. Water Res. 7: 1011-1022.

2. LARMOYEUX, J. D., and R.G. PIPER. 1973. Effects of water reuse on rainbow trout in hatcheries. Prog. Fish-Cult. 35: 2-8.

3. BURROWS, R.E. 1964. Effects of accumulated excretory products on hatchery-reared salmonids. U.S. Bur. Sport Fish. Wildl., Res. Rep. 66, 12 pp.

4. FLAGG, R.M., and L.W. HINCK. 1978. Influence of ammonia on

aeromonad susceptibility in channel catfish. Proc. Ann. Conf. S.E.. Assoc. Fish Wildl. Agencies 32: 415-419.

5. RUSSO, R.C., and R.V. THURSTON. 1977. The acute toxicity of nitrite to fishes. Pages 118-131 *in*: Recent advances in fish toxicology, R.A. Tubb, ed.. Corvallis, OR, U.S. Environ. Protection Agency.

6. CRAWFORD, R.E., and G.H. ALLEN. 1977. Seawater inhibition of nitrite toxicity to chinook salmon. Trans. Am. Fish Soc. 106: 105-109.

7. PERRONE, S.J., and T.L. MEADE. 1977. Protective effect of chloride on nitrite toxicity to coho salmon (*Oncorhynchus kisutch*). J. Fish. Res. Board Can. 34: 486-492.

8. BROWNELL, C.L. 1981. Water quality requirements for first-feeding in marine fish larvae. I. Ammonia, nitrite, and nitrate. J. Exp. Mar. Biol. Ecol. 44: 269-283.

9. RUSSO, R.C., C.E. SMITH, and R.V. THURSTON. 1974. Acute toxicity of nitrite to rainbow trout (*Salmo gairdneri*). J. Fish. Res. Board Can. 31: 1653-1655.

10. FRAKES, T.A. Instant Ocean Hatcheries, personal communication.

11. BOWER, C. E., and D.T. TURNER. 1981. Accelerated nitrification in new seawater culture systems: effectiveness of commercial additives and seed media from established systems. Aquaculture 24: 1-6.

12. SRNA, R.F., and A. BAGGALEY. 1975. Kinetic response of perturbed marine nitrification systems. J. Water Pollut. Contr. Fed. 47: 472-486.

13. ROSENTHAL, H., and G. OTTE. 1979. Adaptation of a recirculating fish culture system to salinity change. Meeresforsch./Rep. Mar. Res. 27: 203-206.

14. KNOWLES, G., A.L. DOWNING, and M.J. BARRETT. 1965. Determination of kinetic constants for nitrifying bacteria in mixed culture, with the aid of an electronic computer. J. Gen. Microbiol. 38: 263-278.

15. BOWER, C.E., and T. HOLM-HANSEN. 1979. An evaluation of commercial test kits for saltwater aquariums. Freshwater Mar. Aquarium 2(12): 10-16; 92.

16. SPOTTE, S. 1979. Seawater aquariums: the captive environment. New York, John Wiley & Sons, 413 pp.

Chapter 6

1. ZERBE, W.B., and C.B. TAYLOR. 1953. Sea water temperature and density reduction tables. Spec. Publ. No. 198, U.S. Coast Geodetic Survey, 21 pp.

2. KWAN, G.C.H. 1980. Chlorine dissipation from tap water. J. Aquariculture 1:50.

3. BOWER, C.E., and T. HOLM-HANSEN. 1979. An evaluation of commercial test kits for saltwater aquariums. Freshwater Mar. Aquarium 2(12): 10-16; 92.

4. ROSENTHAL, H., G. OTTE, and G. KRÜNER. 1979. Long-term operation of a brackish water recycling system: progress report 1978. Int. Counc. Explor. Sea, C.M. 1979/F:12, 8 pp.

5. BOWER, C.E., and D.T. TURNER. Unpublished.
6. KEITH, R.E., 1980. Long term maintenance of the marine aquarium. Freshwater Mar. Aquarium 3(4): 12-13; 79.
7. TURNER, D.T., and C.E. BOWER. Unpublished.
8. SLICHER, A.M., G.E. PICKFORD, and P.K.T. PANG. 1966. Effects of "training" and of volume and composition of the injection fluid on stress-induced leukopenia in the mummichog. Prog. Fish-Cult. 28: 216-219.
9. RUSH, S.B., and B.L. UMMINGER. 1978. Elimination of stress-induced changes in the carbohydrate metabolism of goldfish (*Carassius auratus*) by training. Comp. Biochem. Physiol. 60A: 69-73.

Chapter 7

1. SPOTTE, S. 1979. Seawater aquariums: the captive environment. New York, John Wiley & Sons, 413 pp.
2. ANONYMOUS. 1979. Disease prevention and control. Freshwater Mar. Aquarium 2(10): 29-31; 84.
3. BOWER, C.E., and D.T. TURNER. 1981. Nitrification in closed seawater aquariums: effects of simulated power failures. J. Aquariculture 2: 1-3.

Chapter 8

1. WEDEMEYER, G.A. 1970. The role of stress in the disease resistance of fishes. Pages 30-35 *in*: A symposium on diseases of marine fishes and shellfishes, S. F. Snieszko, ed. Am. Fish. Soc., Spec. Publ. No. 5.
2. MAZEAUD, M.M., F. MAZEAUD, and E.M. DONALDSON. 1977. Primary and secondary effects of stress in fish: some new data with a general review. Trans. Am. Fish. Soc. 106: 201-212.
3. ISHIOKA, H. 1980. Stress reactions induced by environmental salinity changes in red sea bream. Bull. Jap. Soc. Sci. Fish. 46: 1323-1331.
4. FRAKES, T.A. Instant Ocean Hatcheries, personal communication.
5. TOMASSO, J.R., K.B. DAVIS, and N.C. PARKER. 1981. Plasma corticosteroid dynamics in channel catfish, *Ictalurus punctatus* (Rafinesque), during and after oxygen depletion. J. Fish Biol. 18: 519-526.
6. MEYER, F.P. 1970. Seasonal fluctuations in the incidence of disease on fish farms. Pages 21-29 *in*: A symposium on diseases of marine fishes and shellfishes, S.F. Snieszko, ed. Am. Fish. Soc., Spec. Publ. No. 5.
7. WEDEMEYER, G.A., and J.W. WOOD. 1974. Stress as a predisposing factor in fish diseases. U.S. Dept. Interior, Fish Wildl. Serv., Fish. Leafl. No. 38, 8 pp.
8. TOMASSO, J.R., K.B. DAVIS, and B.A. SIMCO. 1981. Plasma corticosteriod dynamics in channel catfish (*Ictalurus punctatus*) exposed to ammonia and nitrite. Can. J. Fish. Aquat. Sci. 38: 1106-1112.

9 . FLAGG, R.M., and L.W. HINCK. 1978. Influence of ammonia on aeromonad susceptibility in channel catfish. Proc. Ann. Conf. S.E. Assoc. Fish Wildl. Agencies 32: 415-419.

10. BURKHALTER, D.E., and C.M. KAYA. 1977. Effects of prolonged exposure to ammonia on fertilized eggs and sac fry of rainbow trout (*Salmo gairdneri*). Trans. Am. Fish. Soc. 106: 119-123.

11. FRAKES, T.A., and F. HOFF. 1981. Effects of high nitrate on the growth and survival of juvenile and larval clownfish, *Amphiprion ocellaris*. *Presented at:*12th Ann. Conf. & Workshop, Int. Assoc. Aquat. Anim. Med., Mystic, CT, May 3-6, 1981.

12. LIEBERMAN, M.T., and M. ALEXANDER. 1981. Effects of pesticides on decomposition of organic matter and nitrification in sewage. Bull. Environ. Contam. Toxicol. 26: 554-560.

13. TOMLINSON, T.G., A.G. BOON, and C.N.A. TROTMAN. 1966. Inhibition of nitrification in the activated sludge process of sewage disposal. J. Appl. Bacteriol. 29: 266-291.

14. HECHT, S.S., C.B. CHEN, R.M. ORNAF, E. JACOBS, J.D. ADAMS, and D. HOFFMAN. 1978. Reaction of nicotine and sodium nitrite: formation of nitrosamines and fragmentation of the pyrrolidine ring. J. Org. Chem. 43: 72-76.

15. WEDEMEYER, G.A. 1971. The stress of formalin treatments in rainbow trout (*Salmo gairdneri*) and coho salmon (*Oncorhynchus kisutch*). J. Fish. Res. Board Can. 28: 1899-1904.

16. SCHRECK, C.B., and H.W. LORZ. 1978. Stress response of coho salmon (*Oncorhynchus kisutch*) elicited by cadmium and copper and potential use of cortisol as an indicator of stress. J. Fish. Res. Board Can. 35: 1124-1129.

17. WILLIAMS, H.A., and R. WOOTTEN. 1981. Some effects of therapeutic levels of formalin and copper sulphate on blood parameters in rainbow trout. Aquaculture 24: 341-353.

18. HETRICK, F.M., M.D. KNITTEL, and J.L. FRYER. 1979. Increased susceptibility of rainbow trout to infectious hematopoietic necrosis virus after exposure to copper. Appl. Environ. Microbiol. 37: 198-201.

19. RØDSAETHER, M.C., J. OLAFSEN, and J. RAA. 1977. Copper as an initiating factor of vibriosis (*Vibrio anguillarum*) in eel (*Anguilla anguilla*). J. Fish Biol. 10: 17-21.

20. KNITTEL, M.D. 1981. Susceptibility of steelhead trout *Salmo gairdneri* Richardson to redmouth infection *Yersinia ruckeri* following exposure to copper. J. Fish Dis. 4: 33-40.

21. ROALES, R.R., and A. PERLMUTTER. 1977. The effects of sub-lethal doses of methylmercury and copper, applied singly and jointly, on the immune response of the blue gourami (*Trichogaster trichopterus*) to viral and bacterial antigens. Arch. Environ. Contam. Toxicol. 5: 325-331.

22. ROALES, R.R., and A. PERLMUTTER. 1980. Methylmercury/copper effects on hemosiderin: possible mechanism of immune suppression in fish. Bull. Environ. Contam. Toxicol. 24: 704-710.

23. WEDEMEYER, G.A. 1973. Some physiological aspects of sublethal heat

stress in the juvenile steelhead trout (*Salmo gairdneri*) and coho salmon (*Oncorhynchus kisutch*). J. Fish. Res. Board Can. 30: 831-834.

24. STRANGE, R.J., C.B. SCHRECK, and J.T. GOLDEN. 1977. Corticoid stress responses to handling and temperature in salmonids. Trans. Am. Fish. Soc. 106: 213-217.

25. ISHIOKA, H. 1980. Stress reactions in the marine fish — stress reactions induced by temperature changes. Bull. Jap. Soc. Sci. Fish. 46: 523-531.

26. GROBERG, W.J., R.H. McCOY, K.S. PILCHER, and J.L. FRYER. 1978. Relation of water temperature to infections of coho salmon (*Oncorhynchus kisutch*), chinook salmon (*O. tshawytscha*), and steelhead trout (*Salmo gairdneri*) with *Aeromonas salmonicida* and *A. hydrophila*. J. Fish. Res. Board Can. 35: 1-7.

27. HUNTER, V.A., M.D. KNITTEL, and J.L. FRYER. 1980. Stress-induced transmission of *Yersinia ruckeri* infection from carriers to recipient steelhead trout *Salmo gairdneri* Richardson. J. Fish. Dis. 3: 467-472.

28. GRAHAM, J.B. 1971. Temperature tolerances of some closely related tropical Atlantic and Pacific fish species. Science 172: 861-863.

29. GRAHAM, J.B. 1972. Low-temperature acclimation and the seasonal temperature sensitivity of some tropical marine fishes. Physiol. Zool. 45: 1-13.

30. REYNOLDS, W.W., and M.E. CASTERLIN. 1980. Thermoregulatory behavior of a tropical reef fish, *Zebrasoma flavescens*. Oikos 34: 356-358.

31. REYNOLDS, W.W., and M.E. CASTERLIN. 1980. Thermoregulatory behavior of a tropical marine fish: *Forcipiger longirostris* (Broussonet). Contrib. Mar. Sci. 23: 111-113.

32. MEDVICK, P.A., and J.M. MILLER. 1979. Behavioral thermoregulation in three Hawaiian reef fishes. Environ. Biol. Fish. 4: 23-28.

33. COATES, C.W., and J.W. ATZ. 1949. Lighting the tank in a public aquarium. Parks & Recreation 32: 480-485.

34. BROWN, T.E., and P.L. SPIER. 1969. Comparative illumination effects on breeding of tropical fish. The Aquarium 2(5): 18-20; 55-58.

35. PERLMUTTER, A. 1962. Lethal effect of fluorescent light on the eggs of brook trout. Prog. Fish-Cult. 24: 26-29.

36. OTT, J.N. 1964. Some responses of plants and animals to variations in wavelengths of light energy. Ann. N.Y. Acad. Sci. 117: 624-635.

37. HOUSTON, A.H., J.A. MADDEN, R.J. WOODS, and H.M. MILES. 1971. Some physiological effects of handling and tricaine methanesulphonate anesthetization upon the brook trout, *Salvelinus fontinalis*. J. Fish. Res. Board Can. 28: 625-633.

38. STRANGE, R.J., and C.B. SCHRECK. 1978. Anesthetic and handling stress on survival and cortisol concentration in yearling chinook salmon (*Oncorhynchus tshawytscha*). J. Fish. Res. Board Can. 35: 345-349.

39. BARTON, B.A., R.E. PETER, and C.R. PAULENCU. 1980. Plasma cortisol levels of fingerling rainbow trout (*Salmo gairdneri*) at rest, and subjected to handling, confinement, transport, and stocking. Can. J. Fish. Aquat. Sci. 37: 805-811.

40. PICKERING, A.D., and D.J. MACEY. 1977. Structure, histochemistry, and the effect of handling on the mucous cells of the epidermis of the char *Salvelinus*

alpinus (L.). J. Fish Biol. 10: 505-512.

41. BOUCK, G.R., M.A. CAIRNS, and A.R. CHRISTIAN. 1978. Effect of capture stress on plasma enzyme activities in rainbow trout (*Salmo gairdneri*). J. Fish Res. Board Can. 35: 1485-1488.

42. FLETCHER, G.L. 1975. The effects of capture, "stress," and storage of whole blood on the red blood cells, plasma proteins, glucose, and electrolytes of the winter flounder (*Pseudopleuronectes americanus*). Can. J. Zool. 53: 197-206.

43. WEDEMEYER, G.A. 1976. Physiological response of juvenile coho salmon (*Oncorhynchus kisutch*) and rainbow trout (*Salmo gairdneri*) to handling and crowding stress in intensive fish culture. J. Fish. Res. Board Can. 33: 2699-2702.

44. BEJERANO, Y., S. SARIG, M.T. HORNE, and R.J. ROBERTS. 1979. Mass mortalities in silver carp *Hypophthalmichthys molitrix* (Valenciennes) associated with bacterial infection following handling. J. Fish. Dis. 2: 49-56.

45. HOSMER, M.J. 1980. Handling as a factor in mortality of trout with or without furunculosis. Prog. Fish-Cult. 42: 157-159.

46. PETERS, G., H. DELVENTHAL, and H. KLINGER. 1980. Physiological and morphological effects of social stress in the eel, (*Anguilla anguilla* L.). Arch. Fischwiss. 30: 157-180.

47. BURTON, C.B., and S.A. MURRAY. 1979. Effects of density on goldfish blood — I. Hematology. Comp. Biochem. Physiol. 62A: 555-558.

48. MURRAY, S.A., and C.B. BURTON. 1979. Effects of density on goldfish blood — II. Cell morphology. Comp. Biochem. Physiol. 62A: 559-562.

49. PERLMUTTER, A., D.A. SAROT, M.L. YU, R.J. FILAZZOLA, and R.J. SEELEY. 1973. The effect of crowding on the immune response of the blue gourami, *Trichogaster trichopterus* to infectious pancreatic necrosis (IPN) virus. Life Sci. 13: 363-375.

50. LAGARDÈRE, J.P., and M. SPÉRANDIO. 1981. Influence du niveau sonore de bruit ambiant sûr la croissance de la crevette *Crangon crangon* (Linné, 1758). Résultats préliminaires. Aquaculture 24: 77-90.

51. LAGARDÈRE, J.P., and M.R. RÉGNAULT. 1980. Influence du niveau sonore de bruit ambiant sûr le métabolisme de *Crangon crangon* (Decapoda: Natantia) en élevage. Mar. Biol. 57: 157-164.

52. KETOLA, H.G. 1979. Influence of dietary lysine on "fin rot," survival, and growth of fry of rainbow trout. Fish Health News 8(2): vi.

53. SNIESZKO, S.F. 1972. Nutritional fish diseases. Pages 403-437 *in*: Fish nutrition, J.E. Halver, ed. New York, Academic Press.

54. ROBERTS, R.J., R.H. RICHARDS, and A.M. BULLOCK 1979. Pansteatitis in rainbow trout *Salmo gairdneri* Richardson: a clinical and histopathological study. J. Fish. Dis. 2: 85-92.

Chapter 9

1. HINTON, S. 1962. Longevity of fishes in captivity, as of September, 1956. Zoologica 47: 105-116.

2. THRESHER, R.E. 1980. Reef fish: behavior and ecology on the reef and in the aquarium. St. Petersburg, FL, Palmetto Publishing Co., 171 pp.

3. RANDALL, J.E. 1967. Food habits of reef fishes of the West Indies. Stud. Trop. Oceanogr., Miami, No. 5, p. 665-847.

4. KELLEY, W.E. personal communication.

5. MYRBERG, A.A., and R.E. THRESHER. 1974. Interspecific aggression and its relevance to the concept of territoriality in reef fishes. Amer. Zool. 14: 81-96.

6. NURSALL, J.R. 1974. Some territorial behavioral attributes of the surgeonfish *Acanthurus lineatus* at Heron Island, Queensland. Copeia 1974: 950-959.

7. LORENZ, K. 1966. On aggression. New York, Harcourt, Brace & World, 230 pp.

8. THRESHER, R.E. 1976. Field analysis of the territoriality of the threespot damselfish, *Eupomacentrus planifrons* (Pomacentridae). Copeia 1976: 266-276.

9. THRESHER, R.E. 1976. Field experiments on species recognition by the threespot damselfish, *Eupomacentrus planifrons,* (Pisces: Pomacentridae). Anim. Behav. 24: 562-569.

10. MAHONEY, B.M. 1981. An examination of interspecific territoriality in the dusky damselfish, *Eupomacentrus dorsopunicans* Poey. Bull. Mar. Sci. 31: 141-146.

11. REYNOLDS, W.W. 1979. Habitat selection and territorial defense behaviors in juvenile Cortez angelfish, *Pomacanthus zonipectus* (Gill). Hydrobiologia 66: 145-148.

12. FEDER, H.M. 1966. Cleaning symbiosis in the marine environment. Pages 327-380 *in:* Symbiosis, vol. 1, S.M. Henry, ed. New York, Academic Press.

13. PETERS, G., H. DELVENTHAL, and H. KLINGER. 1980. Physiological and morphological effects of social stress in the eel, (*Anguilla anguilla* L.). Arch. Fischwiss. 30: 157-180.

14. BURTON, C.B., and S.A. MURRAY. 1979. Effects of density on goldfish blood — I. Hematology. Comp. Biochem Physiol. 62A: 555-558.

15. MURRAY, S.A., and C.B. BURTON. 1979. Effects of density on goldish blood — II. Cell morphology. Comp. Biochem. Physiol. 62A: 559-562.

16. PERLMUTTER, A., D.A. SAROT, M.L. YU, R.J. FILAZZOLA, and R.J. SEELEY. 1973. The effect of crowding on the immune response of the blue gourami, *Trichogaster trichopterus* to infectious pancreatic necrosis (IPN) virus. Life Sci. 13: 363-375.

17. CAMPBELL, G. 1976. Salt-water tropical fish in your home. New York, Sterling Publishing Co., Inc., 144 pp.

18. DE GRAAF, F. 1973. Marine aquarium guide. Harrison, NJ, Pet Library Ltd., Sternco Industries Inc., 284 pp.

19. AXELROD, H.R., and C.W. EMMENS. 1973. Exotic marine fishes. Neptune City, NJ, T.F.H. Pulications, 607 pp.

20. SPOTTE, S. 1973. Marine aquarium keeping: the science, animals, and art. New York, John Wiley & Sons, 171 pp.

21. KUKUDA, S. 1979. On the growth of the file-fish, *Navodon modestus,* in the Seto Inland Sea. J. Fac. Appl. Biol. Sci. Hiroshima Univ. 18: 197-205.

22. HOFF, F. Instant Ocean Hatcheries, personal communication.

23. SCHIOTZ, A., and P. DAHLSTROM. 1972. A guide to aquarium fishes and plants. Philadelphia, J.B. Lippincott Co., 223 pp.

24. COX, G.F. 1974. Tropical marine aquaria, revised ed. New York, Grosset & Dunlap, 160 pp.

25. SIMON & SCHUSTER. 1977. Simon & Schuster's guide to freshwater and marine aquarium fish. New York, Simon & Schuster, 295 pp.

Chapter 10

1. STRANGE, R.J., C.B. SCHRECK, and J.T. GOLDEN. 1977. Corticoid stress responses to handling and temperature in salmonids. Trans. Am. Fish. Soc. 106: 213-217.

2. HOUSTON, A.H., J.A. MADDEN, R.J. WOODS, and H.M. MILES. 1971. Some physiological effects of handling and tricaine methanesulphonate anesthetization upon the brook trout, *Salvelinus fontinalis*. J. Fish. Res. Board Can. 28: 625-633.

3. STRANGE, R.J., and C.B. SCHRECK. 1978. Anesthetic and handling stress on survival and cortisol concentration in yearling chinook salmon (*Oncorhynchus tshawytscha*). J. Fish. Res. Board Can. 35: 345-349.

4. BARTON, B.A., R.E. PETER, and C.R. PAULENCU. 1980. Plasma cortisol levels of fingerling rainbow trout (*Salmo gairdneri*) at rest, and subjected to handling, confinement, transport, and stocking. Can. J. Fish. Aquat. Sci. 37: 805-811.

5. PICKERING, A.D., and D.J. MACEY. 1977. Structure, histochemistry, and the effect of handling on the mucous cells of the epidermis of the char *Salvelinus alpinus* (L.). J. Fish Biol. 10: 505-512.

6. BOUCK, G.R., M.A. CAIRNS, and A.R. CHRISTIAN. 1978. Effect of capture stress on plasma enzyme activities in rainbow trout (*Salmo gairdneri*). J. Fish. Res. Board Can. 35: 1485-1488.

7. FLETCHER, G.L. 1975. The effects of capture, "stress," and storage of whole blood on the red blood cells, plasma proteins, glucose, and electrolytes of the winter flounder (*Pseudopleuronectes americanus*). Can. J. Zool. 53: 197-206.

8. WEDEMEYER, G.A. 1976. Physiological response of juvenile coho salmon (*Oncorhynchus kisutch*) and rainbow trout (*Salmo gairdneri*) to handling and crowding stress in intensive fish culture. J. Fish. Res. Board Can. 33: 2699-2702.

9. TOMASSO, JR., K.B. DAVIS, and N.C. PARKER. 1980. Plasma corticosteriod and electrolyte dynamics of hybrid striped bass (white bass x striped bass) during netting and hauling. Proc. World Mariculture Soc. 11: 303-310.

10. WEDEMEYER, G.A. 1970. The role of stress in the disease resistance of fishes. Pages 30-35 *in*: A symposium on diseases of marine fishes and shellfishes, S.F. Snieszko, ed. Am. Fish. Soc., Spec. Publ. No. 5.

11. BEJERANO, Y., S. SARIG, M.T. HORNE, and R.J. ROBERTS. 1979. Mass mortalities in silver carp *Hypophthalmichthys molitrix* (Valenciennes)

associated with bacterial infection following handling. J. Fish Dis. 2: 49-56.

12. HOSMER, M.J. 1980. Handling as a factor in mortality of trout with or without furunculosis. Prog. Fish-Cult. 42: 157-159.

13. MURAI, T., J.W. ANDREWS, and J.W. MULLER. 1979. Fingerling American shad: effect of Valium, MS-222, and sodium chloride on handling mortality. Prog. Fish-Cult. 41: 27-29.

14. SPOTTE, S. 1973. Marine aquarium keeping: the science, animals, and art. New York, John Wiley & Sons, 171 pp.

15. STRANGE, R.J., C.B. SCHRECK, and R.D. EWING. 1978. Cortisol concentrations in confined juvenile chinook salmon (*Oncorhynchus tshawytscha*). Trans. Am. Fish. Soc. 107: 812-819.

16. McFARLAND, W.N., and K.S. NORRIS. 1958. The control of pH by buffers in fish transport. Calif. Fish Game 44: 291-310.

17. TURNER, D.T., and C.E. BOWER. 1982. Removal of ammonia by bacteriological nitrification during the simulated transport of marine fishes. Aquaculture 29: 347-357.

Chapter 11

1. SPOTTE, S., and G. ADAMS. 1982. Pathogen reduction in closed aquaculture systems by UV radiation: fact or artifact? Mar. Ecol. Progr. Ser., 6: 295-298.

2. TRUST, T.J., and K.H. BARTLETT. 1974. Occurrence of potential pathogens in water containing ornamental fishes. Appl. Microbiol. 28: 35-40.

3. TRUST, T.J. 1972. Inadequacy of aquarium antibacterial formulations for the inhibition of potential pathogens of freshwater fish. J. Fish. Res. Board Can. 29: 1425-1430.

4. TRUST, T.J., and D.C. CHIPMAN. 1974. Evaluation of aquarium antibiotic formulations. Antimicrob. Agents Chemother. 6: 379-386.

5. HERWIG, N. 1979. Handbook of drugs and chemicals used in the treatment of fish diseases: a manual of fish pharmacology and materia medica. Springfield, IL, Charles C Thomas, 272 pp.

6. WEDEMEYER, G.A. 1971. The stress of formalin treatments in rainbow trout (*Salmo gairdneri*) and coho salmon (*Oncorhynchus kisutch*). J. Fish. Res. Board Can. 28: 1899-1904.

7. SCHRECK, C.B., and H.W. LORZ. 1978. Stress response of coho salmon (*Oncorhynchus kisutch*) elicited by cadmium and copper and potential use of cortisol as an indicator of stress. J. Fish. Res. Board Can. 35: 1124-1129.

8. ALDRIN, J.F., J.L. MESSAGER, and M. MEVEL. 1979. Essai sûr le stress de transport chez le saumon coho juvénile (*Oncorhynchus kisutch*). Aquaculture 17: 279-289.

9. BOUCK, G.R., and D.A. JOHNSON. 1979. Medication inhibits tolerance to seawater in coho salmon smolts. Trans. Am. Fish. Soc. 108: 63-66.

10. WILLIAMS, H.A., and R. WOOTTEN. 1981. Some effects of therapeutic levels of formalin and copper sulphate on blood parameters in rainbow trout.

Aquaculture 24: 341-353.

11. VOBORIL, L. Aquarium Designs Ltd., personal communications.

12. KEITH, R.E. 1981. Loss of therapeutic copper in closed marine systems. Aquaculture 24: 355-362.

13. RØDSAETHER, M.C., J. OLAFSEN, and J. RAA. 1977. Copper as an initiating factor of vibriosis (*Vibrio anguillarum*) in eel (*Anguilla anguilla*). J. Fish. Biol. 10: 17-21.

14. HETRICK, F.M., M.D. KNITTEL, and J.L. FRYER. 1979. Increased susceptibility of rainbow trout to infectious hematopoietic necrosis virus after exposure to copper. Appl. Environ. Microbiol. 37: 198-201.

15. KNITTEL, M.D. 1981. Susceptibility of steelhead trout *Salmo gairdneri* Richardson to redmouth infection *Yersinia ruckeri* following exposure to copper. J. Fish Dis. 4: 33-40.

16. COLLINS, M.T., J.B. GRATZEK, D.L. DAWE, and T.G. NEMETZ. 1975. Effects of parasiticides on nitrification. J. Fish. Res. Board Can. 32: 2033-2037.

17. COLLINS, M.T., J.B. GRATZEK, D.L. DAWE, and T.G. NEMETZ. 1976. Effects of antibacterial agents on nitrification in an aquatic recirculating system. J. Fish. Res. Board Can. 33: 215-218.

18. LEVINE, G., and T.L. MEADE. 1976. The effects of disease treatment on nitrification in closed system aquaculture. Proc. World Mariculture Soc. 7: 483-493.

19. CHUN, S.K., I.B. KIM, and D.S. CHANG. 1978. Effects of bacteriocides on the nitrification in the recirculating aquarium. Bull. Nat. Fish. Univ. Busan 18: 69-81.

20. BOWER, C.E., and D.T. TURNER. 1982. Effects of seven chemotherapeutic agents on nitrification in closed seawater culture systems. Aquaculture 29: 331-345.

Chapter 12

1. COWEY, C.B. 1981. The food and feeding of captive fish. Pages 223-246 *in*: Aquarium Systems, A.D Hawkins, ed. New York, Academic Press.

2. CHURCH, C.F., and H.N. CHURCH. 1970. Food values of portions commonly used, 11th ed. Philadelphia, J.B. Lippincott Co., 180 pp.

3. FERGUSON, M. Scripps Aquarium, personal communication.

4. FRAKES, T.A. Instant Ocean Hatcheries, personal communication.

5. PETERSON, E.J., R.C. ROBINSON, and H. WILLOUGHBY. 1966. A meal-gelatin diet for aquarium fishes. *Presented at*: Aquarium Symposium of the American Society of Ichthyologists and Herpetologists, Miami, FL, June 21, 1966. 8 pp.

6. SCIARRA, J.B. 1976. The gelatin diet. Mar. Aquarist 7(1): 39-43.

7. MEYERS, S.P. 1980. Water-stable extruded diets and feeding of invertebrates. J. Aquariculture 1: 41-46.

8. GRABNER, M., W. WIESER, and R. LACKNER. 1981 The suitability of

frozen and freeze-dried zooplankton as food for fish larvae: a biochemical test program. Aquaculture 26: 85-94.

Chapter 13

1. SINDERMANN, C.J. 1970. Principal diseases of marine fish and shellfish. New York, Academic Press, 369 pp.
2. SPOTTE, S. 1979. Seawater aquariums: the captive environment. New York, John Wiley & Sons, 413 pp.
3. HERALD, E.S., R.P. DEMPSTER, and M. HUNT. 1970. Ultraviolet sterilization of aquarium water. Pages 57-71 *in*: Spec. Ed., Drum and Croaker, W. Hagen, ed. Washington, D.C., U.S. Dept. Interior.
4. RICHARDSON, L.B., and D.T. BURTON. 1981. Toxicity of ozonated estuarine water to juvenile blue crabs (*Callinectes sapidus*) and juvenile Atlantic menhaden (*Brenoortia tyrannus*). Bull. Environ. Contam. Toxicol. 26: 171-178.
5. STEWART, M.E., W.J. BLOGOSLAWSKI, R.Y. HSU, and G.R. HELZ. 1979. By-products of oxidative biocides: toxicity to oyster larvae. Mar. Pollut. Bull. 10: 166-169.
6. SPOTTE, S., and G. ADAMS. 1981. Pathogen reduction in closed aquaculture systems by UV radiation: fact or artifact? Mar. Ecol. Progr. Ser. 6: 295-298.
7. BULLOCK, G.L., and H.M. STUCKEY. 1977. Ultraviolet treatment of water for destruction of five gram-negative bacteria pathogenic to fishes. J. Fish. Res. Board Can. 34: 1244-1249.
8. SPANIER, E. 1978. Preliminary trials with an ultraviolet liquid sterilizer. Aquaculture 14: 75-84.
9. TRUST, T.J., and K.H. BARTLETT. 1974. Occurrence of potential pathogens in water containing ornamental fishes. Appl. Microbiol. 28: 35-40.
10. BARHAM, W.T., H. SCHOONBEE, and G.L. SMIT. 1979. The occurrence of *Aeromonas* and *Streptococcus* in rainbow trout, *Salmo gairdneri* Richardson. J. Fish Biol. 15: 457-460.
11. SNIESZKO, S.F. 1974. The effects of environmental stress on outbreaks of infectious diseases of fishes. J. Fish Biol. 6: 197-208.
12. WEDEMEYER, G.A., and J.W. WOOD. 1974. Stress as a predisposing factor in fish diseases. U.S. Dept. Interior, Fish Wildl. Serv., Fish. Leafl. No. 38, 8 pp.
13. SPOTTE, S. 1979. Fish and invertebrate culture: water management in closed systems, 2nd ed. New York, John Wiley & Sons, 179 pp.
14. BOWER, C.E. 1975. The stress-free environment and disease management. Mar. Aquarist 6(9): 38-45.
15. KINGSFORD, E. 1975. Treatment of exotic marine fish diseases. St. Petersburg, FL, Palmetto Publishing Co., 92 pp.
16. DE GRAAF, F. 1973. Marine aquarium guide. Harrison, NJ, Pet Library Ltd., Sternco Industries Inc., 284 pp.
17. VAN DUIJN, C. 1973. Diseases of fishes, 3rd ed. Springfield, IL, Charles C Thomas, 372 pp.

18. DULIN, M. 1976. Diseases of marine aquarium fishes. Neptune City, NJ, T.F.H. Publications, 128 pp.

19. TRUST, T.J. 1972. Inadequacy of aquarium antibacterial formulations for the inhibition of potential pathogens of freshwater fish. J. Fish. Res. Board Can. 29: 1425-1430.

20. TRUST, T.J., and D.C. CHIPMAN. 1974. Evaluation of aquarium antibiotic formulations. Antimicrob. Agents Chemother. 6: 379-386.

21. DEWEY, D. 1980. Disease prevention and control. Freshwater Mar. Aquarium 3(8): 21-22; 86.

22. HERMAN, R.L. 1970. Chemotherapy of fish diseases: a review. J. Wildl. Dis. 6: 31-34.

23. COLLINS, M.T., J.B. GRATZEK, D.L. DAWE, and T.G. NEMETZ. 1976. Effects of antibacterial agents on nitrification in an aquatic recirculating system. J. Fish. Res. Board Can. 33: 215-218.

24. BOWER, C.E., and D.T. TURNER. 1982. Effects of seven chemotherapeutic agents on nitrification in closed seawater culture systems. Aquaculture 29: 331-345.

25. COLLINS, M.T., J.B. GRATZEK, D.L. DAWE, and T.G. NEMETZ. 1975. Effects of parasiticides on nitrification. J. Fish. Res. Board Can. 32: 2033-2037.

26. KABASAWA, H., and M. YAMADA. 1972. The effect of copper sulfate ($CuSO_4$. $5H_2O$) and Negayon on the function of filtering bacteria in a closed circulating sea water system. Rep. Keikyu Aburatsubo Mar. Park Aquarium 1971(4): 18-22 (in Japanese).

27. AMEND, D.F., and A.J. ROSS. 1970. Experimental control of columnaris disease with a new nitrofuran drug, P-7138. Prog. Fish-Cult. 21: 19-25.

28. HERMAN, R.L. 1972. The principles of therapy in fish diseases. Symp. Zool. Soc. Lond., No. 30, p. 141-151.

29. NUSBAUM, K.E., and E.B. SHOTTS. 1981. Absorption of selected antimicrobic drugs from water by channel catfish. *Ictalurus punctatus.* Can. J. Fish. Aquat. Sci. 38: 993-996.

30. PEARSE, L., R.S.V. PULLIN, D.A. CONROY, and D. McGREGOR. 1974. Observations on the use of Furanace for the control of vibrio disease in marine flatfish. Aquaculture 3: 295-302.

31. NUSBAUM, K.E., and E.B. SHOTTS. 1981. Action of selected antibiotics on four common bacteria associated with diseases of fish. J. Fish Dis. 4: 397-404.

32. SINDERMANN, C.J. 1978. Pollution-associated diseases and abnormalities of fish and shellfish: a review. Fish. Bull. 76: 717-749.

33. MURCHELANO, R.A., and J. ZISKOWSKI. 1979. Fin rot disease — a sentinel of environmental stress? Int. Counc. Explor. Sea, C.M. 1979/E:25, 5 pp.

34. KETOLA, G.H. 1979. Influence of dietary lysine on "fin rot," survival, and growth of fry of rainbow trout. Fish Health News 8(2): vi.

35. KETOLA, G.H. 1981. Requirement for dietary lysine and argenine by fry of rainbow trout (*Salmo gairdneri*). Unpublished manuscript.

36. ANDERSON, J.I.W., and D.A. CONROY. 1970. Vibrio disease in marine fishes. Pages 266-272 *in*: A symposium on diseases of fishes and shellfishes,

S.F. Snieszko, ed. Am. Fish. Soc., Spec. Publ. No. 5.

37. MUNN, C.B. 1977. Vibriosis of fish and its control. Fish. Management 8(1): 11-15.

38. UMBREIT, T.H., and M.R. TRIPP. 1975. Characterization of the factors responsible for the death of fish infected with *Vibrio anguillarum*. Can. J. Microbiol. 21: 1272-1274.

39. BROWN, E.M. 1931. Note on a new species of dinoflagellate from the gills and epidermis of marine fishes. Proc. Zool. Soc. Lond., Part 1: 345-346.

40. BROWN, E.M. 1934. On *Oodinium ocellatum* Brown, a parasitic dinoflagellate causing epidemic disease in marine fish. Proc. Zool. Soc. Lond., Part 3: 583-607.

41. NIGRELLI, R.F. 1936. The morphology, cytology and life-history of *Oodinium ocellatum* Brown, a dinoflagellate parasite on marine fishes. Zoologica 21: 129-164.

42. BROWN, E.M., and R. HOVASSE. 1946. *Amyloodinium ocellatum* (Brown), a peridinian parasitic on marine fishes. A complementary study. Proc. Zool. Soc. Lond. 116: 33-46.

43. LAWLER, A.R. 1977. Dinoflagellate (*Amyloodinium*) infestation of pompano. Pages 257-264 *in*: Disease diagnosis and control in North American marine aquaculture, C.J. Sindermann, ed. New York, Elsevier Scienctific Publishing Co.

44. HØJGAARD, M. 1962. Experiences made in Danmarks Akvarium concerning the treatment of *Oodinium ocellatum*. Bull. Inst. Océanogr. Monaco, Num. Spéc. 1A: 77-79.

45. DEMPSTER, R.P. 1955. The use of copper sulfate as a cure for fish diseases caused by parasitic dinoflagellates of the genus *Oodinium*. Zoologica 40: 133-138.

46. CHHAPGAR, B.F., and H.G. KEWALRAMANI. 1958. Copper sulphate in the treatment of diseases of marine fishes. The Aquarium 27: 376-378.

47. DEMPSTER, R.P. 1975. Modern methods of cure. Mar. Aquarist 6(10): 91-94.

48. LAWLER, A.R. 1977. The parasitic dinoflagellate *Amyloodinium ocellatum* in marine aquaria. Drum and Croaker 17(2): 17-20.

49. KEITH, R.E. 1981. Loss of therapeutic copper in closed marine systems. Aquaculture 24: 355-362.

50. KEITH, R.E. Ohio State University, personal communication.

51. NIGRELLI, R.F., and G.D. RUGGIERI. 1966. Enzootics in the New York Aquarium caused by *Cryptocaryon irritans* Brown, 1951 (= *Ichthyophthirius marinus* Sikama, 1961), a histophagous ciliate in the skin, eyes and gills of marine fishes. Zoologica 51: 97-102.

52. WILKIE, D.W., and H. GORDIN. 1969. Outbreak of cryptocaryoniasis in marine aquaria at Scripps Institution of Oceanography. Calif. Fish Game 55: 227-236.

53. DE GRAAF, F. 1962. A new parasite causing epidemic infection in captive cor-alfishes. Bull. Inst. Océanogr. Monaco, Num. Spéc. 1A: 93-96.

54. SNIESZKO, S.F. 1972. Nutritional fish diseases. Pages 403-437 *in*: Fish nutri-

tion, J.E. Halver, ed. New York, Academic Press.

55. GOLDSTEIN, R.J. 1974. *Cryptocaryon* vs. formalin. Mar. Aquarist 5(1): 50-54.

56. GOVEN, B.A., D.L. DAWE, and J.B. GRATZEK. 1980. Protection of channel catfish, *Ictalurus punctatus* Rafinesque, against *Ichthyophthirius multifiliis* Fouquet by immunization. J. Fish Biol. 17: 311-316.

57. CHEUNG, P.J., R.F. NIGRELLI, and G.D. RUGGIERI. 1979. Studies on cryptocaryoniasis in marine fish: effect of temperature and salinity on the reproductive cycle of *Cryptocaryon irritans* Brown, 1951. J. Fish Dis. 2: 93-97.

58. HUFF, J.A., and C.D. BURNS. 1981. Hypersaline and chemical control of *Cryptocaryon irritans* in red snapper, *Lutjanus campechanus,* monoculture. Aquaculture 22: 181-184.

59. JANSSEN, W.A. 1970. Fish as potential vectors of human bacterial diseases. Pages 284-290 *in*: A symposium on diseases of fishes and shellfishes, S.F. Snieszko, ed. Am. Fish. Soc., Spec. Publ. No. 5.

60. DE JONCKHEERE, J.F. 1979. Occurrence of *Naegleria* and *Acanthamoeba* in aquaria. Appl. Environ. Microbiol. 38: 590-593.

61. FAOAGALI, J.L., A.D. MUIR, P.J. SEARS, and G.P. PALTRIDGE. 1977. Tropical fish tank granuloma. New Zealand Med. J. 85: 322-335.

62. WILSON, J.W. 1976. Skin infections caused by inoculation of *Mycobacterium marinum* from aquariums. Drum and Croaker 16(1): 39-42.

INDEX

257

painted (*see Halichoeres pictus*)
pearly (*see Halichoeres margaritaceus*)
red labrid (*see Coris gaimard*)
red-tailed (*see Anampses rubrocaudatus*)
straight-tail razorfish (*see Hemipteronotus martinicensis*)

Y

Yellow water, 62, 108, 120

Z

Zanclus canescens, 151
Zebrasoma flavescens, 147, 192